Teaching Creatively by Working the Word

language, music, and movement

Susan A. Katz

Judith A. Thomas

PRENTICE HALL, Englewood Cliffs, New Jersey 07632

Library of Congress Cataloging-in-Publication Data

KATZ, SUSAN A. (date)
　　Teaching creatively by working the word / Susan A. Katz, Judith A.
Thomas.
　　　p.　　cm.
　　Includes bibliographical references (p. 355) and index.
　　ISBN　0–13–963950–0
　　1. Language experience approach in education—United States.
2. Language arts—United States.　3. School music—Instruction and
study—United States.　4. Poetry—Study and teaching (Elementary)–
–United States.　5. Movement education—United States.　I. Thomas,
Judith A. (date).　II. Title.
LB1576.K36　1992
372.19—dc20　　　　　　　　　　　　　　　　　91–45277
　　　　　　　　　　　　　　　　　　　　　　　　　CIP

Acquisitions editor: Bud Therien
Editorial/production supervision
　and interior design: F. Hubert
Cover design: Ray Lundgren Graphics, Ltd.
Prepress buyer: Herb Klein
Manufacturing buyer: Patrice Fraccio

Credits begin on page 361, which constitutes
a continuation of the copyright page.

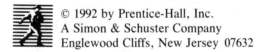 © 1992 by Prentice-Hall, Inc.
A Simon & Schuster Company
Englewood Cliffs, New Jersey 07632

Printed in the United States of America
10　9　8　7　6　5　4　3　2　1

ISBN　0-13-963950-0

PRENTICE-HALL INTERNATIONAL (UK) LIMITED, *London*
PRENTICE-HALL OF AUSTRALIA PTY, LIMITED, *Sydney*
PRENTICE-HALL CANADA INC., *Toronto*
PRENTICE-HALL HISPANOAMERICANA, S.A., *Mexico*
PRENTICE-HALL OF INDIA PRIVATE LIMITED, *New Delhi*
PRENTICE-HALL OF JAPAN, INC., *Tokyo*
SIMON & SCHUSTER ASIA PTE. LTD., *Singapore*
EDITORA PRENTICE-HALL DO BRASIL, LTDA., *Rio de Janeiro*

contents

*Color poems emphasize imagery in poetry using the five
senses. Color terms are a source of movement exploration.*

Chapter 2

The Feeling Poem   33

Feeling poems are used to introduce alliteration and onomatopoeia, and student poems are given rhythmical treatment and extended form.

Chapter 3

The Daydream/Wish/Fantasy Poem   69

Daydream/Wish/Fantasy poems highlight the importance of adjectives, metaphors, similes, and the creation of melodies.

Chapter 4
The When-I-Fall-Asleep Poem 112

When-I-Fall-Asleep poems help define free verse poetry and are used to introduce students to editing techniques. "Found sounds" are discovered in the classroom and used to enhance poetry.

Chapter 5
The How-I-See-Myself/How-Others-See-Me Poem 152

How-I-See-Myself/How-Others-See-Me poems personalize student poetry, and musical and movement skills are synthesized by student/teacher input in a loosely structured format.

SECTION TWO
WORD-WORKING IMPLEMENTATION 197

Chapter 6
Extended Field Trip Experience 200

*Ten-year-old students respond to a sculpture garden field
trip with creative movement, vocal sound, and poetic
expression.*

Chapter 7
Extended Science Experience 225

*The science lesson is extended through language, music,
and movement, resulting in heightened imagination and
more memorable learning.*

Chapter 8
Extended Endangered Species Experience 243

*Student investigation of the animal world, particularly
endangered species, is expressed through music and poetry,
and leads to projects designed to aid wildlife.*

Chapter 9
Extended Math Experience 254

*Numbers in math take on new dimensions when expressed
through movement, poetry, and rhythmic speech.*

Chapter 10
Extended Music-Inspired Experience 265

Listening to masterwork musical compositions, students transform music-inspired images into poetic form.

Chapter 11
Extended Nature and Seasonal Experiences 271

The natural environment and the changing seasons inspire a schoolwide music, movement, poetry program highlighting student work.

Chapter 12
Extended Current Events Experience 292

A wide range of current events topics generate poems, movement pieces, and musical presentations that spiral off in many directions.

Chapter 13
Extended Environment Experience   304

*The far-reaching theme of "This Is My World: I Choose"
becomes a school program for second-, third-, and fourth-
grade students and illustrates how cross-curriculum teaching
enhances the total learning gestalt.*

Appendix   336

Annotated Bibliography   355

Credits   361

Index   363

preface

There are as many ways to teach poetry and music as there are people teaching. The following lessons are channeled toward creating an atmosphere of classroom excitement and rewards that are felt in the "now" of the process. Through language, movement, and music—and all the combinations they imply—we offer this text as one viable approach to teaching poetry and music by "working the word."

The first section of this book contains many sample lessons (scripts), which are reproductions of actual teacher–student classroom interactions. Annotations in the margins of the scripts highlight key situations and provide suggestions on how to handle them.

The sample poetry lessons in this book were developed and applied in the Poet in Public Service Program, 1976–1991, by Susan A. Katz. These lessons were geared toward the fourth-grade level, but were adapted to all ages by upgrading or lowering response expectations. All of the poetry (some in its original form, some edited) appearing in this text was chosen because it best represented the range of students' written responses. The poems which follow were written by students (1976 to 1991) in the following schools in Rockland County, New York:

Birchwood Elementary School

Franklin Avenue Elementary School

Grandview Elementary School

Hempstead Elementary School

Liberty Elementary School (formerly Lakeroad)

Lime Kiln Elementary School

Margetts Elementary School

Merrill Colton Elementary School

New City Elementary School

Suffern Junior High School

Tappan Zee Elementary School

Upper Nyack Elementary School

Woodglen Elementary School

The sample music and movement lessons (some in their original form, some edited) are composites from those developed with Nyack (New York) Public School children from 1976 to 1991, when Judith Thomas served as Arts Resource Coordinator and Orff-Schulwerk Music Specialist for the Nyack District.

LANGUAGE AS THE IMPETUS _____

The various subjects taught in the classroom as individual disciplines are fingers on the same hand. Language is the unifying element and the medium through which we teach *all* subjects. Therefore, it is imperative that we embrace the multiple inherent possibilities within the creative use of language and recognize that words are malleable and can be made to be either holy or humdrum. The process of elevating the ordinary into the extraordinary (in the form of student poems) is where this book begins. The expansion process starts with a stimulus (i.e., colors, feelings, environment, fantasies, etc.) and evolves through a verbal exploration of the subject. Students exchange ideas, react to one another's input, and are then invited to fashion their ideas on paper through imagery (metaphor and simile). Experimenting with the potential power and nuance, sound and substance, of their words through creative selection and juxtaposing, students commit the poems to paper. Students are invited to share their work with teacher and class; and often, this sharing crests in a wave of excitement and enthusiasm. Some may see this as an ending, but for us, it heralds a new beginning.

EXTENDING THE PROCESS OF "WORKING THE WORD" _____

This new beginning further extends the creative process into all areas of the curriculum through the complement of music and movement. Those common, everyday words, which were so painstakingly and thoughtfully selected and which proved to be uncommon (and even memorable) in the context of the poem, now become more than words. Their placement on the page, in the mouth, and within the body takes on additional significance: a new dimension.

Words are found to have depth, height, weight, sound, speed, rhythm, nuance, timbre, form and melody, and take on sensory characteristics. They whisper and scream; smell of spring flowers or ocean spray; they burn, soothe, ooze, melt; they are steps that creak in the night, thunder rolling over the mountains; they are volcanoes erupting, and the softness of cumulus clouds.

SPANNING THE CURRICULUM THROUGH "WORKING THE WORD" _____

Language is active and constantly in motion, refusing to recognize barriers between subjects. Together, teacher and students discover that words need not be confined to paper, or even the mouth, but can be evolved into a rich movement vocabulary of slashes, presses, thrusts, glides, flicks, floats, dabs, and wrings (Rudolph Laban, English educational dance specialist's movement qualities); or that words can be rearranged into movement forms; can be sung, overlapped, layered, whispered, shouted, sped up, slowed down, treated in canon, or accompanied. This book, in this manner, extending language skills into and beyond music and movement, encourages the weaving of the individual strands of the curriculum (various subjects) into a cohesive, whole fabric. Progressive lessons are fashioned to afford students a sense of familiarity with the unfamiliar through language as the bridge; words become user-friendly keys to understanding. The following are examples of what this book is designed to do for students and teachers:

— *Experience science:* Poems wait to burst out of the colors of a prism, layers of rhythms reflect insect calls, and melodies sing to the emergence of monarchs (Chapter 7).

— *Commemorate history:* Poems give personalized, in-depth meaning to the inherent qualities of freedom, and chants redefine the drama of our constitution (Chapter 12).

— *Enhance mathematics:* Poems capture in imagery the circumference of a circle, and movement defines roundness through infinite possibilities of body shapes and floor patterns (Chapter 9).

— *Reflect on the visual details of field trips:* Poems linger over the lines of a Calder monolith and envision the flight of birds or the menace of monsters through imagery in steel structures; movement gives impact and definition to these images (Chapter 6).

There is delight and pride of accomplishment in the finished product; the poem, the extension of the poem, the sharing through music and movement in classroom or assembly forum; but the real *learning* energy is most vividly in evidence during all the various stages of the *process*. It is the exuberant exchange of ideas, the mental muscle flexing, the interplay of input between student/student and student/teacher, which shapes the philosophy of this book. This philosophy is based on the premise that the best learning begins with, and is developed by, the child, with the teacher as facilitator. In this role, the teacher establishes a sense of responsibility for, and ownership of, his or her own ideas within the child, and helps extend these ideas into catalysts for new, ongoing, outreaching, individual and group experiences.

WHO THE BOOK IS FOR

— The classroom teacher, primarily

— The teacher *learning* to be a teacher

— The music specialist

— The curriculum specialist (movement, art, learning disabled, gifted and talented, etc.).

HOW TO USE THE BOOK

1. Classroom Teacher

This book was written as a creative language/music/movement curriculum spanner—to reveal the interrelationship between individual basic subjects. It is meant to provide some new cross-curriculum insights which the classroom teacher can incorporate into his or her own teaching design. While the book was written to encourage one person (i.e., the classroom teacher) to dare to try language arts as a creative springboard and move outward to music and movement, it does not exclude the possibility of utilizing the talents of the school's specialists. Teachers interacting with one another create a positive school happening, incorporating all of the talents within the school which best serve the process. This collaboration can and should create a healthy bond between teachers and teaching areas, as in the following examples:

— A teacher text for developing language arts curriculum (Section One)

— A text for developing movement and music expansion lessons from existing classroom subject matter (Sections One and Two)

— A text for creating expanded field trip lessons (Chapter 6)

— An in-classroom workbook for the teacher (teaching metaphor, simile, etc.) and providing basic theory examples in language arts and in elemental movement and music (Section One)

— A resource book of student poetry and musical examples to share in the classroom and use as inspirations for students (Sections One and Two)

— A departure point for designing and complementing personalized creative teaching experiences (Sections One and Two)

— A map (not fixed or formulized), providing rich and varied landscapes from which to choose personal directions (Sections One and Two)

— An enrichment for the everyday classroom subject areas and events (Sections One and Two)

— A workbook from which materials (examples, ideas, concepts, modus operandi) can be excerpted (Sections One and Two)

— A companion guide for everyday teaching, with its many variables and possible pitfalls ("Troubleshooting," Section One).

2. Teacher Learning to Be a Teacher

For teachers in progress (education students), this text, read in total, will help them assess their future classroom strengths and weaknesses and provide them with good, solid examples of workable techniques. It can further be used as

— A college text for understanding the development and *raison d'être* of creative teaching

— A text that should be read to experience classroom pacing, and for developing an anticipation of possible student reactions

— A guide to actual in-class experience: reaction/response/lack of response, etc., and a guide to ways in which these various responses may be handled (Section One, "Troubleshooting")

— A guide to awareness of the scope of possibility in creative teaching and the acquisition of skills which will facilitate a multiplicity of techniques

— An inspiration to expand those areas which lend themselves to the creative classroom atmosphere.

3. Music Specialist

This book can be used by the music specialist as

— A resource by music specialists who see music as a broad-spectrumed activity, incorporating movement, improvisation, music, body percussion, small percussion, found sounds (i.e., Orff-Schulwerk approach; see Sections One and Two).

— A teaching guide for developing music concepts while using materials, ideas, events, etc. from the general classroom and greater school at large as departure points, thereby teaching in a whole language, holistic, or integrated style, which is desirable for strengthening the cohesiveness of the student's day

— A handbook for ways to draw on words as sources of inspiration for music, and to evoke words which will result in substantial musical creations drawn from field trips, feelings, serendipitous class and school activities, etc.

— An inspiration to make music (and movement) concepts and theory an integrated and essential part of the whole school curriculum.

4. In-School Teaching Specialists

In these multiple areas, this text can be used in any of the ways mentioned previously—and probably the various student responses will be handled selectively, depending on focus, subject area, and individual goals.

GENERAL INFORMATION AND PHILOSOPHY OF THIS BOOK _____

The philosophy of Carl Orff, music educator and composer, spanned an eclectic and broad educational landscape, encouraging and nurturing classroom play, improvisation, and exploration. He believed that "elementary music, words and movement, play, everything that awakens and develops the powers of the spirit, this is the 'humus' of the spirit. . . ."[1] Like Orff, we believe the rewards are enormous in offering students an intensified insight into their own language capabilities. The effects ripple outward to generate musical, rhythmical, and movement potentials.

In keeping with the Orff-Schulwerk philosophy, we believe that the combining of movement, language, music, rhythm, song, improvisation and the playing of elemental instruments form an amalgam that belongs in the *general classroom* as well as the music specialist's room. In his autobiography, *Das Schulwerk,* Carl Orff states that " . . . the place where [the Schulwerk approach] can be most effective, and where there is the possibility of continuous and progressive work, and where its connections with other subjects can be explored, developed, and fully exploited . . . this place is in the school"[2]—the entire school, with its general and specialized classrooms. Importantly, it has to happen

---

[1]*Das Schulwerk,* Carl Orff, published by Schott, 1971, p. 245.
[2]Ibid., p. 245.

early: "It is at the primary school age that the imagination must be stimulated: and opportunities for emotional development which contain experiences of the ability to feel, and the power to control the expression of the feeling, must also be provided. Everything that a child of this age experiences, everything in him that has been awakened and nurtured, is a determining factor for the whole of his life. . . ."[3]

CURRICULUM IMPLICATIONS

We believe, as well, in the rewards to be found in the overlapping of subjects. More and more, classroom teachers are experiencing a crunch of materials and concepts within the limited time frame of the school day. In the most practical sense, overlapping is becoming necessary to facilitate all that is simultaneously going on within the school curriculum. Happily, evidence supports that the learning process is enhanced by the overlapping of subject matter. It has been noted often that children learn best when subjects are integrated. Curriculum directors frequently encourage this kind of holistic teaching, believing that the skills of reading, writing, and speaking should be taught in an integrated way. This is especially apparent in the whole language style of teaching which is child centered, informal, and based on discovery and creative involvement between teacher and student.

Just how this integration is to be accomplished has remained somewhat of a mystery, as few books address the total picture or offer techniques that specifically demonstrate how this fusion is to be attained. There are any number of books on the market which present the magic of children's poetry but offer only cursory explanations of the process used to elicit it. Likewise, few liberal arts college texts give in-depth, easily followed scripting of movement/music/language arts holistic teaching techniques. This book, based on forty-five years of combined language, movement, and music in-class experience and experimentation, reveals pragmatic ways for developing cross-over, evocative teaching skills. It suggests ways to consolidate activities in a cohesive manner without adding more than an introductory amount of content to an already overcrowded program.

SUMMARY

In moving from theory to practice, it is essential that we believe in ourselves as teachers and realize that evocative teaching, while involving risk, opens unexpected doors to unlimited vistas. Like all new experiences, there are

[3]Ibid., p. 246.

moments of exhilarating success, and others which leave us feeling lost and in over our heads. However, even in those moments when we flounder and when the process seems to have failed, the experience is positive because it is one of experimentation and ultimate trust in the creative process.

In our computerized, televised, cable-ized, push-button world, the need for creative expression is volcanic. The child who pushes a computer button needs also to be made aware of the ability to capture, internalize, and re-create everyday experiences through sensory awareness, imaginative effort, and artistic outreach. He or she needs to be taught that *ideas* are the basis for all of our human creations (poetic, scientific, musical, mathematical, etc.) and that ideas are conceived with words, born of language. The classroom needs to be a place of awe, where all things are possible; where learning delights the senses, stimulates the mind, and releases the body. This is the *energized* classroom where the creative essence becomes palpable. It is our sincere hope that this book will offer teachers and their students this expectant and mutually fulfilling kind of environment.

In a very real sense, using creative techniques to teach *and* teaching creative techniques to children is an attempt to provide them ways with which to name their world, and in naming it, expand it. Student word creations, shaped into poems, expanded into works involving movement, texture, form, melody, rhythm, flowing with purpose from subject to subject, are mini-celebrations of self, providing students with the power to unravel the mystery of themselves and the world around them.

> You bend down,
> break a pod,
> and blow unlikely butterflies in the sky's face
> not black and orange like Monarchs, but cloud
> thought white, or like the way I mark my place
>
> when I read your eyes, which witnessing claim:
> This is the world. Try to learn its name.
>
> > Gary Miranda, "Witnessing"—for Patty[4]

[4]Gary Miranda, "Witnessing"—for Patty, *Grace Period*, Princeton, N.J.: Princeton University Press, 1983.

ACKNOWLEDGMENTS _____

Susan A. Katz would like to acknowledge a debt of gratitude to Myra Klahr, Founder-Director, Poets in Public Service, for providing the opportunity to conduct poetry workshops in the classroom and for her support and friendship throughout the years.

Judith Thomas acknowledges, with thanks, the long-term professional interest and support of Bud Therien, Art and Music Editor, Prentice Hall.

For his contagious joy, for his cooperation and involvement, for his superior knowledge and savvy, for his tireless good humor, and for his special rapport with teachers and students alike, we lovingly thank Mr. Barnett Ostrowsky, Principal, Upper Nyack Elementary School.

We jointly express our admiration and respect for the inspiration provided by students and teachers with whom we have "worked the word" joyfully over the years.

We gratefully acknowledge the input received from the following reviewers:

Wendy Sims, University of Missouri–Columbia

Mary Shamrock, California State University, Northridge.

We thank photographer Brad Hess for his commitment and artistry which so revealingly captured the de-"light" in the eyes of our student poets.

Susan A. Katz

Judith A. Thomas

section one
word-working process

DEDICATION:
THE REWARDS
—TO OUR STUDENTS

You collect before us
like drops of dew
on a morning rose
bright in the light
of a new day.

We know your faces
and your names
hauntingly familiar
like the image of oneself caught
beneath the surface
of a still lake.

You have moved us though
we have only met
in passing like a breeze
that turns the leaves showing
them a new view of the sun.

There is a wholeness
in this room as though
something less
than whole had just

completed itself
like a circle closing
like lips forming
circles around words
like words forming patterns
in the mind
poems on paper.

You have led us
time and time again
to that secret place
where children hide and poets
choose to wander
among the hills
of imagination.

Long after your tongues
have forgotten the taste
of our names we will be warming
ourselves beside the flame
we found blazing in your eyes.

Susan A. Katz

INTRODUCTION:
SCRIPTED LESSONS, TROUBLESHOOTING,
TEACHER-AND-STUDENT DYNAMICS _____

This book was written with the intent that it be *primarily* used by *one* person, the classroom teacher. The scripts and information presented, and the techniques suggested, can be applied by the teacher who is interested in exploring and developing the whole language approach to teaching. Indeed, we feel that this book parallels the whole language movement in education, because like whole language:

— It is child oriented and draws from the essence of children's thoughts and interests.
— It places a heavy emphasis on writing and vocalization.
— It uses a variety of learning modes (i.e., poetry, music, movement, etc.).
— It builds a strong bond between teacher and student.
— It provides information for students where needed, in a nurturing and wholly accepting environment.

Further, this book addresses the need to move freely and adeptly through the shifting landscape of the curriculum. It permits and encourages the blurring of lines which separate the individual territories of learning from one another, so there is an integration of curriculum areas. It endorses the belief that there is reward in, and justification for, this type of teacher/learning unification, and complements healthy, child-centered approaches.

ONE-TEACHER APPLICATION;
PROCESS EVOLUTION _____

In examining the reality of a one-teacher approach to the multifaceted demands inherent in this book, it will be helpful for the reader to know how the possibilities came to be, and how they lend themselves to a one-person application. The process espoused in this book evolved over a period of some years and began with the introduction of a language specialist in residence on the elementary classroom level. There was, at the beginning, very little overlap between the poetry workshops and the music and movement activities. The ineluctable problem became how to share most effectively these undeniably worthy student poetry creations beyond the confinement of the individual classroom. The works were shared (within this limited classroom context) at the conclusion of each writing workshop, and the students' reactions to their own poetry and one another's was so intense that very often *they* posed the question: "Can we put our poems up in the hall on the bulletin board? . . . read them in other classes? . . . draw pictures to go with our poems?" etc.

It became apparent that the inner needs of the students for sharing deserved a broader showcase. It was at this point the music teacher was invited to develop a 45-minute assembly focusing around the poems created during the poetry workshops. Now the problem became a programmatic one: how not to bore—for no matter how vibrant the student writing, the sheer numbers of students involved would make for a one-dimensional and numbing kind of presentation. Clearly, more had to be accomplished than a marathon poetry reading.

This realization prompted the music teacher to return the students' poems to them for further consideration and reshaping. This meant reexamining them for rhythm and speech-play potential, for possible reforming, for movement possibilities, or for locating those student poems which would be enhanced by melodic treatment. The subsequent reworking (by students, individually and in groups with teacher input), resulted in original poems which then were ready to *move* across the stage as well as be heard . . . be *sung* and overlapped in canon rather than just spoken, and be *enhanced* by small percussion and body percussion accompaniment.

Now with rich word imagery, music, and movement evident within the student works, the process of creation was moving in concentric circles between the language arts class, where editing and rewriting was going on; the poetry workshops, where new techniques and skills were being learned and honed; the homeroom, where time was being given for further refinement and brainstorming; and the music room, where extended developments were being created.

The resulting assembly was a delight to the senses. It captured the imagination and held the attention of both those presenting and their audience. In analyzing the success of the presentation, we were struck by the diversity of input, and we concluded that curriculum layering enhances the individual effort and makes for an enriching experience.

What was not apparent at that time, but later revealed itself, was that this experience was memorable for the students themselves in the language and music areas. Of equal merit was that poetic techniques and skills were now appearing in daily classroom and musicroom work (i.e., metaphors and similes were being used routinely in student writing; and movement and music exploration took on a new depth and richness). Having had the experience of applying these techniques to their works, students were now able to utilize them in analyzing masterwork poetry.

Another unexpected dividend was the discovery that the language arts specialist was using movement and music layering in the poetry workshops— both to enhance student work and to inspire it. The music teacher was helping students create original poetry complementing sculpture graphics (see "Extended Field Trip Experience," Chapter 6) and classroom teachers were utilizing newly learned student skills to accelerate enthusiasm for the extension process. Metaphors and similes taught to enhance poetic imagery now became devices to describe science experiments, current events, environmental issues, etc.; a nature study of leaves became an impetus, opening itself to movement lessons; and fall became a seasonal inspiration for reflective poems and musical modes that paralleled them. And so the process went.

Increased administrative and parental enthusiasm and encouragement developed for this kind of teaching, which produced outstanding creative results (i.e., poetry anthologies; poetry/movement/music assembly showcases; poetry/art ongoing bulletin board themes; enriched writing skills, cutting across the curriculum; cooperative all-school writing focuses; classroom/school/community poetry publications; and poetry books created for fund raising, etc.). As well, much of the inspiration for themes and focuses began to come from the classroom teachers (see Section Two, Chapter 13, "Extended Environment Experience," Marion Anderson, Upper Nyack Elementary), and much of the work was being done by them within the framework of their own prescribed curriculum. This resulted in an increased flow of ideas and interaction from student to student, class to class, teacher to teacher, and subject to subject.

The evocative process took on a life of its own with a much greater teacher investment and ownership. And so it is today as we present this book, confident from our experiences that a one-teacher application is indeed both possible and educationally sound.

WHO THIS BOOK IS FOR _____

To reiterate, this book is mainly for the *classroom teacher;* but not exclusively. The *music teacher* will find the level of music demand easy and applicable; while perhaps growing and benefiting most by the less familiar skills covered in the poetry section. The *student teacher* in a college classroom or in the field will find the whole book useful, particularly as a projected vision of actual classroom interactions, and as an introduction to the evocative process. The *experienced teacher* may wish to use this text in consort with ideas and applications of his or her own, or mix and match—or perhaps simply to experiment with material and formats presented in this book. The *gifted and talented teacher* may use this book selectively to spark ideas, or as a supplementary text for developing new and extended projects with his or her students. In the special case of the totally *nonmusical teacher,* the book's nonmusical sections may still be effectively used by calling in a music specialist to apply the more technical musical aspects. The *language specialist* will find application of creative techniques valuable in enhancing language skills and promoting enthusiasm for language development. The *art specialist* will find rich art resources in the words and movements of children, and should be able to more fully integrate the art experience into the total school experience.

   If you believe, as we do, that the creative classroom is the ideal classroom, then there is something in this book for you.

SAMPLE LESSONS: HOW TO USE THEM

Scripting, in any text, is simply a way to illustrate teacher-and-student interaction in a format which may guide other teachers in the creation of their own lessons. No one can plan ahead (or script) the definitive lesson or predict the infinite number of student responses; but studying scripting can build a volume of confidence in the lesson orchestration.

   Sample lessons may be used as outlines for actual in-class presentation: teachers and student teachers may wish to practice possible classroom scenarios by paralleling sample scripts with scripting of their own design, tailored to their specific classroom needs. As well, these scripts may be studied for possible problem areas. Lines of questioning and commentary may be lifted from scripts for application in appropriate classroom settings. And, finally, scripts may be used as maps to chart directions and ultimate destinations of lessons.

chapter 1

the color poem

IMAGERY: THE COLOR POEM

Often, the success of teaching poetry in the classroom is achieved through imagery. This introductory lesson needs to provide students with an insight into their own creative depths, helping to establish their "eye for resemblances."[1] Further, we need to create the *sense* of language as a visual medium. Defining a relationship between the *image,* and the *art,* is the key to explaining how everyday words can be patterned to create memorable language experiences (i.e., poetry). We need to move away from the notion that the idea is where the poem begins. Poems do not begin with ideas so much as they begin with words that are developed into language patterns which create imagery.

> Give the word the fresh scent of ripe corn
> swaying in the wind of a hopeful field,
> tasty as the rare bread of my hungry childhood.
>
> Oh let the word ride endlessly, fantastic
> speak face to face, heart to heart
> with your neighbor of the farthest century.

> Menke Katz
> (Excerpted from "A Word or Two Against Rhyme,"
> *Aspects of Modern Poetry—Poet Lore)*

In poetry, each word is of monumental importance. The goal is to create the most potent visual sensory images possible. Out of imagery is born the poem, and a new understanding of, and delight in, language. This experience leads to a new

---

[1]Aristotle: "The greatest thing by far is to have command of metaphor. This alone cannot be imparted to another; it is the mark of genius, for to make good metaphors implies 'an eye for resemblances.' "

insight into one's own possibilities. Like fingerprints, each individual is capable of creating unique images that incapsulate personality, psyche, memory, experience: *self.*

In this first lesson we introduce imagery using colors[2] and the five senses.

SAMPLE LESSON: POETRY

TEACHER: Today we are going to be talking about poetry. Who knows something about poetry?

STUDENT: Poetry uses rhyming words.

T: Always? Does a poem always have to rhyme?

S: No, not always. But most of the time it does.

T: It's true that most of the poetry, limericks, and nursery rhymes that we study and read in class do rhyme. However, poetry that is being written today, and much that has been written in the recent past by those we call *contemporary poets,* for the most part, does not rhyme.[3] It may have a rhyme inside the poem, and we call that *internal rhyme,* or it may have a line or two that rhymes, but the poem, overall, is written in what we call *free verse.* Free verse allows us, among other things, not to rhyme. We'll be getting quite familiar with free verse once we begin to write our poems. Does anybody else want to tell us what poetry is?

[2]Kenneth Koch, *Wishes, Lies, and Dreams: Teaching Children to Write Poetry,* Vintage Books/Chelsea House Publishers, 1970.

[3]For example, Theodore Roethke, "Orchids," from *The Collected Poems of Theodore Roethke,* A Doubleday Anchor Book, 1975.

They lean over the path,
Adder-mouthed,
Swaying close to the face,
Coming out, soft and deceptive,
Limp and damp, delicate as a young bird's tongue;
Their fluttery, fledgling lips
Move slowly
Drawing in the warm air . . .

S: Poetry tells a story.

T: Sometimes. But again, not always true and in fact, the type of poetry that tells a story has a very specific name. It's called a *narrative poem.* Has anybody ever heard the word *narrator?*

S: Yes.

T: What does a narrator in a movie or on television do?

S: Tells the story of what's happening.

T: Right. So a poem that is a narrative is the kind of poem we would want to write if we wanted our poem to tell a story. The kind of poetry we are going to be writing today is not going to be narrative. Today we are going to be most concerned with the *words* themselves. In poetry, words are often *more* important than the idea. Let's explore poetry a bit, by trying to define what makes a poem a poem. If we were going to bake a cake, for example, what ingredients would we need?

STUDENTS: Flour . . . sugar . . . milk . . . eggs . . .

T: Right. And we might also want to add a bit of salt, some butter, and maybe top it all off with some chocolate icing. Now, if we want to "make" a poem, we need to know what ingredients go into the poem. The first and *most important* ingredient, like the flour in our cake recipe, is a small word. It comes from the larger word *imagination.* The small word we are looking for is the word *image.* An image in poetry is what we call a *word picture.* We will explore how word pictures work in a few moments. The second ingredient is almost as important. Without it there is no poetry. I'll give you a clue: We laugh or we cry, we yell or pout or kiss and hug, depending on how we . . .

S: Feel.

T: Yes, feel. *Feelings* are the second ingredient in our poetry recipe . . . *how* we feel about what we are writing. We need to put ourselves into our poems. We need to try to make the reader understand our emotions and feelings so that when they read our poems they will be able to feel and understand what we felt when we wrote them. Our goal, in poetry, is to capture our own personal energy and to project our

In this particular form of questioning, specifically using the word ingredient, *the intent was to give the students something familiar with which to name the less familiar subject, poetry. The technique of linking familiar to unfamiliar is extremely helpful when introducing new ideas or new subjects.*

The teacher is attempting to build a foundation of ideas which will clarify the terminology to be used, and in this case, illuminate, in understandable language, the essence of poetry. As in all of the scripting, the emphasis is on a kind of repetitive reinforcement of newly presented ideas and upgrading of vocabulary.

By encouraging students to draw on their own views of the world, we are providing them with a means of personalizing their feelings through poetry.

very own personal feelings. How do we know how we feel about something? From where do feelings come?

S: The heart.

S: The brain.

T: Yes, but how do we know, for example, that we like chocolate cake, but dislike spinach (or like spinach and dislike chocolate cake)?

S: Because we've tasted them, and chocolate cake tastes better than spinach.

T: True for most, and this tasting is what we call *experience*. Drawing on this experience is what we call *memory*. So, feelings can be said to come from experiences and memories. When you are writing a poem and are looking for an image or word picture to describe the beach, let's say, and you, Barbara, went to the beach once and found a shell with a pearl inside—and you, Neal, fell asleep in the sun and got a terrible sunburn, do you think you would use the same images or word pictures, or put in the same feelings when writing your beach poem?

S: No.

It is also a way of subtly reassuring them that their responses at whatever level will be neither right nor wrong, but rather a projection of their creative use of words flavored by their experiences. The teacher is therefore constantly creating this accepting environment which will allow for the greatest freedom of ideas. Note also that the teacher presents image examples (modeling).

T: No, of course not. One image might be: A day at the beach is as shiny and pink as the inside of a shell and white and brilliant as a newly formed pearl. The other image (word picture) might be: A day at the beach is red and hot and painful as a blister. Both images convey the visual impact of a word picture, and both draw on memory and experience. Each image is a very personal statement, and each image tells us something about the poet who wrote it. Do you begin to see how images and feelings work in poetry?

S: Yes, but how do you really know what a day at the beach is like?

T: A day at the beach is like the poet who writes about it. That's why, if we chose today to write about the beach, there would be as many different views of the beach as there are students writing, and that's what makes writing poetry so exciting. It gives us each a chance to be who and what we are through our poems, and to explore our own very personal feelings about things.

Inventing the "poetry recipe" through class discussion.

Let's move on now to the final major ingredient. This ingredient, like the eggs and the salt in our cake, completes the main part of our poetry recipe, and it is *the subject:* what it is that we are writing about. Most people would think that the subject would be the most important ingredient, and if we were writing a book report or term paper, it would be. But in poetry we are concerned with language, words, what we can do with them, and what we can make them do for us. So far, then, this is what our poetry recipe looks like:

The Poetry Recipe
How ⎰ 1. Images—Word pictures
   ⎱ 2. Feelings—emotions (memories and experiences)
What—3. The subject

T: The image and the feelings are what we will call the *how* of poetry. How do we put words together to form pictures? How do we shape those pictures by using feelings and emotions? And the subject is the *what* of poetry. What are we writing about? Now we have a basic understanding of what goes into "making" a poem. There is still one more thing we need to include if our poem is going to come to life. It's something you have five of, and it isn't your fingers and it isn't your toes. What else do you have five of?

S: The five senses?

Learning to use the senses: Touching.

Learning to use the senses: Touching.

Learning to use the senses: Smelling.

T: You're right. The five senses. Let's list them on the board.

See—how things *look*
Hear—how things *sound*
Taste—how things *taste*
Touch—how things *feel*
Smell—how things *smell*

Emotions—how things make us feel inside

You'll notice that I added an additional sense. It's not a physical sense, but it is important in writing the poem. Now that we have all these ingredients, let me give you an example of how they work. Suppose I wanted to describe the color of my blouse without ever using the color word in my poem. I might write something like this:

My blouse is the color
of midnight, of bats that flap

their wings on Halloween, of the
sleek limousine that cruises
down the street. My blouse is
a color that smells like smoke
drifting up from a campfire in
the woods and the rich, dark
smell of chocolate melting
in a pot. My blouse is a color
that tastes like licorice
and burned marshmallows and steak
cooked on a grill. My blouse
is a color that feels bumpy
and rough like coal or sticky
and bubbly like tar on a summer
day. My blouse is a color
that is frightening like stairs
that creak in the middle of the
night. It is a lonely color
like a sky without stars or a
room without lights.

T: What color was I describing?

S: Black.

T: Did you see the word pictures? Could you have drawn pictures of the images I used? Bats on Halloween? Smoke drifting up from a campfire? A sky without stars?

S: Yes.

T: Did you hear the five senses in the poem? Can you give me an example of one of the five senses?

S: You can *smell* smoke.

S: You can *see* a limousine on the street.

S: You can *feel* sticky tar.

S: You can *taste* chocolate.

T: Good. What about an emotion? Did I use an emotion to describe the color black?

S: Yes, you said it was frightening.

S: And lonely.

T: I can tell you were thinking and listening very well. So now, we begin to see how images—word pictures—work, and also how we use our five senses to create images. It's important to remember that this was *my* black poem. Your black poem would have been different because you would have had entirely different *memories* and *experiences* to draw on. Let's work on a poem together before we try our individual poems. Let's use the color red and try to describe it, through poetry, using all we now know about poetry: images, word pictures, feelings (red is the subject) and emotions; and let's try to bring our own personal memories and experiences into our images. Now. What does the color red look like?

S: An apple.

T: I can see that. An apple. Let's take that a bit further to find the word picture. Where is the apple? Is it in a bowl or on a tree?

S: On a tree.

T: On a tree. What time of year is it?

S: It's fall.

T: I see. Is the apple ripe?

S: Yes.

T: Tell me more about it. Describe this apple, this particular apple on this particular tree on this particular fall day. Describe it.

S: It's shiny.

S: It's round.

S: It's juicy.

T: Those are fine descriptive words which tell us something about the apple. Let's put them all together and see what we have:

Red is a ripe, juicy, shiny,
round apple on a tree
in fall.

What else does red look like?

S: A fire engine.

T: Ah ha! A fire engine. Describe it.

This illustrates the process of creating an image, and extending it through the use of adjectives. The teacher acts as the extractor of ideas by using a technique of quick, insistent questioning. This type of lesson needs to move quickly, and the teacher should be constantly aware of pacing. *Note also how the teacher adds weight to the student response by thoughtfully and reflectively repeating it, indicating to the class that he or she is a truly attentive and involved listener. In doing this, the teacher is modeling the listener role, so important to any class dynamic.*

S: It's long.

S: It's fast.

S: It's sleek.

T: Where is the fire engine? What is it doing?

S: Racing to a fire.

T: *Racing* is a good word choice. All right, let's put it together:

Red is a long, fast,
sleek fire engine racing
down the street to a fire.

T: What does red sound like? Is it loud or soft? Does it scream or whisper?

S: Red sounds like the siren on a fire engine.

T: I can almost hear it. What does the siren on a fire engine sound like? Find a word or combination of words that describes that very particular sound.

S: It's very loud.

S: It's also a very long sound. It goes on and on.

T: Good. What time of day do you think the siren sounds the loudest? Day or night?

S: It sounds loudest at night when everything else is quiet.

T: That's good, and that tells me you've listened to the sound of fire engines. Then our image or word picture for the sound of the color red might be:

Red is the loud, long sound
of a fire engine siren
at night.

T: A good device you can use to help yourself come up with images is to list words that go along with the five senses and emotions. List *see* words or *sound* words or *touch* words. How about the feel of the color red? Let's start out by listing *feel* words.

S: *Hot* is a *feel* word.

S: *Cold.*

S: *Sharp.*

S: *Sticky.*

S: *Bumpy*.

T: Good words. Which ones, or perhaps others we haven't mentioned yet, might best describe the feel of the color red?

S: *Hot.* Red is definitely a hot color.

T: Hot as what?

S: Hot as a fire.

S: Hot as an oven.

S: Hot as a fire in the woods on a cold winter's night.

T: Now we're beginning to see how to extend the image. Make it more visual, a better word picture. So then we might say that

Red feels hot as a fire
in the woods
on a cold
winter night.

T: How about some more *feel* images?

S: Red is hard as a rock.

T: What kind of a rock?

S: A volcanic rock.

T: Interesting! What else might red feel like?

S: It might be dry.

T: Dry as what?

S: Dry as a desert sun.

T: Yes! Good image! What does red smell like? What is the scent, the fragrance, the aroma of the color red?

S: Red smells like a rose.

T: Where is this particular rose? Your particular rose? In a vase by the window? In the garden? Where?

S: In the garden.

T: What time of year is it?

S: Springtime.

T: What time of day is it?

S: Morning.

T: Now put it all together and tell me what we have.

S: Red smells like a rose in the garden in the morning in the springtime.

T: It works! What else might red smell like?

S: Smoke.

S: Perfume.

T: Fine. Let's take one of these at a time and make them into word pictures. Let's do the perfume first. Tell me about it. Whose perfume is it? What does it smell like? What does the fragrance remind you of?

S: It's my mother's perfume, and it smells like flowers.

T: Red is the flowery smell of my mother's perfume. Good. Now, what about the smoke?

S: Red is the smell of smoke from a campfire in the woods on a snowy night.

T: Very effective string of words. That's putting it together! What does red taste like?

S: It tastes hot.

T: Hot as in temperature or spicy hot?

S: Spicy hot.

T: Like what?

S: Pizza.

S: Hot peppers.

S: Spaghetti sauce.

T: Put it together.

S: Red tastes spicy hot like pizza and hot peppers and spaghetti sauce.

T: What emotion does red make us feel? Happy? Sad? Lonely? Excited?

S: Red is brave.

T: Brave as what?

S: Brave as a soldier in war.

T: What else?

S: Happy. Red is happy as a birthday party or a clown.

T: That's really good imagery, and it's a good place to end our red poem. Let's go over it and see what we have:

RED

TO SEE
> Red is a ripe, juicy,
> shiny, round apple
> on a tree
> in fall.
>
> Red is a long, fast,
> sleek fire engine racing
> down the street
> to a fire.

TO HEAR
> Red is the loud,
> long sound
> of a fire engine siren
> at night.

TO FEEL
> Red feels hot
> as a fire
> in the woods
> on a cold
> winter night.

TO SMELL
> Red smells like a rose
> in the garden
> in the morning
> in the springtime.
>
> Red is the flowery smell
> of my mother's perfume and the smell
> of smoke from a campfire in the woods
> on a snowy night.

TO TASTE
> Red tastes spicy hot
> like pizza and hot
> peppers and spaghetti sauce.

EMOTION
> Red is brave
> as a solider
> in war and happy
> as a birthday party
> or a clown.

T: Good poem. Let's see if we can put together everything we know and everything we've experimented
with today and write our own color poems. I want
each one of you to choose a color (the subject) and,
using images and feelings and the five senses (plus

emotions), describe that color for me through free
verse poetry.

student poems[4]

WHITE

White feels like two people getting married.
White smells like peppermint candy
getting ready to be eaten.

White looks like clouds in the sky.
And white feels like white roses growing
in a garden.
White tastes like a white ice cream cone.
White feelings are comfortable.

                        A. D., 3rd grade

YELLOW

I look like the sun,
In the sky,
Dandelions, melting butter,
And corn on the cob.
I sound like someone whispering,
And fire cracking.
I sound like someone yelling.

I taste like corn on the cob,
Lemonade and butter.
I feel like sticky bubble gum,
Watery lemonade,
And a smooth pencil.
I smell like flowers,
Fire and sweet candy.

                J. T., 4th grade

PINK

I sound like
a small meek voice in the distance,
a little baby crying at night.
I sound like
anything young or a cat's meow.

I smell fresh but not crisp
I smell calm
I smell of talcum powder
and a clear river just at the harbor.

I look small
I'm pale and in the distance
I look light but not bouncy
I'm calm.

I feel smooth like
a baby's skin
I feel soft like
a new pillow
I feel like
a light colored fabric.

I taste almost like
nothing, like an old piece of paper,
a dried up piece of meat
I taste like
seltzer with the fizz all gone.

I taste calm.

                    K. R., 6th grade

[4]Throughout the text, student poetry appears exactly as it was written by students, without teacher correction or editing, unless otherwise indicated.

VIOLET

I smell like a violet
Blooming in the Spring.
I taste like grape juice.
I am the sound of an opera singer.
I feel sticky—like crushed grapes.

B. R., 2nd grade

LAVENDER IS A LILAC

Lavender is a soft lilac,
Sitting between the roses,
And the daisies.

It looks beautiful as
It shimmers in the sun.
The water drips down,
Off the petals
From last night's rain.

The lilac smells
Sweet and romantic,
Like a cool spring day.

It feels soft and weak,
As it opens wider and wider,
And it sounds so, so quiet,
As the wind blows past it.

As I look at it,
I get a taste in my mouth,
Like a big juicy grape.

F. M., 6th grade

YELLOW

Yellow is as bright as
the sun, it is as soft
as a feather and
it sounds like a
falling star, it
smells like a
flower, and tastes
like a lemon, it
shines all day,
and glimmers
in the weather.

M. K., 3rd grade

RED

I feel hot as sunrise
and soft as a bird's feathers
I taste like strawberries
and ketchup on hot dogs.
I smell like strawberry pie.
I sound like cardinals.
I look like a rose.

C. S., 3rd grade

PEACH

Peach reminds me of a cool summer morning
The shape of it is long and bold
    with many curves.
It is like a sculpture of an Oriental woman
    warming peach juice for her baby.
It smells of natural qualities
It sounds like fur brushing by a new leaf.
I believe it is very relaxing.
It tastes of peach cobbler
I feel peach as a child
    with a freckle on her nose
Sleeping under her mother's smile.

D. P., 5th grade

I AM THE COLOR GREEN
(GROUP POEM)

I smell like lemons and limes and juicy leaves
    and grass and ripe peaches.
I taste like bananas when they're not ripe
    and grapes and grass and papaya, salad and peas.
I am soft as cotton and comfortable as playing
    in the leaves, cold as ice, squishy as peas.
I am the color of the Hulk
    and leaves in the spring and grass in the summer,
    dinosaurs, apples, caterpillars.
My voice is the sound of grass swishing in the air,
    wind blowing very hard through the trees.

                        Class Poem, 3rd grade

SUMMARY: POETRY

In this introductory poetry lesson, we provided some simple writing tools for our students. These tools enabled them to explore new language possibilities. By asking them to enter an arena that had no definitive borders, no hard-and-fast rules for right and wrong, we asked them to take new, and perhaps, uncomfortable risks. Praise, encouragement, and emphasis on the positive were the essentials.

Each group of students (on any given day) generates its own very personal energy source. It is this energy, this spontaneity and sense of sharing, that cannot be captured in print. What is lacking is the laughter, the giggles, the de*light* in students' eyes when confronted with the wonder of words (their own and others'). The exhilaration, exuberance, and sense of accomplishment that comes from the metamorphosis of red into an apple, an apple into a bloody moon, and the moon into an angel's pillow, is memorable. Each creative strand becomes a part of a fabric that is woven of words, conceived joyously one at a time.

But the real moment of truth is the time of sharing. The poem, personal and personified, is given as a gift and, more often than not, accepted in the same spirit. The enthusiasm with which the poems are read and greeted readies the group for further word–music–movement exploration.

MOVEMENT: THE COLOR POEM

While imagery seems to lead naturally to a richer vocabulary and lends itself to the creation of the poem, *movement* also provides a natural starting place, both for teacher and for student. Because movement does not have to be learned, it is a good first way to extend the poem beyond the page.

Analyzing some of the preceding poems with the kind of vision mentioned earlier, we first find the common denominator, color. The *names* of colors, in and of themselves, provide a possible beginning for group movement exploration and a necessary first flexing of movement imagination which gives students the confidence and skills to apply to their own creations.

For example, the *onomatopoeic*[5] qualities of the word *pink* express a light, quick sound in the mouth which might be equated in movement with the flick of the hand, the toss of the head. In its brevity it requires *quickness* and *lightness*. Two of the three possible elements of movement are already evident:

Time—how long a movement takes

Weight—the light or heavy quality of that movement

Space—where in space the movement happens: high, low, behind, under, through, around, in opposition.

Take another word—*red*. *Red* might be defined as a word in transit—powerful, bright, possibly increasing in speed as it goes, ending with an explosion. *Brown* suggests a dark quality—and thus might call for a heavy, ponderous accompanying movement. *White* has air in its body, and glides in the mouth as it would in space, except for the little catch at the word's end which brings it to a delicate stop. All these sounds and the sounds of thousands of other words can become the reason for first explorations in movement.

While the sounds of the color words dictate the time and weight of the movement, it is necessary for the beginning explorer to have the teacher suggest *which* body parts to use, and *where* to place the movements in space. It works well to start the group exploring any movement from seated positions (floor or chairs), moving gradually to an upright position, and finally involving forward movement (locomotion). This sequence gives the student a greater sense of security in what may feel like a new experience, and also gives the teacher time to isolate the task, making refinement possible for both. When choreographed, these simple movements can lead to surprising artistic results.

SAMPLE LESSON:
MOVEMENT

Introducing new
concepts in ways that

T: You've recently created some wonderful color poems. Let's explore these colors in yet another way. In

---

[5]Onomatopoeia: "the coining of use of words that imitate the sound of a thing: . . . also refers to sound symbolism which does not approximate a precise echo, but is strongly suggestive of the thing suggested." Babette Deutsch, *Poetry Handbook: A Dictionary of Terms*. Barnes & Noble, 1957.

demand involvement and thought by students is always desirable. Here, it becomes a guessing game of how to link the abstract movement with the sound of a color. The teacher had the particular color red in mind, but accepted the related colors offered as possibilities.

Modeling first, asking the class to try the demonstrated movement, then moving to students' own ideas provides a sure and comfortable framework. Asking students to model other student ideas is another technique for showcasing originality and giving weight and credence to student input.

Starting a movement from a stationary spot is a way to provide students with a comfortably restricted area. It also ensures that the inexperienced or overly exuberant student will be more likely to stay on task and not take the lesson in an unwanted direction.

More difficult to control and to accomplish with merit

a moment I'm going to communicate to you in the language I would like us to use. I'll say the name of a color in this new language. See if you can guess the color *and* the new language. [T makes strong, upward motions, first with one fist, then the other.] First, can anyone guess the language?

S: Movement.

T: Right . . . a language we use to communicate with much of the time, right along with words and facial expressions. Anyone know the color I was moving?

S: Probably yellow.

S: I think orange.

T: You were both on the right track with your bright colors . . . I was thinking of red. From your seats, would you all make my motions as you say the word *red* . . . say the *r* very strongly . . . right . . . thrust up and outward . . . do it as often as you wish but say the word with each motion. Stop when you feel your red piece is ended. Is there any other way we could move the word *red?*

S: You could sort of twist your body and bring your arms around . . .

T: Would you stand and show us what you mean? . . . Could everyone stand and copy Neal's motion when I say *begin?* Each time you say the word *red,* you are going to accompany it with a strong twisting motion. . . . *Begin.* Now we have two ways to move *red.* Could anyone think of a way to move *red* which would take us into the room—moving forward?

S: You could take a slow step and raise your knee on the *r*—then on the end of the word stamp your leg down.

T: Demonstrate it please. We'll watch. Class, was this a strong or a weak motion? Yes . . . it almost had a pressing quality, and had great weight behind its slowness. Try pressing the word *red* with your arms outward this time . . . upward . . . [say the word each time] . . . a harder one—press your back into space . . . and stop. I liked your concentration.

You've all moved *red* in three ways—thrusting, twisting, and pressing it in all directions. Could you now combine these three versions into one movement

is movement which moves into the room (i.e., locomotion), and thus it should follow those movement tasks which are static.

The insistence for concentration is a

piece called "Red," accompanying your own movements with your voice throughout? Let's let half the room demonstrate while the other half observes. Observers be ready to tell us who had good concentration, who had motions with the greatest variety, who used their space in an interesting way (high, low, middle), who connected the movements into a convincing whole. Performing group, begin, and freeze when you are finished.

priori *when working with* all *levels of children—if the task does not involve vocal sound, the movements should be done in concentrated silence. Recognition of those children who can accomplish a task with a kind of single-mindedness and unawareness of the group is one way of reinforcing these goals and ensuring a more interesting movement result.*

At the bottom of page 23, the teacher has summed up what has been observed in the student movements and

T: Who saw someone whose movement they liked?

S: Neal looked good. I liked his concentration.

T: That's very important in being convincing in movement. What else?

S: I liked the way Betty went from one version to the next and sort of connected it into one idea. I liked when she kneeled down.

T: Good. A movement can start from any position: standing, sitting, kneeling.

S: I liked the way Bob said the word as he moved. He really looked in movement like his color sounded.

T: Your comments will help the next group! Switch roles please. [Other half of the group explores and is critiqued in a positive way by peers (e.g., "what did you like about . . .)]

T: Before we try another color, let's see what we've learned so far:
— That movement can begin with any part of the body, from any position, and happen in any part of space possible.
— That the word *red* called for a heavy, pressing kind of movement quality and was slow.

labeled them using movement vocabulary. These words now become a handle for both student and teacher, for future movement use and analysis.

In the situation of peer evaluation, it is the teacher who defines the parameters wherein the discussion will take place (exhibiting a strong teacher presence). These margins delineate the goals of the exercise, as well as suggest what qualities the observing group should be looking for. This tactic can successfully sidestep any negative-comment tendencies of the group or individuals, and again make the experimental zone a safe haven for trying.

The summation of any task in effect headlines for students those salient bits which are to be remembered— and hopefully reapplied.

— That all movement has three qualities: time, weight, and length (duration).

With that information, let's explore another color: pink. Sit down, please. As I say the color randomly, *think* how the word makes you *feel* like moving . . . only move mentally. Now from your seats, will you *show* me what you imagined, as I say the word. If I'm silent, you're to be without motion. If my voice is high, show me in space where that would be:

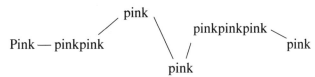

I enjoyed watching your responses! I saw quite different movements this time . . . flicks, quick light motions. Antionette, you moved your shoulders quickly . . . Rob, you moved disjointedly, like a robot. All your movements reflected the weight and time of the word *pink*. Good. Everyone please stand and let's practice this quick flicking with all parts of the body. Let's see you flick . . . with your nose. Flick . . . with your hips . . . one knee . . . one foot . . . your hands . . . a shoulder . . . flick with your hands *and* your head! *That's* interesting. Instead of *saying* the word *pink* this time, I wonder if we could find a sound in this classroom which sounds light and . . . pink. [T taps metal cabinet with ruler] . . . Pink sound?

S: How about this? [Runs pencil up spiral back of notebook]

S: I have a better one—the bell on your desk!

T: [Playing bell] Do the rest of you like that sound for pink? Then that's the way it will be. As I play the bell, I'll suggest body parts and places in space in which to move.

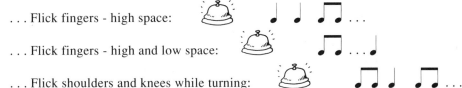

This time, can you make up—*improvise*—a flick piece with any body parts of your choice—but always look in the direction of your movement. (Your eyes are like a flashlight that illuminates your movement.) Excellent. That little trick of looking in the direction you are moving makes your improvisation look very convincing. It made me want to look at you. Shall we divide up the class again and watch each other? Which student would like to play the bell? Remember, this time it is the *bell* which is the leader of your movement, so you will have to listen carefully to know when to move. Be ready to say what you liked!

♩ = bell sound

All of this lesson is geared toward building experiences in actual movement, and in labeling what is being done—for later, more sophisticated application within the color poetry itself. It is, if you will, a playing with the elements of an idea before putting it into a more complex structure. To have started with the color poem might have been to invite shallow and tentative results,

T: Pink got us into movement qualities which are light and fast—these are named flick and dab. Let's try the word *brown,* and this time I would like you to choose movement qualities from this list that you think best express brown. [T lists on board.][6]

SLASH, PRESS, PUNCH, GLIDE,
WRING, FLOAT, FLICK, DAB.

S: I think *brown* has to have a slower movement, so I choose *glide.*

S: I think *glide* is too light for brown . . . I pick a slow, heavy one: *press.*

[6]Rudolph Laban, *Modern Educational Dance,* MacDonald & Evans, Ltd., London, England, 1963.

because that task could have been overwhelming. Thus, it is helpful for students first to isolate elements, regardless of what they are, before fixing them into a more involved form.

T: Other ideas?

S: Well . . . it's definitely not flick . . . what about *wring*? Is that like *twist*?

T: Exactly—imagine your whole body is a large, wet towel which you are wringing out—takes a heavy, weighted movement and lots of time to get the water out. Then most of you agree with *press, wring,* and possibly *glide?* Fine. Will you divide into two groups, five people each of pink and five brown—pinks over by the windows, browns near the door. I have a picture I would like you to move. Can you tell what will happen as you study this drawing?

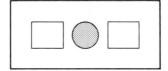

Which shape do you feel represents pink best? Then this means the pink group will begin, followed by the brown group, resuming (and concluding) with the pinks. Will the groups ever be moving at the same time?

Who would like to play the bell sound for the pink group? Browns, yours will be a vocal sound—let me hear you say BROWWWNNNNN, and make it sound like the color it is. Fine. Harry, you are the leader of the brown group—when Harry starts, pinks stop. Ready to do a color movement piece in A-B-A form? Begin. [Critique for concentration, interaction of group, letting eyes move in the direction of the gesture, using space in a varied and interesting way, using parts of the body in a varied way.]

This next color will take us to A. D.'s poem called, "White." Say the word *white* and feel it in your mouth. It has air at the front end, and a *t* stop sign at the end . . . and in the middle? Show me the middle. Yes . . . a long glide motion does nicely. We may then need to combine some movement qualities to meet the needs of *white*. Try *dab . . . glide . . . flick.* Repeat this and on the *glide,* move forward in the room. Nicely done. Find a new starting position for the word *white* . . . yes, it could certainly be twisted with arms extended . . . and I see you want to start the word from low space. All these ideas are equally good. You've shown me a good beginning vocabulary of movement, so I think we are ready to try A. D.'s poem. Read it to yourself from the board. May I hear some ideas about how we might move her first line, "White feels like two people getting married"?

S: We could have a few people move the word *white* and let others say the part about getting married.

T: Yes, and you're controlling your giggles very well. How many people do you think should be in each group?

S: Let everybody except two people do *white* and freeze their last movement, while the two getting married say and move their part.

T: Volunteers for the couple? Volunteer for the *white* leader who will breathe just before beginning? The class will watch and listen for that breath and thus know when to start. Will you lead, Joe? Breathe a beginning for us and see if the group can come in wordlessly with you. Nice leading—your group came in beautifully! Can the two people getting married invent a movement which suggests they like each other? No? Anyone suggest something for them?

S: They only have a short line and not much time, so maybe they could just raise their arms into an arch.

T: Good point. Please try it so far. Look to your breathing leader to know when to start . . . speak as you move . . . ready? [Group tries first line]

That was the idea. Let's go on further. There's another *white* at the second line: "White smells like peppermint candy getting ready to be eaten." Should the larger group do this? Divide off? Have a solo? What do you suggest?

S: I think the whole group should do *white* again and have a solo on the candy.

T: Right. Volunteer for the solo? Perhaps you can think of a shape of a peppermint candy in a state of readiness, and use that as your movement when you say your line. Let's all try it from the beginning . . . married couple ready? Candy? Listen for the breath from your leader. Well done. Going on . . . "White feels like clouds in the sky." Any movement ideas for that line?

S: We could have some separate clouds like we had the candy and the couple.

T: If we do that, what movement quality do you recommend . . . is it the same glide for *white* or is it a press/float/dab . . . what does the key word *cloud* suggest to you, and where should the movement take place?

S: I think the movement should be a light one. A float maybe. And since it's sky, we should use high space.

T: Would you all try this idea of the larger group again saying *white,* then completing the line with a float on "looks like clouds in the sky?" Begin. It's looking nice. Let's continue. What are the key words in the next line, "And white feels like white roses growing in a garden"?

S: Roses.

T: Another?

S: Growing.

T: Would you all try to move a "growing rose" please . . . where will you begin in space? Right . . . low, so you have somewhere to grow. Be aware of how you are moving, sensing in your muscles the feeling of this movement. Begin. Most of you floated slowly, upward. Some of you also pressed your flower open, which was effective. Will the whole *white* group perform this?

S: I think three people should be roses.

T: Three volunteers please? Let's now get the couple, the candy, and the rose people placed in a way that makes the visual arrangement of our movement piece look interesting. Any suggestions?

S: The solo people should be off to the side.

T: Agreed? Let's then try to go from the beginning. Give me a piece of quiet, and when the sound paper is blank, your leader will breathe the lead breath. It's beginning to look convincing, and we're almost through . . . ready?

That was good so far. Our movements have been

mostly slow and light . . . but here comes a ''white ice cream cone'' and those words speak something different. Can the whole group find a way to move ''white ice cream cone'' *as a floor pattern* . . . making the shape of the object on the floor as you move it in space? I saw some people moved forward . . . a few to the side . . . one person moved very lightly side to side, hopscotching the cone shape . . . I especially liked that because it changed the speed of the movements we have been moving and added *contrast*. Variety is good. Consider now the last line of A. D.'s poem: ''white feelings are comfortable.'' Ideas please?

S: I think only a few people should do the ice cream part so we can all do the last line.

S: I do too.

T: OK. Let's try it. Three volunteers for the side-to-side ice cream cone movers. What, then, will the whole group do to look comfortable?

S: Lie down.

T: I know you were being funny—but that's really not such a bad idea. What if we didn't go clear to the floor, but got into comfortable low shapes? Everyone . . . show me a comfortable shape . . . I see people with their elbows up on each other's shoulders, leaning, slouching. OK . . . we'll try these, but can you *get* to these positions in a slow-motion float? As you say ''white feelings'' from this point on, move as slowly as you can until you come to the words *are . . . com . . . for . . . table,''* and be ready to hold your final pose (freeze). You should relate to each other as if a photographer placed you for this final picture.

S: Can I end up kneeling?

T: Certainly. In fact, why don't we have about three of you end up in a kneeling position—levels are always more interesting than everyone being the same height. Can you end with your elbow on your knee and fist on your chin? And would one of you end up in a delicious stretch, using your high space? This variety should look good. Hold the final picture for three slow counts. Let's just practice the ending. Remember—*everyone* is doing the last line. Ready?

Speak the words of the last line very slowly . . .
*White . . . feelings . . . are . . . com . . . for . . .
table* " (1-2-3) . . . and relax. Bravo. Shall we take it
from the top? A. D., we are honored to be celebrating
your choice poem in movement, and we will try to do
it as beautifully as you wrote it!

S: If it's good, can we do it for the class across the hall?

WHITE

White feels like two people getting married
White smells like peppermint candy
    getting ready to be eaten,
White looks like clouds in the sky.
And white feels like white roses growing
    in a garden.
White tastes like a white ice cream cone.
White feelings are comfortable.

                A. D.

SUMMARY: MOVEMENT

Successful movement lessons have some givens:

— A room or space big enough for movement exploration

— Clearly defined movement tasks for exploration with time for trial and mutual reflection

— Clear signals on how to begin and end movement efforts

— Reinforcement of the need for concentration on the task at hand

— A trusting, accepting class atmosphere *consciously nurtured by the teacher,* where risk is comfortable and critiquing always positive by both students and teacher

— A teacher willing to model movements occasionally and explore along with students

— A nonthreatening lesson progression for the inexperienced which moves from small movements at the lesson's beginning and later spirals to more complex tasks which use the whole body, space, and locomotion

— A process which is accomplished by a combination of the students' improvised ideas and suggestions, joined with light input and gentle shaping by the teacher

— Movement lessons accomplished either with provided sound, self-sound, or in silence, *but always without conversation.*

Any introductory movement lesson, whether taught early in the "working of the word" or later, serves as an invaluable tool for subsequent movement involvement with poetry. Whatever time is taken isolating qualities and playing with the ideas of time, weight, and space will pay enormous dividends in helping children adapt movement to their own poetry. Nor is this kind of specific movement focus limited to older children—in shorter working spans, young children benefit just as much from analyzing movement qualities, along with the less abstract kinds of movement more commonly associated with the young.

Movement can be an important keystone to all your creative word works. Its sources are many: vocal sounds, the sounds of words,[7] word meanings, musical instruments or "found sounds" (see Chapter 4) along with the whole area of visual motivation which is not covered in this book: graphics, paintings, children's art works, or combinations of aural and visual stimuli.

Movement helps bring "shape to joy, . . . and release to tension."[8]

[7]Barbara Mettler, *Materials of Dance as a Creative Art Activity,* Mettler Studios Publication, Tucson, Ariz., 1960.

[8]H. Ginott, *Between Teacher and Child,* Macmillan, 1972.

chapter 2

the feeling poem

EMOTIONAL INPUT THROUGH ALLITERATION AND ONOMATOPOEIA: THE FEELING POEM

Poetry speaks of our lives, of the holy and humdrum aspects of our lives. And although some poems may elude us, there are those that can make us gasp with recognition, that can make us say, "Yes, that's me." And, "Yes, oh, yes, that's how it feels." And, "Yes, that's what happened."

> For poetry knows our black despair . . .
> And poetry knows our lush, untamed exuberance . . .
> And poetry knows we never recover from love . . .
> And poetry knows how we sometimes recover.

> Judith Viorst,
> "Some Simple Praise for the Poetic
> Response to Life"[1]

We have explored poetic expression through utilization of sensory perception and imagery, and are now ready to evoke emotional input through "the feeling poem." During this lesson, students will be asked to identify feelings and internalize them for the sake of the poem. Because feelings cause us to react with intensity, students may need something in addition to words with which to express themselves. This lesson, therefore, provides a comfortable opening for the introduction of poetic devices such as *alliteration* and *onomatopoeia*. By utilizing sounds of words and series of sounds to help intensify and dramatize the

---

[1]Copyright © 1982 by Judith Viorst. Originally appeared in *Redbook*.

poetic impact of the feeling, students achieve a greater understanding of the relationship between the poem and its emotional effect (on their classmates). This search for "sound" words (onomatopoeia) also helps them to identify more clearly for themselves exactly what it is they are trying to express. By asking them, as well, to call on their own memories and experiences (the source of feelings) for their images, we afford them the opportunity to deal honestly and intimately with their own emotions.

SAMPLE LESSON: POETRY

In this instance the teacher is relying on the repetition of ideas and concepts to make them familiar to the students, and easily accessible as a resource. This repetitive beginning to the lesson acts, as well, as a platform from which to reach for the next plateau *in the sequence of poetry exploration. Sequential teaching has the advantage of nurturing itself and expanding the learning process in a natural and ever-widening spiral.*

T: In our first poetry lesson, we learned how to create images (word pictures). We used our five senses when writing a poem. In fact, if you remember (and I'm sure you do) we put together a "poetry recipe" and discussed the ingredients that go into "making" a poem. Would someone like to remind us what those ingredients are?

S: Images and word pictures are the first ingredients, and feelings were the second, and the subject was the third.

T: That's right. So we know that if we want to write a poem we need to use images/word pictures; and we practiced using word pictures by writing what kind of a poem?

S: A color poem.

T: That's right. A color poem. And along with our images/word pictures, what else did we use in writing that poem?

S: The five senses.

T: Yes, the five senses. How things *look* to us, *sound* to us, *taste* to us, *smell* to us, *feel* to us. And what "sense" did we add to the five senses—does anyone remember?

S: Our emotions. How we feel inside about things.

T: That's correct, and I'm especially glad that you remembered because today's poem is going to be dealing with that subject. Feelings are the subject of today's poem. What exactly are feelings?

S: Feelings are stuff going on inside you.

T: What kind of stuff?

S: Good stuff, bad stuff. That kind of stuff.

T: I guess *stuff* is kind of a vague word. Not much of a word picture. Let's see if we can zero in on *stuff* and come up with some examples. What are some feeling words?

S: *Happy* is a feeling word. So is *sad*.

T: That's the idea. Let's see how many "feeling" words we can come up with and let's list them on the board. More "feeling" words, please.

S: Excited.

S: Angry.

S: Furious.

S: Lonely.

S: Scared.

S: Brave.

S: Proud.

S: Bored.

The teacher needs to know when to jump in and take control by saying, in essence, "Enough is enough." To allow the students to continue offering feeling words would be to threaten the pacing of the lesson, and thereby weaken the structure.

T: I think it's becoming obvious to us that there are many "feeling" words, and we could probably go on thinking them up all day. In our first lesson we talked about the fact that "feelings" come from memories and experiences. Do you remember the example we used?

By setting up a concrete example *through imagery (using memories and experiences), the teacher is demonstrating how to* internalize *the subject that will ultimately become the poem. While the teacher example is an*

S: We talked about two people who go to the beach and each one has a very different experience. One person has a good experience, and one has a bad experience.

T: That's right . . . and what did we say that would mean in terms of the kind of poem they would write about the beach? What kinds of images would their poems have?

S: The person with the good experience would have happy images, and the person with the bad experience would have unhappy images.

T: That's exactly right. Therefore, when we write our

invention, it suggests that the students should reach within themselves for a "real" response, while at the same time giving students a form to follow and helping them to articulate their own memories and experiences through imagery.

We have examples again of teacher modeling, and reinforcement of student responses by providing immediate, positive feedback. This kind of enthusiastic teacher response encourages students to vocalize in the discussion and makes learning playful, giving students an opportunity to feel good about their contributions.

feeling poems today and we draw on our own memories and experiences, those memories and experiences will really decide for us whether or not our images will be joyful ones, sad ones, moody ones, or humorous ones. So it is especially important today for us to get in touch not only with our feelings, but with specific feelings about specific moments in our lives. From those very personal memories we will be creating poems that are uniquely our own . . . in much the same way that our fingerprints are uniquely our own. No one has the same set of fingerprints that you have, and no one has the same sets of memories and experiences that you have. So when you honestly bring your own memories and experiences, through imagery/word pictures, into your poem, you create something that no one but you could have created. You also give us—your classmates, and those people you will choose to share your poem with—a very real and a very meaningful insight into the person you are.

This is a very good place for us to talk a little bit about a couple of devices that we use in poetry to make our poems more dramatic, to enhance not only the imagery, but the meaning as well. They also, happily, add a rhythmic and musical quality to our poems. The two devices I'm talking about are alliteration and (a long, funny-sounding word) onomatopoeia. Has anybody ever heard either one of those words before?

S: No.

T: I think if you had heard onomatopoeia before, you probably would have remembered it. It means, simply, words that sound like, or are imitations of, the sounds they are describing . . . words like *buzz, hum, crackle, roar, rage, boom.* Do you get the idea? Could you give me some examples of onomatopoeia?

S: How about chuckle?

T: Yes indeed. I think that's a great one. Some more, please.

S: Screech.

S: Scratch.

S: Gurgle.

S: Burp.

At this point in the lesson, the teacher is simultaneously attempting to broaden the pleasure of words and to give students another "choice source" for selecting words that will enhance and enrich their poems.

S: Groan.

T: Those are all marvelous words, and I wonder if we say them again, this time trying to make them sound like what they are describing, if we won't get an even better idea of what onomatopoeia is all about. Let's say the words again and try to be dramatic about it. OK. Let's go.

CLASS: Screeeeeeeeech. Scraatch. Guuuuuuurgle. Buuuurp. Groooan.

T: That's the idea. Those are words that feel good in your mouth. Don't you agree? They enable us to create very strong and very meaningful images. The other word or device that I mentioned was alliteration. Alliteration is simply the repetition of the same initial sound or beginning letter. For example: The Silent Sun Set Slowly. How about giving me an example of alliteration?

S: The Grey Ghost Gurgled Gleefully.

T: A special pat on the back for using what? What did Evan just use along with alliteration?

S: He used *gurgled,* which is an example of onomatopoeia.

T: Right! And for that he deserves a bonus. How about letting Evan be the first to share his feeling poem today? Now see if we can, using *everything* we now know about poetry, do a group feeling poem. Let's do a happy poem. What does happiness look like? (Remember please, alliteration, onomatopoeia, word pictures/images, and certainly we want to put *feelings* into our feeling poem.)

S: Happiness looks like a Big, Beautiful, Breathtaking Butterfly.

T: Wonderful. What else does it look like?

S: Happiness looks like a Fragile Flower Fluttering in the wispy wind.

T: You are all Exceedingly Expert Example givers. What does happiness sound like?

S: Happiness sounds like the Chittering, Chirping and Chuckling of birds in the summer time.

S: Happiness sounds like Big, Booming Bells.

While these are examples of teacher modeling, more importantly they are examples of a teacher getting involved in the process on the same level as the students. This is done subtly

*without calling
attention to the fact
that the teacher has
chosen to participate in
the exercise, and in the
process of doing this,
the teacher takes risks
and becomes
vulnerable along with
the student. There is
also a lessening of the
usual distance which
separates teacher from
student.*

*In this exchange, the
teacher relinquishes
some of the decision
making to the class,
relying on leaders to
point the way, but
leaving the matter
undecided. This acts as
further reinforcement
for the concept that
there will be no
judgment here. That
the teacher is indeed a
filter for ideas, letting
them flow through him
or her, back to the
group. Students are
allowed to have some
control over the
direction the lesson will
take.*

*This poem is a
compilation of
individual responses
(thus becoming a group*

T: Fantastic. What does it smell like? And remember, let's try to personalize our images. Remember to draw on your own memories and experiences. The smell of happiness is . . .?

S: Christmas Candy Canes.

S: My Mother's Marvelous Muffins.

T: Those are wonderfully, workable images. What does happiness taste like?

S: Sunday Supper.

S: Tasty Turkey on the Thanksgiving Table.

T: More marvelous images. What does happiness feel like?

S: Happiness is as Soft as my baby Sister's Skin.

T: I love that one. How about another?

S: Happiness Feels Fluffy as a kitten's Fur. Is *fluffy* an example of onomatopoeia?

T: What do you all think? Let's say the word aloud together and let's say it in a dramatic sort of way. Together now . . .

CLASS: Fluffffffy.

T: What do you think?

S: I think it does, because it sounds like something soft.

S: I don't think so, because it doesn't sound as much like what it's describing as the word *gurgle* sounds like gurgling.

T: It's good to have a difference of opinion. It points out that poetry is not set in stone, something that is either right or wrong, but rather a poem is something that is creative and personal and, by its very definition, has a strong emotional impact on the reader. It also points out to us that any single poem may mean different things to different people, because the reader brings something of himself or herself to the poem . . . and that's the way it should be. Let's remain undecided about fluffy, and look at our happy poem.

HAPPINESS IS

Happiness looks like a big, beautiful
butterfly and like a fragile flower
fluttering in the wispy wind.

poem). The creation of this poem represents the immediate coalescing of individual ideas into a finished product.

This is an important end result because it is a model for what the students are about to be asked to do (write their own poems); it gives added meaning to what they have been doing by collecting the disparate images and turning them into a finished product; and it is simply good teaching to demonstrate how a variety of disparate ideas can be fashioned into a complete and excellent piece of work.

Happiness sounds like the "chittering," chirping and chuckling of birds in the summer time and like big, booming bells.

Happiness smells like Christmas candy canes and my mother's marvelous muffins.

Happiness tastes like Sunday supper and tasty turkey on the Thanksgiving table.

Happiness is as soft as my baby sister's skin and feels fluffy as a kitten's fur.

T: That is really a fine poem! It contains all of the elements that we have been talking about and gives a very clear picture of what happiness is to us, in this class, on this day. Finally, I would like to finish with an image that deals with the emotion itself. For example: Happiness is my birthday party—or a hard hug from my marvelous mom, or the song we sing softly in church on Sunday. What I want is something personal, something that expresses your very own definition of the *feeling* happiness. Someone, please?

S: Happiness is the Hard, High Home run I Hit in my Little League game.

T: That's the idea. Another one, please.

S: Happiness is the Soft, Slippery, Sweet-Smelling Sheets on my bed when I crawl into it on a Stormy, Snowy, winter night.

S: Happiness is the Feeling of Finding no F on your report card.

T: Those are exactly what I was looking for. I think we're ready to move on to today's assignment. I want you to choose a feeling, one of the ones we've listed on the board, or one of your own, and write a poem using all that you know about poetry: images/word pictures, feeling (putting yourself into the poem through memories and experiences), the five senses, and onomatopoeia and alliteration when you feel it will contribute to the intensity and the emotional impact of your poem. If there are no questions, let's begin writing.

_____ **student poems** _____

TRAPPED

When I go to school I feel
trapped, like a frightened fish
out of water, gasping.
I'm always thinking of getting
out running leaving all my
worries behind, like a baby bird
in flight, winging over vast fields,
looking for a place to get away.
When the last bell rings, I
feel like someone is opening
the door, and I'm flying out.

> Anon., 4th grade

FEELINGS

I feel like a dog sleeping in the sun,
I feel as clumsy as a clown,
I feel like a mudpuddle,
    To tell you the truth I feel
        HORRIBLE.

> R. P., 4th grade

THE BLACK STREAM

A deep, lonely, black colored stream of
Water dripping causing circles to flow.
The reflection staring you in the face
Like death staring at an old man.

Everything is calm
Yet too calm to be calm
The black trees surrounding you
As if you were caged in
Yet let free to go.

Animals surrounding you,
Staring at you
Acting scared but not
Noises endlessly chirping
As if a million miles away
Yet still a few feet away.

The water rushing against
the rocks as if fighting each other
but at the point of going crazy
daybreak appears relieved now of
the darkness and loneliness
of the Black Stream.

> E. S., 5th grade

EXCITED

Excited is
as crunchy as
a girl playing
in the leaves in
Autumn. It is as beautiful
as a pumpkin
with a flower
on its stem,
as juicy as a sloppy,
gooshy piece of watermelon
right out of the garden.
It is a balloon popping
right out of your hand.
As wiggly as a person
dancing in a special
dance.
It is as special as
your mom giving you
a kiss before bed.

           M. K., 3rd grade

DEATH: AFRAID

Death—the beginning
or end, floating, floating
in black like a long, long
hallway with no end to
it, it goes on and on with
nothing to stop you. Stars
like fire in the night. You
fall in black, but you don't
stop because there is no end.

           R. P., 5th grade

BRAVE

Brave is
A tiger and lion
Growling and fighting
On a misty night.
A man
Going into
A dark and gloomy
Cave,
A creepy, crawly
Crab on a great beach,
Or linguini
For an
Easter dinner,
As fast as
A fish of
The sea,
A polar bear growling
As loud as an ocean
breeze.
BRAVE IS A DARK COLOR.

           J. A., 3rd grade

HAPPY

Happy looks like a rose from a bush.
Happy looks like someone smiling
and singing a song.

Happy sounds like two people talking
and a band playing in the street.

Happy feels like me roller skating
in the street and like me at my
aunt's house swimming.

Happy tastes like sweet candy hearts.
Happy tastes like fresh pancakes.

Happy smells like sweet maple syrup and
a sweet plum.

           B. P., 3rd grade

CLOSING IN

I feel like a bird flying in a
dark forest.
The path that I have chosen
is leading to a black bottomless pit.
I call for help, but no one answers.
I can see the arrows, pointing many
different directions.
When I walk, I can't go anywhere.
When I run, I bump into a wall.
I'm living in a box with not
enough air.
I have to climb out, before it's
too late.

L. K., 6th grade

WHAT AM I?

I am the soft sound
of a faint foghorn
and a boat whistle.

I sound like the city
when all the cars honk—
honk—honk
their horns and the trains
whizz and rattle by.

I look like a rotten
apple, brown and bruised,
and taste like beans, burned
burgers and broccoli.

I feel like "oooozy" tar
and I smell like peppers
and onions.

What am I?
ANGRY!

C. P., 6th grade

HAPPINESS

I am like children playing in an open field,
and dogs and cats
licking people's hands and fingers,
and when you go on a trip to
see old friends and relatives,
and when you go to the beach.

Children laughing and eating candy
and sweet things,
and like beautiful butterflies landing on
stumps of trees,
and birds chirping when they fly over tree tops,
and sweet sticky taffy being stretched,
and people having a good time at the park.

Seeing, and petting animals at the zoo,
eating popcorn with butter,
and flying a kite on a cool day,
and petting your dog, and seeing your
Grandma and Grandpa.

French toast with syrup and melted butter,
flying in a balloon high over the clouds,
roses and hot pretzels, and cotton candy.
Luscious lollypops in your mouth,
and sweet sticky bubble gum crackling
as you blow bubbles,
steak and candy apples,
and melted butter with pancakes
and sweet candies.

B. T., 5th grade

HAPPINESS

Happiness is a smile
Happiness is a birthday present
Happiness is hearing a humming bird hum,
Happiness tastes like a ripe cherry
Happiness smells like a rose
Happiness feels like a smooth piece
of paper and a
rose petal.

W. S., 3rd grade

ANGER

You hear people,
yelling at you,
running at you,
with mad faces,
with weapons.

It tastes like,
a bad bitter lime.

It feels like,
gravel and rough red dirt.

It smells like
smoke and gas,
from an exhaust pipe.

                    E. G., 3rd grade

THE NAG

There's somebody in this
classroom that is like a coyote
always howling. He is like
a knife at somebody's back. Everyday it's
like your hands are being frostbitten.
He nags you like a real estate salesman
and he never stops. He's like a bull
running rampant in the city. Every time
he speaks it's like a whip being "slayed"
on a horse. I think of him as an ice storm,
but I don't know what everyone else
thinks, because I have got the worst
of him.

                    F. K., 5th grade

SUMMARY: POETRY

In reading the students' poems, we are aware that not all of them use all the elements that have been discussed. Still, something of great importance has been used, and that is honest, introspective reflection. There is a sense of self in the poems that goes beneath the surface to illuminate unexplored depths. Within the safe, yet limitless, boundaries of the poem, students explore anger, fear, frustration, death, and loneliness, and linger with a dawning sense of wonder over the delights of love, friendship, and happiness. Without being directed, they seem naturally to move themselves into the poem (the feeling) that will be the most satisfying for them to explore.

At the conclusion of the lesson and the first presentation of their poems to their classmates, I generally ask students, "When is a good time to write a poem? What is a good emotion to write about?" In most cases, having experienced the cathartic effects of exploring their own emotions, they respond, "*All* the time! *All* emotions!"

SPEECH AND RHYTHM: THE FEELING POEM

Previously, we focused on movement, where the student's word choices prompted a variety of physical responses. In this chapter we'll analyze some of the original poems for *speech* and *rhythm-play* possibilities.

Speech and rhythm are as naturally elemental as movement. They are areas where children are at home, because it is where they *are:* Rhythmic repetition of words, of body movement, is common and comfortable. Using only the sounds and words that can be created with our mouths, and claps, leg slaps, finger clicks, stamps, facial taps, etc. (body percussion), plus the idea of pulse or heartbeat, a simple foundation can be laid on which countless variations can rest and with which we can further "work the word."

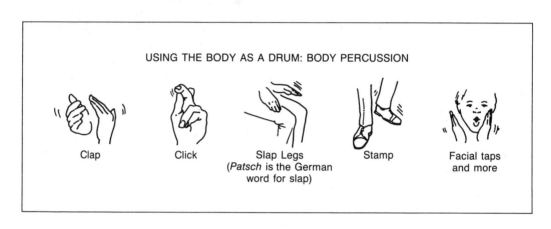

Pulse, sometimes called the heartbeat, is a constant beat. It can be felt most easily in examples of poetry which have been written in a metrical style, such as follows. You might want to try speaking them as you patsch the beat on your legs:

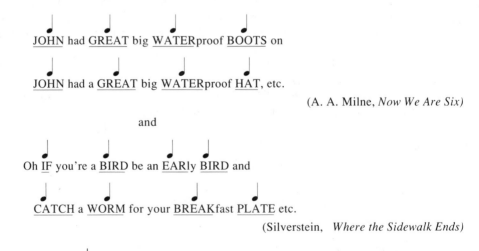

JOHN had GREAT big WATERproof BOOTS on

JOHN had a GREAT big WATERproof HAT, etc.

(A. A. Milne, *Now We Are Six*)

and

Oh IF you're a BIRD be an EARly BIRD and

CATCH a WORM for your BREAKfast PLATE etc.

(Silverstein, *Where the Sidewalk Ends*)

Notice: ♩ = one beat (quarter note) and will represent the heartbeat in this material.

Both these examples clearly demonstrate beat, and this particular feeling—straight, march-like—can be counted off in twos or fours. This type of metrical feeling is called *duple* meter. Later we will examine student examples which will call for a different kind of rhythmical feeling or meter.

Notice, too, that though both examples had the duple feel of meter in their straightforwardness of rhythm, one started *on* the beat, and one started *before* the beat. Music or a word that starts before the heavy downbeat is called an *upbeat* or *anacrusis:*

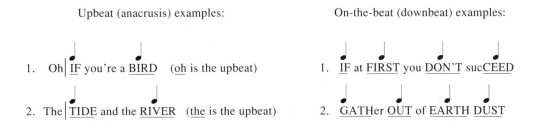

Upbeat (anacrusis) examples:

1. Oh| IF you're a BIRD   (oh is the upbeat)

2. The |TIDE and the RIVER   (the is the upbeat)

On-the-beat (downbeat) examples:

1. IF at FIRST you DON'T sucCEED

2. GATHer OUT of EARTH DUST

When you are analyzing poetry for speech and rhythm possibilities, it is often important to know whether you are dealing with an upbeat situation or a downbeat, as it can affect the naturalness with which you treat words; for example, without allowing for the upbeat in example 2 you get: *THE* tide *AND* the *RIV*er.

The poetry assignments which have been used for the previous lessons did not impose meter requirements, primarily because we are working in free verse, which is the least restrictive poetic form for young children; but the reality is that *all* writing contains elements of meter. Words themselves are often rhythmic and metered, as follows:

(upbeat) I FEEL like a BIRD   FLYing in a DARK   FORest . . .

Closing in, L. K., above

Thus, pulse can be imposed on essentially nonmeasured verse. Rapping, a fad that goes in and out of the pop music scene, is a good example of rhythmical treatment of nonmetered speech.

How then does one identify the type of student-written poem which will lend itself to rhythmic treatment? You first look for poems which have a bounding, driving quality about them and which, because of the mood or subject matter, might be enhanced by shaping them into frameworks with a heartbeat—poems which lend themselves to something ongoing and constant. The exploration which will uncover this type of poem can be done by the teacher alone or jointly by students and teacher.

SAMPLE LESSON:
SPEECH AND RHYTHM

The earlier poem, "Happy" (p. 41, B. P.), falls into a rhythmical category: The word content is joyful, and the mood gives way easily to rhythmical interpretation. One way of approaching heartbeat exploration with students is to suggest that the beat should fall on the most important words, here shown in caps, underlined, with the beat appearing as quarter notes.

T: Class, can you keep a "heartbeat" going with both hands on your legs while I read the first stanza of a student's poem? Remember, the beat once established will be constant and unchanging.

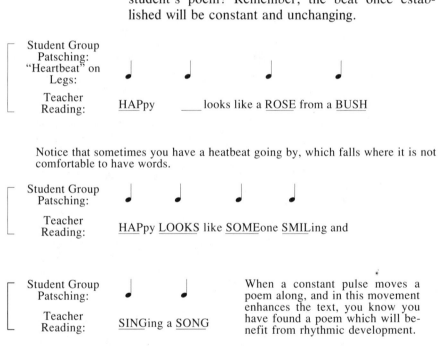

Student Group
Patsching:
"Heartbeat" on
Legs:

Teacher
Reading: HAPpy   looks like a ROSE from a BUSH

Notice that sometimes you have a heatbeat going by, which falls where it is not comfortable to have words.

Student Group
Patsching:

Teacher
Reading: HAPpy LOOKS like SOMEone SMILing and

Student Group
Patsching:

Teacher
Reading: SINGing a SONG

When a constant pulse moves a poem along, and in this movement enhances the text, you know you have found a poem which will benefit from rhythmic development.

T: How about taking the poem "Anger" and seeing if we can put a pulse under the important words? Ethan, would you try, please? We'll all keep the beat going, and you read it, making the strong words fall on the beat where you think it sounds best. [The student experiments.]

At the onset of this lesson, many examples of reading a poem within the framework of a heartbeat were given by the teacher, and time was given for students to try the same. At this point, the teacher needs to have some concrete ideas as to how to enhance that linear presentation:

1. Reading the poem, but changing (thickening) the texture by adding something:
a. little pieces of the lines repeated (ostinati)

Adding Speech Ostinatos to Create Texture and Complementary Rhythms

T: Right now this poem is linear—one line happening at a time. I wonder what it would sound like if we made the piece have more than one thing happening—if we thickened the texture by adding words against the original poem. It might be interesting. Would you like to try? Please read E. G.'s poem once more to yourself, and find some words which could be repeated effectively. Jerry?

S: Anger . . . anger.

T: Fine. Some others?

S: Yelling at you.

T: Both ideas would work. When you say that phrase repeatedly, wouldn't you agree it's fairly hard to say continuously, and perhaps not terribly interesting either? What would happen if we put three rests or silences after each outburst, like this:

Heartbeat:

Spoken: Yell-ing at you   Yell-ing at you

b. silence (rests)
2. Variety of word rhythms (spoken quickly, slowly).

Trial-and-error becomes an important technique in sampling ideas volunteered by students, and verbal traffic management definitely comes into play.

Ways must be explored for deciding which possibilities are to become the final

When a pattern repeats itself, it's called an *ostinato.* Your *yelling at you* created an interesting speech ostinato. I especially liked that the speed (tempo) of the ostinato is faster than in the original poem. When this happens, we say the rhythm ostinato complements, or improves, the original text rhythm. It enhances the original by being different. Later we might try adding a second complementary ostinato. Tell me how you all liked the sound of the three beats of silence (rests) following the ostinato.

S: I thought it was OK.

S: I felt like something should be happening.

T: Silence can be very effective; but you also have the option of filling those silences with sound. What might we use?

choices: teacher's say, class vote, or combination; but most important is that the ideas, in their student forms, be tried.

S: Claps—or better, stamps. The words kind of make me want to stamp.

T: Can you demonstrate, please?

S:

Yell - ing   at   you   (stamp)   (stamp)   (stamp)

T: I like it. Can we try putting the first ostinato pattern with Ethan's first stanza?

Both the group doing the ostinato and the poem group should keep the heartbeat going as you speak. Ready? Begin.

Both Groups Speaking Simultaneously

T: How many of you heard both parts going on? It was good!

For those readers less experienced in what music looks like on the page, the following symbols have been used thus far:

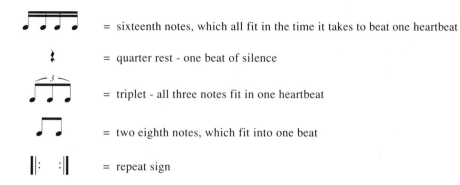

= sixteenth notes, which all fit in the time it takes to beat one heartbeat

= quarter rest - one beat of silence

= triplet - all three notes fit in one heartbeat

= two eighth notes, which fit into one beat

= repeat sign

It is again important to point out that none of the above has been notated during the process of creation with the students, and it is rarely necessary to do so.

**SAMPLE LESSON:
CONTINUED**

The teacher is as much a part of the warp and weave of this fabric as the students, and should an idea occur to him or her, the teacher has a right to express it—and the class a reciprocal responsibility to try the teacher's idea.

Other possibilities to facilitate this multifaceted creative process are:

1. An awareness of the need for contrast. This means that word rhythms which may be

T: I remember another word someone excerpted earlier as a possible ostinato—*anger!* Just how did you say that, Ben?

S: Anger . . . anger.

T: . . . as if you're taking a breath—or a rest—in between. Can you all do it with Ben?

Class Chanting:
ANger   ANger

T: Let's see how that fits with the first ostinato—this half of the room you're anger—the other half, *yelling at you*—all groups feel the heartbeat first. Ready? Begin. Interesting! Can anyone think of another word or combination to try?

S: What would happen if we did one pattern of *yelling at you* followed by the *anger* pattern?

ongoing at the same time as the original poem will be different, *and thus enhance the original and not* cover *it. The term for this is*

Yell-ing   at   you   (clap)   (clap)

to complement.

   2. An awareness of the variety of dynamics to suggest to students: loud, soft, gradually getting louder, gradually getting softer, suddenly louder (f, p, cres., dim., subito, etc.).

T: We'll try it—first tell me what happens to the rests after *anger.*

S: This time let's clap on the three beats following *yelling at you* and stamp on the rests in between *anger.*

T: Let's try it:

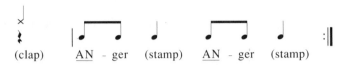

(clap)   AN - ger   (stamp)   AN - ger   (stamp)

T: What happened is you've made an even more interesting ostinato, because it has more variety, less predictability, and gives more contrast to the ear. Can you suggest how you imagine the loudness or softness—or the *dynamics,* using musical term?

S: I think it should all be fairly loud.

T: Forte it is then. Everyone ready to try it with E. G.'s first line?

It is always the combined artistic discretion of both student and teacher which determines when something should stay the way it is, or change. It is the teacher and students who in combination decide if another part is to be added, or if the majority feel the creation seems right. Sometimes a vote clears the question.

   If the group could handle a third complementary part, it might be one with dramatic dynamics which starts softly and gradually gets louder (crescendo). (It is always helpful to start with the heartbeat to help stabilize the pattern.)

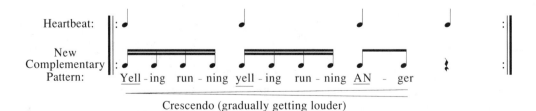

Crescendo (gradually getting louder)

Other musical terms for dynamics:

f = forte = loud

p = piano = soft

pp = pianissimo = very soft

ff = fortissimo = very loud

m = mezzo = medium

crescendo = gradually getting louder

decrescendo = gradually getting softer

Were you to see the original poem plus the two ostinatos plus the heartbeat happening at the same time in score form, it would look like this:

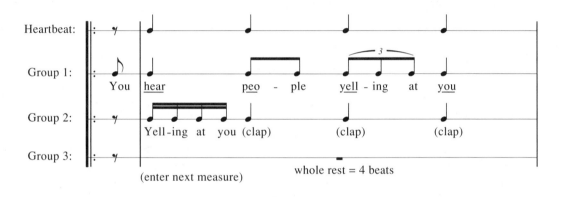

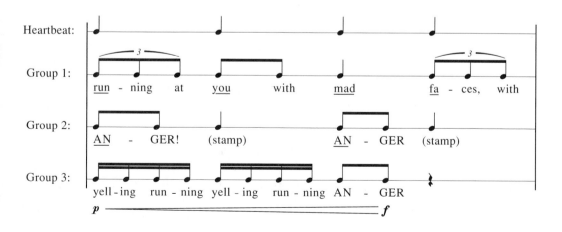

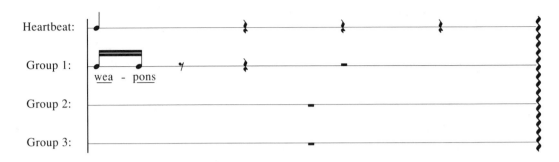

Heartbeat:

Group 1:

wea - pons

Group 2:

Group 3:

**SAMPLE LESSON:
CONTINUED**

Introductions and Codas

*A piece can be
expanded by the
addition of an
introduction and a
coda, or by students
improvising rhythms in
interlude sections.*

T: Sometimes a piece wants something to happen before
the main event . . . something which relates to the
original, but introduces the listener to what is about to
happen. This is called an introduction. As with the
ostinato, excerpting phrases and ideas from the poem
is a good way to find material for an introduction. In
"Anger," the part group 3 performed might become
an introduction if spoken twice before the original
work began. Try it.

Yell -ing   run - ning   yell -ing   run - ning   AN - GER

You | hear people yelling at you, running at you with
mad faces, with weapons, etc.
  We are beginning to build a form. You can tell from
the picture I've drawn on the board which is the
introduction and which is the main body; thus the
form is as follows:

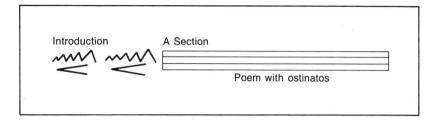

T: If the following is added to the picture, what do you think has happened to the form?

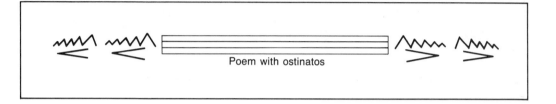

T: You're observant. The material used in the introduction appears to have made it to the end . . . but now it is called a *coda,* which means a final, finishing section; a rounding out of ideas—coming to a final point. But is it exactly like the introduction?

S: The crescendo mark is going the other way.

T: Right! Which means, just as it looks, we're getting softer, or decrescendoing. Class, please say the coda with me and see if you can decrescendo. [Class responds.]

Working for Contrast

T: Another important element in manipulating speech and rhythm is that of *contrast*—the art of creating the unexpected. Contrast of sounds, rhythms, and texture keeps the participant and the observer interested. Contrast can also occur through varied dynamics, as well as in the number of voices involved (sometimes many, sometimes few, sometimes solo), and in the form of the piece. In the middle section of "Anger" there is an opportunity to savor the different *vocal timbres* or qualities of voices if the lines were assigned like this:

Student 1: "It tastes like a bad, bitter lime."
Student 2: "It feels like gravel and rough red dirt."
Student 3: "It smells like smoke and gas from an exhaust."

"Anger"'s form would now look like this [putting the graphic on the board]. Shall we try the whole thing?

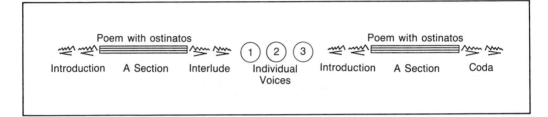

The life of E. G.'s original work has been extended through *repetition*. Student poems are often too short and need this kind of extension. The possibilities are literally endless. In this short poem, only a handful of ideas have emerged through layering one group texture over another, each complementing the other, one a heartbeat with the original poem text, the others contrasting rhythmic ostinatos. The musical elements have added up, as teacher and students expressed and put into practice dynamics, form, ostinatos, increased texture, and body percussion to complement the original work. While maintaining the integrity of the original, the class has had the fun and excitement of seeing a new work emerge, one in which they all shared the joy of creation and performance.

The Process Applied to a Poem in Compound Meter

All the poems we've worked have had a duple-meter feel. This student's (E. G.) choice of words is more naturally spoken and played with in a new-feeling meter called *compound*. Say the first lines of "Humpty Dumpty sat on a wall," and you will immediately be in this meter. It is a rhythm that has hidden rhythms within it, because its beats can be felt in two groups of three:

(in this case a two beat is felt) or three groups of two:

(in which case three groups of two are felt). This rhythmical optical illusion reveals rhythm within rhythm and thus is named compound meter.

SAMPLE LESSON: CONTINUED

T: Let's work through one more poem, applying the ideas of layering speech with body percussion ostinatos. "Happiness" (p. 42, B. T.) rollicks along and is a good choice for rhythmic treatment. As before, could one person volunteer to read his or her version over the heartbeat the group will provide?

S:

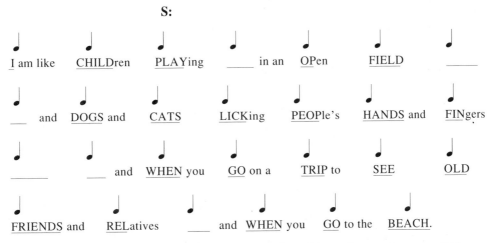

T: A fine interpretation. [Note that again you will have beats going by without words, which helps the poem feel more natural.]

T: Next, as with the previous poem "Anger," let's add a complementary rhythm pattern. To help get the feel of this pattern, which has a different rhythmic feel than E. G.'s, say these words after me:

‖: HUMPTY DUMPTY FELL :‖

In the same rhythm, say these excerpted words from "Happiness":

‖: DOGS AND CATS AND FRIENDS :‖

This new meter is called ⁶⁄₈, and it is very familiar to you from many children's poems and nursery rhymes. Try clapping it as you say the words.

DOGS   AND   CATS   AND   FRIENDS

Rather than just being clapped, it might be transferred to different places on the body for a variety of sound colors. Who could make a body percussion out of this clapped rhythm—perhaps even using two or more sounds?

S:

Pattern 1

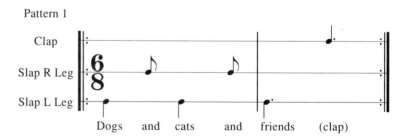

T: That feels very comfortable. Let's call that pattern number 1. Can this half of the room patsch the heartbeat while saying B. T.'s poem, while the other half does pattern 1, "dogs and cats and friends"? If we hear both parts clearly we can invent another complementary layer for further interest. Ready? Here's the heartbeat. Begin. [Students try two parts together.] Fine. Would anyone like to excerpt another idea from the poem to add as another rhythmic pattern? Eric, why don't you try it?

S: How about, "when you go to the beach"?

T: I liked the way you kept the heartbeat under your reading. Can everyone say those words in the rhythm Eric used? Who can invent a way of putting them on the body with a body percussion?

S: Clap . . . . . clap . . . . . slap R, slap L, slap R, slap L. (when   you . . .   go   to   the   beach)

Pattern 2

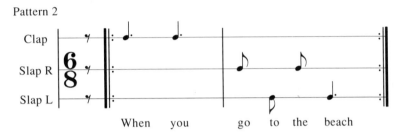

T: Try that one, class. Is it the same as "dogs and cats and friends" rhythmically, or different? Paul? You're right, it is different, and therefore complements the original set of words and the first pattern. Let's divide into three groups and try the text with the two additional patterns and see how it sounds:

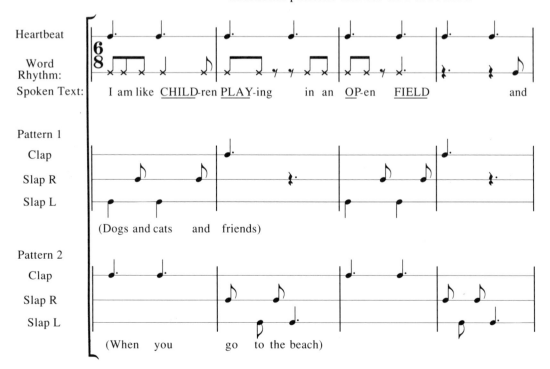

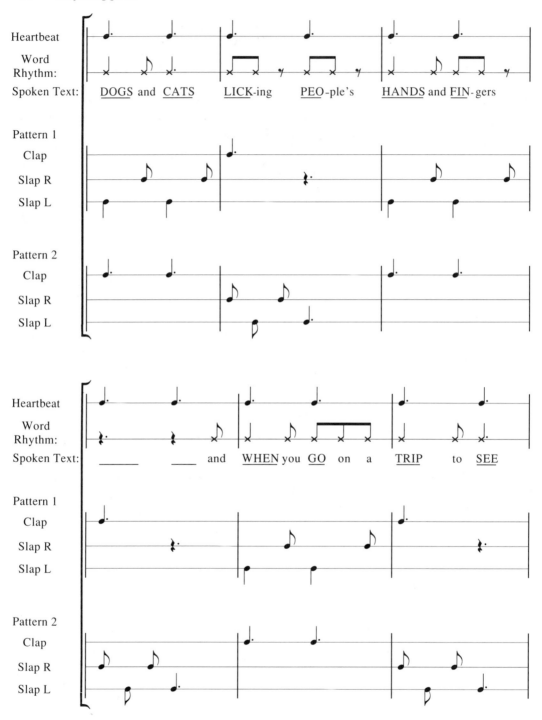

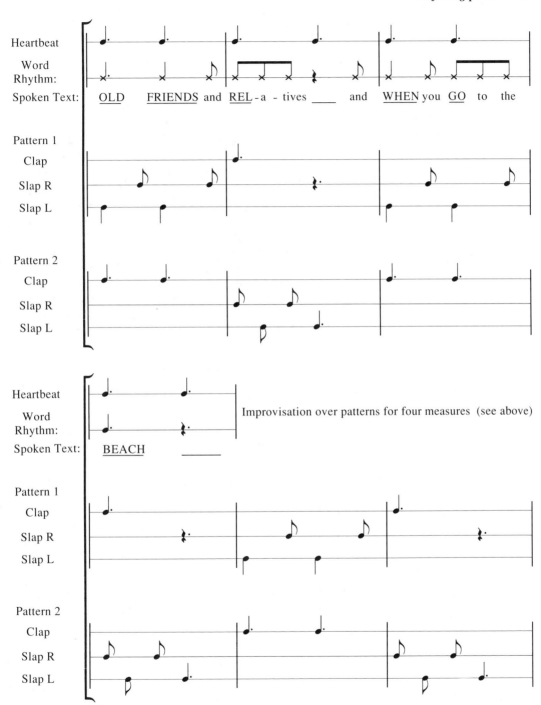

Contrasting Interludes Through Improvisation

T: Rather than going immediately on to the second stanza of the poem "Happiness," something happening next could provide a *contrasting interlude*. The two ostinato patterns could continue under an improvised clapping section. An improvisation is something made up spontaneously. It is not at all preplanned, and is new and different every time. It depends entirely on the inspiration of the moment. The only aspect the improviser has to take into consideration is where the heartbeat is, so that the speed (tempos) and rhythms relate to that heartbeat, making the solo effective. Improvisations can be measured in length (as in "so many beats of improvisation") or unmeasured, where the soloist goes until finished and in some way signals the end. Let's get our improvisation rhythms warmed up through this echo game. I'll clap some made-up patterns the length it would take you to say, "Humpty dumpty sat on a wall" (two measures, twelve beats).

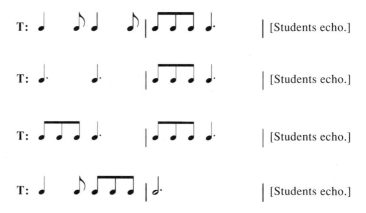

T: May we have a student volunteer to lead some more patterns with this compound-meter feel (p. 54)? [Students volunteer.] We're almost ready to use these ideas in B. T.'s poem (p. 42). One more rhythm game. This time, instead of copying my rhythm or echoing me exactly, will you all make up (invent, improvise) your own pattern which will answer mine. I will clap you the question, and you invent the rhythm answer. Here's the question:

T: (question)

S: (answer)

(Variations to this game: Have one student be the question, another the answer—or have one person be both question *and* answer.)

I think you will have some good ideas when we come to the improvisation interlude in B. T.'s poem. Here's what the form looks like so far:

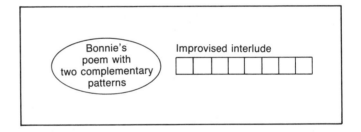

CANON

The second stanza of B. T.'s poem has such nice word-rhythm contrast, that it would work well in *canon*.[2]

Children laughing and eating candy and sweet things, and like beautiful butterflies landing on stumps of trees, and birds chirping when they fly over tree tops, and sweet sticky taffy being stretched, and people having a good time at the park

[2]A poetry piece can be enhanced through canon.

A canon is a technique of overlapping, and is related to a round: One group begins a rhythm or song, a second group enters later with the same rhythm or song, and a new rhythmic or tonal complexity results, and a new texture as well. Canon can be applied to speech, song, movement, instrumental rhythms, or body percussion. Visually, a two-part canon might look like this:

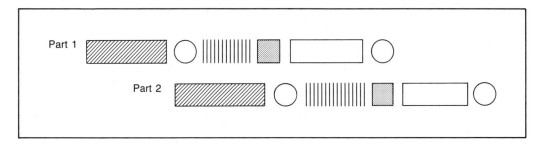

After exploring and agreeing on a way to read the second stanza consistently, again making the important words fall on the heartbeat, the group could be divided, to decide where the second part would enter. A possible entry would be at the second measure, that is,

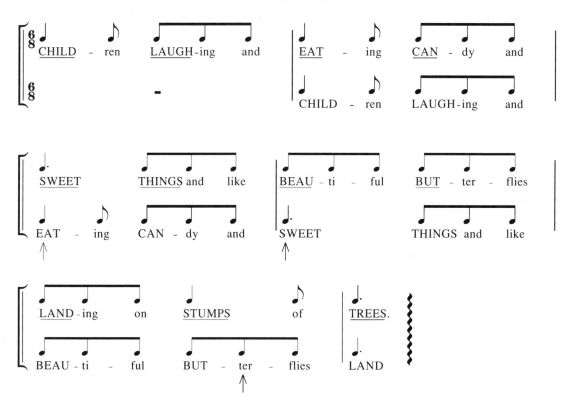

The arrows show where the contrast is the best in this canon. Where measures are the same, there is doubling and thus no contrast. The canon should create two separate, distinctive rhythms when it is at its best. If it is not possible to write out a canon to see this distinction, you will hear it on performing the canon aloud.

Were a canon to be used in B. T.'s poem, a change of ostinato running under it would be good for contrast. The onomatopoeia of "beautiful butterflies" might sound effective fluttering under this canon, but in a two-measure form. (Were you to repeat the pattern without stopping, it would be too relentless and too difficult to sustain with both the body percussion and the spoken poem.)

The form of happiness now looks like this:

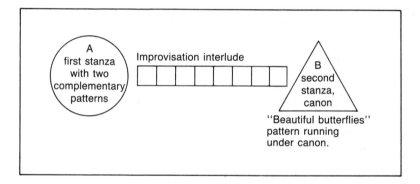

Repetition of sections or recurrence of patterns helps solidify the form of any piece. It would therefore be appropriate to bring back the improvisation interlude once more, over the original complementary patterns 1 and 2:

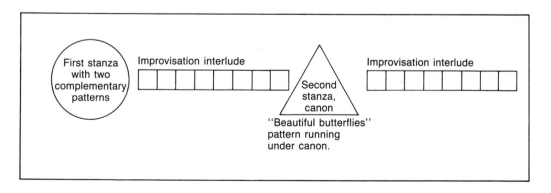

The form is beginning to resemble a *rondo,* which is as follows: same, different, same, still different, same, or:

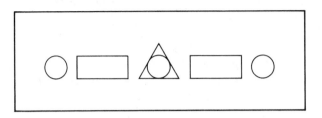

The circles refer to the poem's verses, the rectangles to the improvisation. A literal rondo form would look like this:

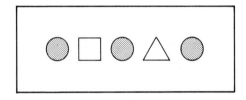

(ABACA form, or rondo form).

B. T.'s poem is one example of a fairly lengthy and complex work. If a poem happens to be of this type, it might benefit by excerpting. (Earlier, the opposite problem of brevity in elemental forms was mentioned.) In "Happiness," skipping to the last stanza would result in a finished and satisfying completion of form.

> Luscious lollypops in your mouth and
> sweet sticky bubble gum crackling
> as you blow bubbles.
> Steak and candy apples and
> melted butter with pancakes and
> sweet candies!

Since we have used a rhythmical treatment so far in this poem, the contrast of letting students read at their own unmeasured speeds would be welcomed. Nowhere in the poem have we had the singular sound of one voice speaking, to appreciate the individual timbres and colors of voices, so this would be an appropriate way to go.

> Student 1: Luscious . . . lollypops . . . in your mouth . . .
>
> Student 2: and sweet . . . sticky . . . bubble gum . . . crackling as you blowwww bubbles
>
> Student 3: Steak!

Student 4: And candy . . . apples . . .

Student 5: And melted butter with pancakes . . .

Student 6: and sweet candies!

THE CODA: AN ENDING

Now the piece needs to return to something familiar to pull it all together and make it feel cohesive. We need to feel the earlier heartbeat and hear the earlier patterns:

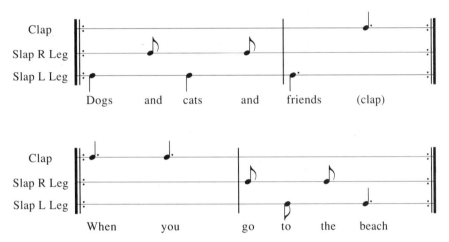

SAMPLE LESSON:
CONTINUED

T: If we came in with those familiar rhythms immediately after Amy says, "and sweet candies," can anyone think of a word or phrase which might sum up the poem for use in a coda?

S: What about the title—"Happiness"?

T: Fine. When should it happen, and how loud do you want it to be?

S: Three times, getting louder.

T: Three times with a crescendo. OK. Let's try it at the beginning of each pattern. Here's the heartbeat [demonstrates]. Group 1, begin your pattern:

S: Dogs and cats and friends [clap] . . .

T: Keep it going . . . group 2, now add yours.

S: When you go to the beach . . .

T: Both groups . . . now add the word *happiness* at the beginning of each pattern, every two measures. Here's the beat. Now begin.

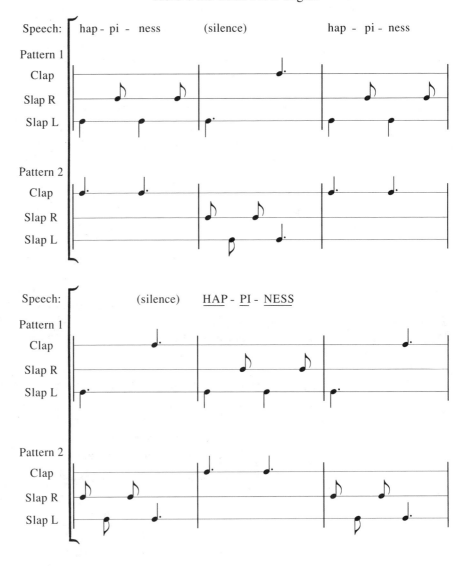

T: A very effective coda. Let's put the whole piece together now. We'll need two small groups for pattern 1 and pattern 2. In the second stanza these same people can do the accompaniment for "beautiful butterflies." May I have six solo volunteers for the C section of our piece? Look at the final form I've drawn on the board. Here's what the poem has been transformed into:

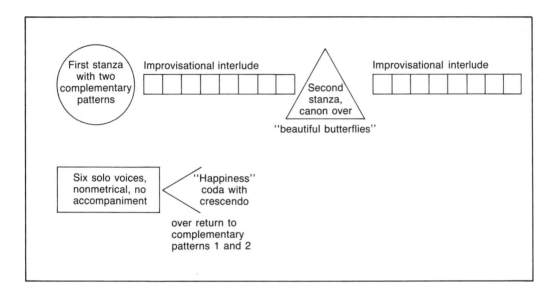

T: Poet B. T., would you please announce the title?

SUMMARY: SPEECH AND RHYTHM

Although it's probably obvious, it still should be pointed out that this process does not happen at one session. Time permitting, it is desirable to savor and revise the experience in installments. The pieces when finished become part of the group repertoire, along with the songs students may share or poetry they have memorized; they can be reviewed with immense student and teacher pleasure throughout the school year.

In Chapter 2, patterns, repeated ostinati, dynamics, form, word coloring, timbre, duple and compound meter, heartbeat, and canon have been explored and applied to children's poetic works. We've seen how ideas can come from excerpting the originals, and we've observed the need for contrast between complementary patterns for maximum interest.

Through all this, an equality and ongoing creative dialogue has been established between student and teacher by each empathizing with the intuitive reactions and spontaneous input of the other.

chapter 3

the daydream/wish/fantasy poem

METAPHOR, SIMILE, AND USE OF ADJECTIVES:
THE DAYDREAM/WISH/FANTASY POEM _____

Poetry implies an adventure beyond formats, beyond limits, beyond restrictions. It offers students the exhilaration of creative flight. It says, "Give in to inspiration; fly with your ideas; be willing to be outrageous." Because we all want to be right and dislike being wrong, we need, as teachers, to find ways to make *limitless* more desirable than *limit* and *outrageous* more fun than *safe* thereby eliminating the concept of right or wrong. One way to accomplish this is to initiate an assignment which will be accepted in the spirit of fun. The daydream/wish/ fantasy poem[1] provides this kind of creative abandon. We can (and do) daydream or wish for anything, and our fantasies are, after all, supposed to be farfetched and beyond the realm of possibility.

The element of personal investment in the poem still needs to be stressed. Simply because we are wishing and fantasizing does not mean we are entitled to forget or forgo the need for self-involvement. These are *our* daydreams, *our* wishes, and *our* fantasies, and while they may be absurd, we need to approach them seriously. We need to explore what it is we would wish for if wishes came true, and where we would let our fantasies take us if we had access to a flying carpet.

The image, even in a daydream/wish/fantasy, begins with an original point of inspiration and then blooms, through comparison and the use of adjectives, into something extended, enhanced. If we fantasize a tree, it's just a tree until we imagine it as something else: a soldier, for example. Through the use of adjectives *(tall* and *proud)* we extend the image further into the visual dimension. "The tree stood tall and proud as a soldier." We offer a view of *our* tree, as we see it, leaving

[1]*Wishes, Lies and Dreams,* p. 66, Kenneth Koch, Vintage Book / Chelsea House Publishers, 1970.

room for the reader to do some creative interpreting on his or her own. The process of choosing the comparison and the adjectives which will make it work should be a highly selective one. It should reflect individual perceptions and personalities and mark the poem with the poet's signature.

In the preceding chapters, we developed an awareness of the basics of poetry writing. We introduced students to the *ingredients* that go into "making" a poem. We investigated the importance of the image and the use of the five senses. We explored, as well, the need for emotional input and the need to stamp our individual identities on the poem through the use of personal memories and experiences.

In this chapter, we define the types of images and establish a process for selecting adjectives. At no time is it more appropriate to be crafting visual comparisons (word pictures) that help bind the unfamiliar to the familiar than when we journey to the farthest corners of imagination. If we wish for gold, is it a pile bright as sunlight, high as the far side of clouds, shiny as a full moon, heavy as Santa's sack? If we fantasize a journey to the stars, is the way as long as an endless tunnel, as frightening as walking blindfolded into a damp cave, a miracle of lights, like birthday candles on a cake? The image becomes the anchor, a point of reference, that transforms the unimaginable (through metaphor and simile) into the imaginable.

SAMPLE LESSON: POETRY

T: In our previous two poetry sessions we learned how to write a poem using our five senses, imagery, feelings, onomatopoeia, and alliteration. Today we are going to expand our poetic experience by writing a poem that will stretch our imagination to its limit. How many of you are good at daydreaming? . . . ah, lots of hands are up. I think daydreaming is something we *all* spend a lot of time doing, sometimes when we should be doing something else. But there are good times to daydream and one of those times is when we are writing poetry. What kinds of daydreams do you have? Will someone share a daydream with us? John, how about you?

S: I like to daydream about sports.

T: In what way?

S: I don't know, different kinds of things. Hitting a home run in the World Series. Winning an Olympic Gold Medal. That kind of thing.

T: Interesting. Anyone else want to share a daydream with us? Betsy?

S: I daydream about being a rock star and making a video and singing on MTV.

T: Sounds exciting. What is another word for daydreaming? Can anyone think of a word that really explains what daydreams are or where they come from?

S: Imagination.

T: Absolutely. Daydreams are our imagination at work. Another word to explain that function of our imagination might be *wishing*. Wishing is a big part of daydreams. Daydreams are perhaps our wishes in a moving-picture form; and fantasy, perhaps, when we wish for something that doesn't really have much chance of coming true or happening—but we see it in our imagination as if it were real. "I see myself crossing the finish line first at the Olympic marathon. I see myself being the first poet in space. I see myself sliding like a cloud across a summer sky." Daydreams born of wishes? Like moving pictures they travel across our mind and become a part of our private fantasy world.

How many of you wish for things or fantasize the impossible in your imagination? Good. All the hands are up and waving. Daydreams, wishes, fantasies are the subject of today's poem. But before we begin exploring this subject on the page, I'd like to help you stretch your imagination to its absolute limit as you reach for those secret places in your mind.

In a moment, I'm going to speak two lines very slowly. Listen *very, very* carefully. At first, they may sound very much alike, but there is a difference between them. *Listen* for that difference. "The soft, white snow was like a sheet settling over the land." "The soft, white snow was a sheet settling over the land." Evan, did you hear the difference between the two versions of that image?

S: Yes, I think so. In the first image you said the snow was like a sheet settling over the land. In the second image you didn't use the word *like*.

The teacher is layering ideas and poetic concepts in an attempt to establish a firm foundation of skills from which students may draw when writing their poems.

By reviewing terms and ideas previously learned, the teacher is also subtly saying that learning is an additive process and "I expect you to remember and call on what was learned in the preceding lessons." In the classroom jargon, this is called student accountability. The only way that a teacher can ensure that these skills (or any skills) become a part of the students' intellectual persona is to consciously and repeatedly provide a framework in which these skills may be used.

T: Good for you. You caught the difference. In the first image I said, "The soft, white snow was *like* a sheet settling over the land." That is what we call a simile. I compared one thing to another using the word *like*. I could also compose a simile using the word *as*. I might have said, "The snow was as soft as a sheet settling over the land." That would still have been a simile. The second image, "The soft, white snow *was* a sheet settling over the land," is what we call a metaphor. It compares one thing to another by saying one thing *is* another. In the second version of the simile I could change it into a metaphor by saying, "The snow *was* a soft sheet settling over the land." I hope everyone is beginning to see the difference between the metaphor and the simile. Just to make sure, let's do some more examples. "The trees stood still as soldiers." Metaphor or simile?

S: Simile.

T: Why?

S: Because you used the word *as*.

T: Right. By the way, I used something else you should recognize. Listen to the sound of that simile. "The trees stood still as soldiers." Did you hear it? What is the poetic term that describes the choice of words in that simile?

S: Alliteration?

T: Exactly. I'm delighted you remembered. It's important for us to understand that we are *adding* new ideas and increasing our poetry skills, not replacing one with the other. So, "The trees stood still as soldiers" is a simile *and* it uses alliteration. Would someone try and turn that into a metaphor? Gregg?

S: The trees stood . . .

T: Let me write the image on the board.

The trees stood still as soldiers.

Learning to create metaphors and similes.

Study it a moment and then decide what word or words may need to be taken out or changed for this simile to become a metaphor.

S: The trees were soldiers?

T: Yes. You transformed the simile into a metaphor. Does anyone else see another way of doing it?

S: The trees were still soldiers.

T: Well done. Let's try another.

The sun is as bright as a giant eye.

Metaphor or simile?

S: It's a simile.

T: Why?

S: Because you used the word *as*. You used it twice.

T: So I did. Who would like to try and change our simile into a metaphor?

S: The sun is bright . . . the sun is . . . a giant eye?

Learning to create metaphors and similes.

T: Absolutely. Someone else see another way it might work? What word was left out that might be included?

S: Bright?

T: Yes. Would you like to try creating the metaphor and include the word *bright?*

S: The sun is a bright, giant eye.

T: Nicely done. One more example. Metaphor or simile?

Her eyes shone like stars
out of the pale moon of her face.

Please study this one carefully. Let's say it aloud . . . now, metaphor or simile?

S: I think it's a simile because you used the word *like*.

T: Is Evan right or wrong? I see we have a difference of opinion. Bobbi, why do you think Evan is wrong?

S: Because you said her face *is* a pale moon. So I think it must be a metaphor.

T: Do you agree or disagree with Bobbi?

S: I think they are both right.

T: Could you explain?

S: Well, because half of the image is a metaphor and half of it is a simile.

T: You're absolutely right. We have a simile and a metaphor happily snuggled up together. Let's look at it again. "Her eyes shone like stars out of the pale moon of her face." Do you all hear it now? Let's diagram it on the board.

Her eyes shone like stars . . . Simile (eyes *like* stars)
Out of the pale moon of her face . . . Metaphor (face *is* pale moon)

Someone please give me a metaphor for the sun.

S: The sun is a yellow balloon.

T: I like that. Another one?

S: The sun is a burning ball of fire.

T: We can picture that. However, scientifically, the sun is a burning ball of fire. It's actually more like stating a fact than creating a metaphor or simile. Do you want to try another?

S: The sun is a gold coin?

The gentle rebuke steers the student back toward a more viable vantage point and also says, "It was OK to miss the target—but try again."

Occasionally the teacher must point out that an error has been made in order to clarify what is sought. In this case the correction was done quickly, without fuss, without calling attention to the student, and an explanation was given for why the answer didn't work.

The teacher reinforces use of sensory imagery by responding with the word tasty *to the student image.*

The students are given the opportunity to demonstrate their listening skills by being asked to analyze and evaluate the qualities of the student image.

T: That's a very nice image. How about a simile for the moon?

S: The moon is like a clean plate.

S: The moon is as pale as milk.

S: The moon is like a buttermilk pancake.

T: Those are extremely effective, and they used, consciously or unconsciously, some of the five senses. I'd like for us to remember the other skills we've learned—alliteration, onomatopoeia. Remember, alliteration is the repetition of beginning sounds of letters and onomatopoeia is a word that sounds like what it is. So we want a metaphor or simile, using the five senses, alliteration, and onomatopoeia. That, I think, requires some time for thought. Please take a few moments, and when you're ready jot your image down on paper. . . . Ready? Liz?

S: The moon is yellow as melting mozzarella cheese on a sizzling meaty hamburger.

T: What a tasty image. Did Liz use all the required elements?

S: Yes, I think she did.

T: Would you explain, please?

S: She created a simile by saying "the moon is yellow *as* . . ." She used the letter *M* to create alliteration, and she used the sense of taste. Also, *sizzling* sounds a lot like what it is.

T: You did a very fine job with that. And the image, itself, was wonderfully done. While we are creating our images, our metaphors and similes, we need, as well, to be thinking about adjectives. Adjectives are those picturesque words that describe things, making them real for us. We've already learned that poetry needs to say as much as possible while still choosing words sparingly and with great care. When we choose an adjective for our image, it needs to be just the right adjective (or adjectives). The adjective must add something positive to the image. I think of adjectives as adding color to our poems, so I've come up with something I call my *rainbow of images*. Let me give you an example on the board. Let's use the sun as our subject.

```
┌─────────────────────────────────────────┐
│                                         │
│                                         │
│    SUN ─────────                        │
│                                         │
│                                         │
└─────────────────────────────────────────┘
```

Now, what shall we compare the sun to?

S: A red balloon.

```
┌─────────────────────────────────────────┐
│                                         │
│                                         │
│    SUN _____  RED BALLOON          │
│                                         │
│                                         │
└─────────────────────────────────────────┘
```

T: What I would like for you to do now is to think about what the sun and a red balloon have in common. What is it about the sun (our subject) that made us think of a red balloon (our comparison)?

S: They're both round.

T: Good.

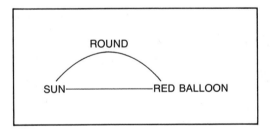

T: What else do they have in common?

S: They both are bright.

S: Yes. I'll add that to our growing rainbow.

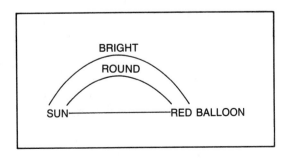

T: Can you think of more words that describe the sun and a red balloon?

S: Shiny.

S: Hot.

S: Sparkling.

T: Those are all fine descriptive words, and we are in the process of building a beautiful word rainbow.

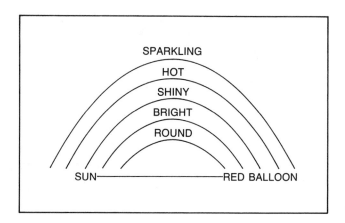

This is an exercise in selectivity, the lesson being that more is not necessarily better. The teacher hopes to show, in the resulting responses to this assignment, that there are many workable images possible; that poetry is an individual, creative effort and reflects the responsive "soul of the poet."

Now, we need to be selective. Remembering that we are poets, we need to choose just the right adjective or adjectives to make a powerful personal metaphor or simile. Ben, would you like to be the first to select the word or words for your metaphor or simile?

S: The sun is a shiny, bright red balloon.

T: Good selecting. Jane, is that a metaphor or a simile?

S: A metaphor. But I would rather use the word *round* because then you are using alliteration, too.

T: Let's hear your image for the sun, using the word *round*.

S: The sun is like a round red balloon.

T: Metaphor or simile?

Class: Simile!

T: You've convinced me you know the difference between the metaphor and the simile. Let's work a bit more on building word (adjective) rainbows. Begin this time with clouds (the subject.)

```
CLOUDS ————————
```

What shall we compare them to?

S: How about cotton balls?

T: That works. I'll diagram it on the board.

```
CLOUDS ———————— COTTON BALLS
```

T: How high can we build our word rainbow? Descriptive words, please. Words that tell us what clouds and cotton balls have in common.

S: They're both soft.

S: They're white.

S: Fluffy.

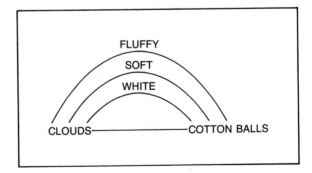

T: Reach inside yourselves for those words that others may not think of. When creating an image, strive to make it unique, to make it *yours*. More words, please.

S: How about *feathery*?

T: That's a playful one.

S: *Gentle.* Or how about *weightless?*

T: Excellent. Let's see what we have.

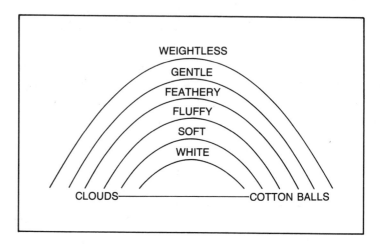

T: Please take a moment to study the rainbow on the board. Think about the words—what they mean, how they relate clouds to cotton balls. Close your eyes and picture the clouds . . . your clouds . . . now see them as cotton balls. Place the picture firmly in your mind. Then carefully, thoughtfully, creatively craft your metaphor or simile. Who's ready to try? Karen?

S: The soft, white clouds are fluffy and feathery as cotton balls.

T: Very nice. You chose to describe your clouds twice. First, as soft and white and then as fluffy and feathery. It really worked for me. Anyone else?

S: The clouds are gentle cotton balls.

T: You chose to be very selective, but the image works. It's interesting to see how many different ways there are to describe clouds. Let's try one more.

S: Clouds are white, weightless cotton balls.

T: I like that one, too. You chose the two *w* words and added a bit of alliteration, and it worked very well as a metaphor for clouds. Those *w* words almost feel like clouds in your mouth. Everyone together . . . slowly . . . savoring the sound . . . say the image aloud.

Class: Clouds . . . are . . . white . . . weightless . . . cotton . . . balls.

T: It sounds and feels soft on your tongue. Poetry should feel good when you speak it aloud.

I think we are quite comfortable with the selection of adjectives and the creation of metaphors and similes. What I'd like for us to do now is start thinking about our daydream/wish/fantasy poem. When we are doing our writing today, we will be trying to bring together all of the elements of poetry we have been learning. For now, let's see what kinds of imagery express our daydreams, wishes, and fantasies. A wish image, please.

S: I wish I were rich.

T: Is that an image?

S: No.

T: I don't think so, either. Is there some way we can help John turn his wish into an image?

S: I wish I were rich as a King.

T: Yes, that's better. You chose to turn John's wish into a simile. Is there anyone else who would share a wish or fantasy with us? How about something in the realm of a fantasy journey you might take or a place you might like to visit? Anyone?

S: I am swimming beneath the ocean in a dark, dreary, drab wet world.

T: That's an excellent one. Good use of alliteration. Someone else.

S: I wish I were a long lightning bolt booming across the sky.

T: What elements of poetry does that image contain?

S: Alliteration.

T: Yes, it most certainly did. Did it contain anything else? Poetry needs to be written very carefully. It also needs to be read and listened to very carefully, because *every* word is so important. Please speak your image again.

S: I wish I were a long lightning bolt booming across the sky.

T: Did you hear it this time? A word that sounds like its meaning?

S: Booming?

T: Would you all agree that booooming sounds a lot like what it describes?

S: Yes. How about *bolt?*

T: Good question. What does everyone think? Does the word *bolt*—everyone say it out loud, *bolt,* again, *bolt*—sound like what it is? Raise your hand if you think it does. Well, everyone seems to think so, so let's include *bolt* in our praise of the poet's use of onomatopoeia. More wishes or fantasies or day-dreams?

S: I wish I were the sound of silence in the sleepy summer night.

T: Very nice. It's fun to experiment with alliteration and we are aware, I hope, that your very complete image included the sense to hear. How about a scent image?

S: I wish I were the smell of smoke rising slowly in the starry sky.

T: A simply sensational image. You certainly used your imagination and lots of alliteration. How about a tasty wish or fantasy?

S: I am the pretty pink roses on a chocolate-covered birthday cake.

T: That tells us something about you. That you like chocolate cake and pink roses, perhaps. How about one that uses the sense to feel?

S: Moonbeams are smooth ladders I climb to reach the stars.

T: What a lovely image. Let's take what we've created thus far and put it into a group poem. While we're doing that, let's also remember that we don't always use *all* of the poetry ingredients *all* of the time. Some of the time we will be using alliteration, some of the time onomatopoeia, but most of the time we will be creating powerful metaphors and similes. This is, after all, where the poem *happens.* As I write the poem on the board, I want you to study it. Read it line by line, remembering all we now know about poetry. Is there a spot, for example, where we can make a comparison, create a metaphor or simile, select an additional or more effective adjective, use alliteration or onomatopoeia?

GROUP DAYDREAM/WISH/FANTASY POEM

I wish I were rich
as a King.
I am swimming beneath
the ocean in a dark
dreary drab
wet world.
I wish I were a long
lightning bolt booming
across the summer sky.
I wish I were the sounds
of silence in the sleepy
summer night.
I wish I were the smell
of smoke rising slowly into
the starry sky.
I am the pretty pink
roses on a chocolate
covered birthday cake.
Moonbeams are smooth
ladders I climb
to reach the stars.

T: Suggestions, please, to improve our poem.

S: How about swimming like a mermaid?

T: Fine. We'll add that to our poem. Other ideas?

S: Booming like a jet plane.

T: Great. Another one?

S: The smoke was rising like a shadow.

T: That works very nicely. By adding those few word comparisons, we've created some very powerful word pictures. Let's look at the poem again, with the additions.

GROUP DAYDREAM/WISH/FANTASY POEM
REVISED

I wish I were rich
as a King.
I am swimming like
a mermaid beneath
the ocean in a dark
dreary drab wet world.
I wish I were a long
lightning bolt booming
like a jet plane
across the summer sky.
I wish I were the sounds
of silence in
the sleepy summer night.
I wish I were the smell
of smoke rising like a shadow
into the starry sky.
I am the pretty pink
roses on a chocolate
covered birthday cake.
Moonbeams are smooth
ladders I climb to reach
the stars.

T: I am delighted with the reach of your imagination.
Remember when you are writing your personal poems
today, the only limit you must face is that of your own
imagination. You have the words (the poet's tool).
Take out clean paper and begin, please.

————————— **student poems** —————————

THE WHOOPING CRANE FANTASY

I'm a whooping crane
at a clear blue lake
on a warm, clear
summer day catching golden
sunfish with my
long sharp beak at noon time.

I'm a green plant with
many daffodils with the regal
sun bathing my leaves
with golden sunshine.

> W. P., 5th grade

FANTASY

I wish I was far away in a dream
of paradise fantasy of Hawaii; and
beside the richest and most powerful
millionaire in the richest robe,
with the richest of jewels, like the
twinkle of an outstanding diamond
of yonder.

Walking along the coast of an island
beside a gorgeous stream, or wonder-
waterfall in a garden, with a tulip
in my mouth.

My wholesome dream would be to
live in a mansion
with every feeling in me,
with relaxing moments,
and everything I would want
in my entire, exciting, emotional
life.

> M. C., 5th grade

FANTASY

I could see large
dark horses galloping
as fast as they could.

I could hear them galloping
their hoofs
banging like
an exploding
earthquake.

I could taste all
the dust coming at
me just like an
exploding earthquake.

I could touch their
silky hair when they stopped
like a squeaking car.

> B. R., 5th grade

WISHING

Oh, I wish a BIG, BIG wish . . .
But, what can wishing do?
I wish I were a puppy
and I wish I were a guppy.
I wish I were a kitten
and I wish I were a mitten.

I wish I were a hunter bold
to make the tiger run.

I wish I were a circus clown
to make the people laugh.

I wish that wishes
would come true.

> W. D., 1st grade

MY FOUR WISHES

I wish I could be
a soldier
in the Revolutionary War
so I could be famous.

I wish I could be
a hero and save
a person
because I want
to help people.

I wish there was
no school and you could
still get a good
education, because
I want to be SMART.

I wish these three wishes
would come true and turn
into four.

V. B., 5th grade

I AM BLACKNESS (A FANTASY)

I am dark as night
and like the color of ink
I sound as silent as death
for you can't hear me.
I am the fragrance of charcoal
burning on a fire.
I am the taste of smoked ham
and overcooked marshmallows.
I am the feel of fingers running
through my hair
and the burnt butt of a
cigarette.

A. M. R., 6th grade

MY ULTIMATE FANTASY

When I sleep
I become as rich as
a King and as powerful
as an Emperor.

I drown in my
power and riches.

I have anything
I want to have.

In the red hot
summer I have
a cool refreshing
swimming pool.

In the ice cold
winter I have a warm palace
away from all the
ice and snow.

I have a limousine
that takes me
anywhere I want to go.

But then my
palace suddenly
crumbles.

All my riches
are stolen.

All my power
is taken away.

Everything I had
is gone.

Everything I bought or was
given is now gone, gone until . . .

A. U., 5th grade

MY FANTASY

Peaceful, like drifting off to sleep
on a soft feathery pillow.
That's the way I WISH it was.
Quiet, like a forest after a hard rain,
not one word.
People, with endless faces,
just drifting.
People drifting through puffy, white clouds,
like birds,
endlessly
not seeming to go anywhere.
Sadness, like tears rolling on a cheek
or the clouds raining as if they're
crying.
Never heard of it,
and then,
reality.
Reality of that there will never be
a place like that of my knowledge.
Wishes,
that's all it is,
just . . . wishes.

                    S. K., 6th grade

FANTASY GOING AWAY

When I dream a dream of
going away far like going
to Alaska and jumping
in the snow that is very
high and throwing snow
balls and making snow
men I feel very cold
like freezing icicles
that are skinny and tall
and my fingers and toes feel
like they are coming off
my cheeks and face are
as red as fire.

                    K. R., 6th grade

WISHING

I wish I was blue as the sky.
I wish I was white as the clouds.
I wish I was an apple so everybody would
eat me.
I wish I was in a yellow forest.
I wish I was brown as a big boat.

                    G. P., 3rd grade

FLOATING

I'm floating through
an endless spaceship
alone
floating through
the brain of the ship
in the engine
parts of the engine
are gleaming beautifully
they jump out at me
like thousands of grasshoppers
jumping through the grass
just jumping out at me.

                    T. D., 3rd grade

IMAGES

It is a clear night as clear as glass.
The crickets are playing like an
orchestra of violins.
Birds are humming as softly as a pillow.
A spaceship is taking off like a bullet
out of a gun.
The night is whispering a tune like a
happy bird.
The trees sway back and forth like
hula dancers.
The stars are falling out of the sky
like snowflakes.
The wind whips by like a speeding
car.

                    D. R., 5th grade

I WOULD LIKE TO BE SNOW

I would like to be snow
where children play
and sleigh ride.
Every winter year there is a Christmas show,
but when the sky turns blue,
and the sun comes out,
I feel like the wicked witch because I melt
away.
But when the winter comes
I start all over again.

M. W., 3rd grade

I WISH

I wish I was a feather
flying freely in the wind.
I wish I was a bird
gliding through
the sky.
I wish I was a tree
swiftly shaking
in the wind.
But I am me.

C. T., 4th grade

FANTASY

When I dream, I dream I am a
hawk flying over mountainous peaks
and sloopy hills, I dream I fly
over the hottest desert and the
coldest snow.

I dream I am perched up on a
tree or flapping my wings. The
sweet smell of the wind or the
darkness of night go by, I dream I
see my prey scampering along and
then I dive down and get the
little animal.

I dream I am the strongest bird
and I rule the sky, I dream I
fly proud and all birds obey me,
I dream I am supreme and all
beings like me. Once in a while
I fight with an eagle and watch
it fall to the ground.

D. G., 6th grade

I WISH

I wish I could be
as beautiful
as a rose
and as smooth
as a piece of glass.

I wish I could fly
like a bird swirling
up and down.

K. S., 2nd grade

SUMMARY: POETRY

It is often the case that the lines spoken aloud in class exhibit a greater scope of imagination, freedom, and adventure than when the poem is committed to the page. In "fixing" the poem, the student claims permanent responsibility and feels the need to be more cautious. On occasion, the desire to create the image results in lines that have little or no logical meaning. In these early stages of creative experimentation, the emphasis should be on positive verbal rewards for exciting, innovative, successful imagery. It is helpful, however, to suggest that the students return to their work and assess its clarity of idea and meaning.

While the sample poems in this section may use metaphors and similes, adjectives, alliteration, and onomatopoeia sparsely, they are stunning in their spirit and zest. There is a burgeoning pleasure in the limitless possibilities of language. Students may have some difficulty in sustaining poetic form, but *they are attempting it* and their poems display a gleeful spontaneity and inventiveness, as in the following examples:

wonder-
waterfall in a garden
with a tulip
in my mouth.

the feel of fingers running
through my hair.

hoofs
banging like
an exploding
earthquake.

feather flying
freely in the
wind.

clouds raining
as if they're
crying.

quiet like a
forest after a hard rain.

as beautiful
as a rose.

as smooth
as a piece of glass.

they jump out at me
like thousands of grasshoppers
jumping through the grass.

crickets are playing like an
orchestra of violins.

stars are falling out of the sky like
snowflakes.

the night is whispering a tune like a
happy bird.

Language has become something more than individual words strung casually together. It has evolved into word combinations, word patterns that create images so real they can be seen, smelled, tasted, touched, heard, and *felt*. Words which seemed flat and lifeless on the page have suddenly taken on shape, become lively and animated, and the poems themselves are malleable material ready to be re-created through movement and music. In the ongoing lesson, the emphasis is on "making the words sing."

MELODY: THE FEELING POEM

As with most activities, the greater the initial preparation and stirring of ideas, the richer the response. To request suddenly that a student try singing one of his or her poem lines would probably not produce a satisfying result. Thus, these next lessons back into the idea of melody, starting with the basis of inflection and nuance. The lessons work toward melody through:

— Word interpretation

— Phrase interpretation

— Melodies that are sung as conversation

— Spontaneous melodies using limited pitches (improvisation using simple five-tone pentatonic scales)

— Melodic shapes observed as they occur in common examples, which influence meaning (melodic contour)

— More advanced concepts of combining melodies, creating melodic texture or harmony

— Melodic canon.

Creating good melody deserves the exploration of these types of musical experiences.

With younger children it may be appropriate to go only as far as nuance and recitative in this sequence. The following lesson covers this aspect, and then goes even further, addressing the older student.

SAMPLE LESSON: MELODY

Inflection, Nuance, and Accent

In this reflection over past explorations, the teacher is pointing out to the students that (as with language) musical extensions also are layered, and that there is a sequence of anticipated difficulty.

This sequence is one for the reader to note as well when using this text: Movement exploration is perhaps

T: Looking back over our work, we have applied movement to your poems, letting the words take us into space. We have added word patterns, created forms, added body percussions, and experimented with canon. Let's now involve our voices, not just in speech, but in song. Let's see how we can develop ideas toward setting the lines of poetry you have written into melody, and observe what that involves.

You are singing, *slightly,* even when you are talking! If you listen, your voice has high and low sounds in it as you speak . . . or as I am speaking now. This singing sound that enters your speech, even when you are not actually singing, is called *inflection,* or *nuance* of speech.

the most imminent and readily available aspect in the classroom. It requires only space (which can be created logistically) and students, and so is a workable departure point. Adding sounds which bodies can tap, slap, clap, stamp, shout are also "born of the body." The texture, becoming more complicated, now includes complementary rhythms, form, and combined ostinati, deepening the musical observation while keeping the level of complexity operable. Melody involves more specificity both for teacher and student, and so is a realistic additional layer at this point for both.

Try this: Read the following words out loud and try not to put any changes in your voice at all—no rise or fall of inflection:

grasshopper . . . snowflakes . . . feather . . . beautiful . . . waterfall

T: You sounded somewhat like mechanical people. Now read them like you would normally say them and be aware of the rise and fall of your voices—the nuance and inflection:

Generally, where a word is accented is where the rise of the voice comes, as in

con – sti – TU – tion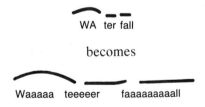

Try graphing some words of your own choosing. Who has a suggestion? [Children can notate their inflections on the board.]

T: To take those words one step toward song, you simply have to hold onto the vowels a little longer:

WA ter fall

becomes

Waaaaa teeeeer faaaaaaaaall

Try singing this while moving your hand high and low with the inflection. You should be able to hear a little melody. When people write for the voice, they consider a word's natural nuance and where the accent or stress falls naturally on a word. For fun, try saying, then singing, *waterfall* putting the stress on *fall:*

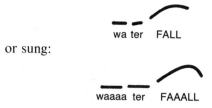

wa ter   FALL

or sung:

waaaa ter   FAAALL

It felt wrong, didn't it? It wouldn't work because *the natural inflection of the word is changed or distorted.*

Let's take some words from the poem "I Wish I Was Rich as a King" created by the group. Try the word *swimming:*

Natural word stress: SWIM ming

Unnatural word stress: swim MING

If we were to sing *swimming* and observe its natural inflection, *swim* would be higher in pitch than *ing.* The same is true of *mermaid, ocean, lightning, summer, shadow, starry, pretty,* and *moonbeams* within this poem as well.

Sung Conversation: Two-Note Recitative

With nonrhyming verse, it is especially effective to sing lines using only two pitches, saving the higher sound for the nuance that needs emphasis, and the lower for those word parts which are not stressed. This technique has been used for thousands of years, dating as far back as the Greek tragedies. Operas call this style of sung talking *recitative.*

SAMPLE LESSON:
CONTINUED

T: I'm singing two sounds:

Higher Sound
Lower Sound
G   E

[How does the teacher find those pitches, or a related shape as notated above? One way is to have an elemental, portable instrument such as a glockenspiel in the general classroom with letters on the keys. Another is to sing the universal teasing chant heard around the world—the first two notes are the minor third needed.]

Na   na na na   na

T: If I were singing the first line in recitative, I might do it like this: [demonstrates]

| High sound | WISH | | RICH | |
| Lower sound | I | I were as | | as a King. |

If I wanted more stress on *rich* and *King,* I might do it like this:

| High sound | | RICH | KING |
| Lower sound | I wish I were as | as a | |

Whenever the extended task involves melody, the most critical point of the lesson is at the beginning where the students must hear, repeatedly, whatever sets of pitches (key center, i.e., la pentatonic, do pentatonic) will be the sounds used in the melody (or improvisation).

The un-self-conscious response of the student is in direct proportion to the amount of time and clarity with which the teacher is willing to sing/speak using those tones.

So depending on where you choose to put the higher sound as an emphasis, you can affect the interpretation of a line. Here is where the poet really has to say what his or her intent is, and to choose the way that best fits those intentions.

Putting the importance of the rising sound on *wish* and *rich as a,* it would look like this in music:

I   wish   I   was   rich   as   a   King.

Going on with the poem, the next phrase might be sung like this, giving importance to *swimming, mermaid,* and *world.*

*fermata: Hold the note as long as you wish.

[Since wishing is so important in this poem, try isolating the *I wish* part, letting the group all sing that particular thought together, in between solo voices on the recitative.]

The final expansion of this poem, using recitative and the idea of the rising and falling inflection as it relates to words and their accents, might look like this from the students' ideas:

Group: I wish . . .

Solo 1: I wish I was rich as a King . . . I am swim - ming like a
mer - maid be - neath the o - cean in a dark drear - y drab wet world . . .

Group: I wish . . .

Solo 2: I were a long light - ning bolt boom - ing like a jet
plane a - cross the sum - mer sky

Group: I wish . . .

Solo 3: I wish I were the sounds of si - lence in the
sleep - y sum - mer night . . .

Group: I wish . . .

Solo 4: I wish I were the smell of smoke,
ris - ing like a shad - ow . . .

Group: I wish . . .

The variety resulting from children's individual vocal timbres (qualities) coupled with the group sound, while very simple, can still be extremely effective. Music thus adds leaves to the winter tree, making it still the tree, but new.

Three- or Four-Note Recitative

Let's move toward a slightly more complex melody by adding tones. You've been working with children and the idea of a two-tone recitative, using the two tones just presented (named minor third or falling third, because of the downward movement and the particular space between the tones—the interval between tones).

Another space, or interval, which is commonly used for recitative is five notes apart, and is thus called a fifth. You can find it by singing

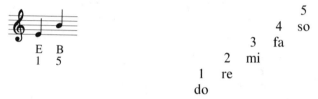

```
                                        5
                                  4  so
                               3  fa
                       2  mi
              1  re
              do
```

E   B
1   5

Adding the lower tone below the fifth, we now have three sounds which work well in a recitative style as before:

← Reciting tone

With these three tones, the reciting tone will mostly be the fifth, using the lowest tone (1) almost as one uses a period in a sentence—when things come to a stop.

**SAMPLE LESSON:
CONTINUED**

[Nothing substitutes for modeling by the teacher. Thus, edging into these three tones in a recitative style, "My Ultimate Fantasy" by A. U. might begin like this:]

T: I'm going to play [or sing] three sounds to explore for a melody setting of "My Ultimate Fantasy" by A. U. Listen to these three sounds [plays/sings: 1, 4, 5]. I'm going to start on tone 5 and make up a melody for "When I sleep, I become as rich as a King." I will use tone 4 and 1 as well. See if you can tell which tone I end on:

B   A   E
5   4   1

[Teacher invents:]

When I sleep,   I be - come as   rich   as   a   King.

The acceptance of many ideas on the same phrase gives credence to the fact that within the structure, there are many right ways.

Did anyone notice which tone I ended on for *King:* 1, 4, or 5?

S: 1.

T: Good ears. And ending that way was intentional. Perhaps you could hear how it made *King* sound final. The first tone of any scale has that characteristic. If you want to sound final, you end on tone 1. Would anyone else try making up a three-tone melody for that phrase using [teacher sings/plays again: 1, 4, 5, 1]?

S:

When   I   sleep I   be - come as   rich   as   a   King.

T: Another good possibility.

Melodic Ostinato

In the previous poem, the idea of wishing was heightened by having the group sing the recurring *I wish.* The same kind of returning to group thought works well in this poem with the phrase "rich as a King."

Rich   as   a   King.

By repeating this, you are creating a melodic ostinato much like you did earlier with rhythm. Putting the two parts together, you have a very simple harmony. In notation, with the group and the solo singing at the same time, it would look like this:

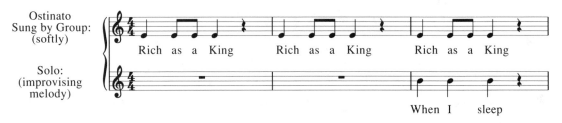

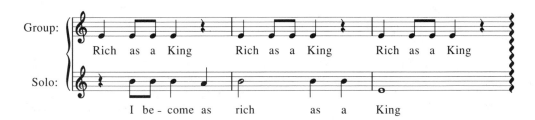

An easy addition of tone is accomplished by going to the leading tone to 1, which is called 7. In this case it would be

A variation of the melodic ostinato could then be

Have a soloist try another improvisation over the classes' new ostinato variation.

Five-Tone Pentatonic Melodies (la)

The addition of the G in the D, E, A, B series gives further opportunity for melodic interest. It increases the tones in use to 5, which is called a pentatonic scale or mode. This particular flavor of pentatonic is called *la* because it is based on the sixth tone of the scale, do, re, mi, fa, so, *la,* ti, do. The scale now looks like this, with E still being 1, or the home tone:

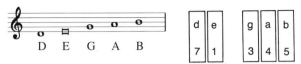

While this set of tones can sound cheerful given a fast tempo, it lends itself especially well for regal, pensive, lonely, mystical moods, and thus is a good one for "My Ultimate Fantasy." Again, one of the best ways to get into any set of tones is by the teacher modeling these sounds in recitative. If the goal is to get a student to improvise in *la* pentatonic in a recitative style, just the sounds of those tones sung or played by the teacher is a start, or an echo game where the class echo sings what the teacher is singing.

SAMPLE LESSON: CONTINUED

T: [Plays on an elemental instrument, i.e., recorder, glockenspiel, E G A B D B A G E D E; then sings in recitative using those tones.]

T: Does anyone recognize their poem?

S: That was the first part of "My Ultimate Fantasy!"

T: Yes! And wouldn't it be the ultimate if we could turn your poem into a sung/spoken piece! We've experimented with word nuance and turned it into two-note songs.

We've explored different words and their natural inflections and turned them into mini-melodies. Now we have a new scale today, which will get us even closer to what you generally call melody . . . but this is not anything you will have to remember or write down, because every time you perform it, you will spontaneously create a new melody for the words. This is what improvisation is all about. The sounds will be the same five tones [teacher plays five sounds again], but the way you arrange them will differ every time you improvise. Let's use the idea of melodic ostinato as we did earlier.

Could this group over here keep the ostinato going that I'm about to sing? Echo me, please:

[Group echos "when I sleep."]

Fine. Now can we keep this going while Alice improvises using A. U.'s words? [Class tries.] Lovely. Will another student try improvising using the *la* pentatonic and A. U.'s words? [Class begins ostinato, and soloist improvises over.]

Looking through the poem, is there any place where it might be more effective to *stop* this ostinato?

S: Where the mood changes . . . down at "but then my palace suddenly crumbles."

T: The mood is definitely shattered there. Perhaps at that spot the soothing repetition of "when I sleep" should stop. Let's try it again, eliminating the ostinato at that point. Andrew has volunteered to be the soloist this time, and he will be using all he has learned so far about the rise and fall of words, of natural word nuance; and the new idea he is trying to use is keeping those five tones in his recitative. [Teacher again reinforces E, G, A, B, D, B, A, G, E and restarts the ostinato group.]

Here is A. U.'s hypothetical improvisation, riding under the group's melodic ostinato:

The following silences (rests) are used:

= four beats of silence, whole rest
= two beats of silence, half rest
= one beat of silence, quarter rest

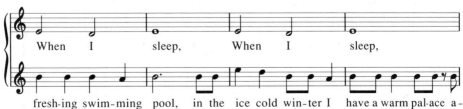

Group
Ostinato

When   I   sleep   When   I   sleep

Solo
Improvisation

way from all the   ice and snow . . . I   have   a   lim-ou-sine that

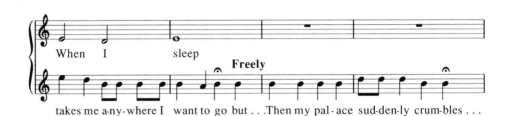

When   I   sleep

Freely

takes me a-ny-where I   want to go but . . . Then my pal-ace sud-den-ly crum-bles . . .

All   my   rich-es   are sto-len . . .   Ev - ery-thing I   had   is   gone.

E - very-thing I   bought, or   was giv-en, is   now gone . . . gone   un-til

Slowly

When   I   sleep,   When   I   sleep

When   I   sleep

Still using the *la* pentatonic set of tones, another student, another day, might give yet another interpretation of this poem, improvising a new melody above the group-sung ostinato. Such pieces are simpler to do than to notate. They tend to look more complex on paper in notation form than they are in actual practice. Even the teacher with a limited background in music should not fear this type of exploration. The rewards are great.

Touching on Form in Melody

When students repeat phrases in their improvisations, using similar melodies for different phrases, this presents a good opportunity to talk about form in melody. The main distinction between recitative and song is form. The latter often purposely repeats phrases, creating a predictable and purposeful kind of framework for a melody. The best melodies have not only a good melodic form, but are shaped to best serve the nuance of the word and phrase, thus enhancing the song's meaning. Notice the improvised phrase in the previous example, "in the red hot summer, I have . . ." "and in the ice cold winter, I have." The student sensed the parallel nature of the text and automatically sang these two phrases in a similar way, creating a repetition that hinted of form.

Older students may enjoy analyzing familiar songs to get a feeling for like, unlike, and similar phrases. Drawing these forms is a helpful way to visualize what is heard. This kind of observation of folk songs and familiar simple melodies strengthens understanding of how repetition creates structure in songs. For example,

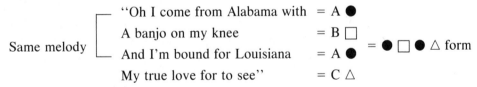

The same form is found in the first part of Beethoven's "Ode to Joy" from the Ninth Symphony.

There are many other song forms, and while it is not important to go into these in detail, it may be helpful in refining the task for the older student to be made aware of form. This understanding might allow K. S. to hear her two stanzas in a similar way, thus creating a form of ABAC for her poem (still using *la* pentatonic):

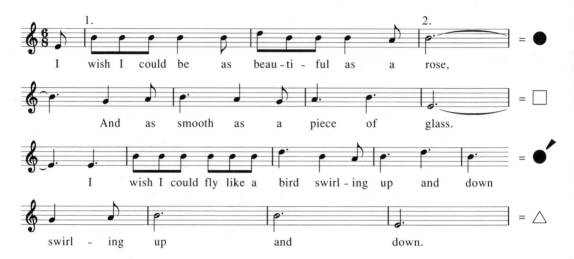

The A sections are not *exactly* the same, so this form would be A B A' C.

Melodic Canon

The pentatonic scale is very functional as a musical tool with which to create because of its simplicity and absence of half-steps, which can cause notes coming together to sound wrong. With the half-steps missing, the scale's tones are spread more evenly over the eight-note span (octave); therefore, one of the other good features is that the notes blend. This makes the pentatonic scale useful when creating canons. Many pentatonic melodies will work as canons, such as the preceding melody. Try it with two groups entering at points 1 and 2, for a two-part canon.

When a child constructs a melody with a form, one to be remembered, the tape recorder becomes essential to the mildly musical teacher who would not be expected to notate it. The repetition afforded by the tape recorder makes hanging onto melodies, such as the preceding one, possible in the regular classroom.

The "Shapes" of Melodies (Melodic Contour)
and Relation of Sound Duration
and Choice of Interval to Word Meaning

It can be interesting to observe the shape of a melody as an indication of its worth. Notice in "The River Is Wide" how the melody actually widens with a long-held note, and on a higher pitch, then how it descends with the thought of "not being able to get across it." Notice the beautifully shaped arch the outline of the melody creates with a gentle ascent and descent:

American Folk

In "Swing Low, Sweet Chariot," notice how *low* moves literally to a lower pitch, and how the phrase then soars upward to the high point of the idea, "home." Also observe the varied contour created from the melody outline:

Spiritual

In the example "This Land Is Your Land," notice how the word *your* is emphasized by the placement of notes and of *my* in the next phrase. Notice the phrases which are the same in melody, thus creating another example of the ABAC form shown earlier.

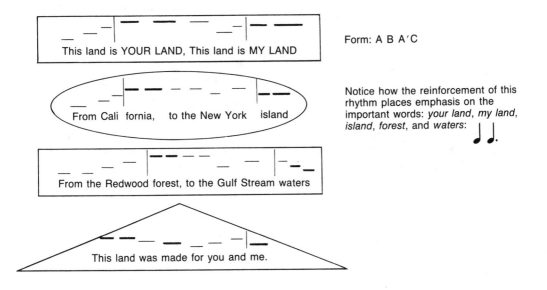

This land is YOUR LAND, This land is MY LAND

From Cali fornia,   to the New York   island

From the Redwood forest, to the Gulf Stream waters

This land was made for you and me.

Form: A B A'C

Notice how the reinforcement of this rhythm places emphasis on the important words: *your land*, *my land*, *island*, *forest*, and *waters*:

In "America the Beautiful," notice how the attention is turned to the words *beautiful* and *spacious* by the contour of the melody as well as attention to the nuance of the word:

Oh   beau - ti - ful   for   spac - ious skies . . .

In the American folk song, "Cindy," note how the word *wish* jumps out because of the high melodic placement:

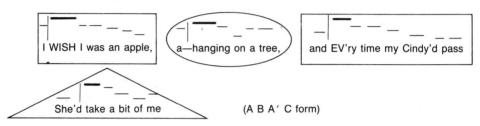

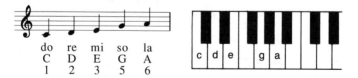

(A B A′ C form)

Taking songs common to a group of older students and letting them observe the ups and downs, nuances, and contours of these melodies strengthens their awarenesses for their own creations.

Using do *Pentatonic, the Major Five-Tone Scale*

There is another five-tone elemental scale useful for setting student poems into melodic pieces: *do* pentatonic, so named because it starts on *do* of the scale. Written on C, it looks as follows:

Because of the way the tones are arranged, this mode creates a brighter mood owing to the interval between C and E, called a major third. This mode is thus called a major pentatonic, unlike *la*, which was minor, and is darker in sound.

A way for the less experienced reader to hear that scale is to sing the first two phrases of "Oh Susanna," which outlines it perfectly:

Foster

Oh I   come from Al - a - bam - a   with   a   ban - jo   on   my   knee . . .

Getting the sounds of that mode into the students' ears becomes the task before asking them to create in that scale. Again, teacher-sung conversation, using these notes, will help prepare them.

**SAMPLE LESSON:
CONTINUED**

Freely

T: C. T. I've cho-sen your poem be-cause it's care-free... I

have a new set of sounds which I'm sing-ing...may we set your song us-ing these

sounds? Sing me your an-swer... [C. T.]: Yes, you may use my poem.

T: Class, as you read the first line of C. T.'s poem, will you make a gesture with your arm which looks like her words sound? [They read: "I wish I was a feather flying freely in the wind," and gesture.] Your arms rose and fell, much like the feather in her line.

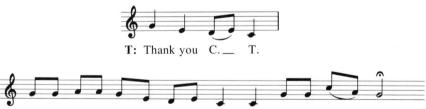

T: Thank you C.__ T.

T.: Who will try to sing me what your arms moved us-ing C. T.'s words?

[A relaxed pause here is essential to make time for the melodic ideas to happen in the students' minds. The teacher's body English and relaxed manner wordlessly say, "There is no doubt that someone will come up with something." If the pause is inordinate, the teacher can sing encouragement such as,  (singing) Can someone help with only the first two words, *I wish?* If the courage thermometer is low that day, the teacher can start the *I wish* and ask for someone to go from there.]

S:

I wish I was a feath-er...

T: Can everyone sing that line as I tape it? I like the way your melody makes *feather* important, and also helps insure the natural word accent: FEATHer. Who can continue that phrase? Everyone sing their ideas at once and use your arm movement again to give you melodic ideas. Begin. [Whole group explores.] Will one person share his or her idea? I'll sing the first part, and you raise your hand if you would like to sing your continuation. [T. sings: "I wish I was a feather."]

S:

...fly - ing free - ly in the wind...

S: Could the whole group echo that after the solo sings it?

T: Try it. C. T., would you sing the solo?

S:

[Solo] I wish I were a feath-er fly-ing free-ly in the

wind... [group] Fly - ing free - ly in the wind...

T: That was a good idea—it sounded fine. Perhaps the other lines would lend themselves to that kind of echo. Will someone please sing an idea for the next line?

S:

I wish I were a bird, fly-ing through the sky...

Here the teacher points up a form that was created when the student sang the second line almost like the first. The observation of the student's slowing of the rhythm pointed out the appropriateness of time to word meaning and spoke to the sensitivity of the student who instinctively did the artistic thing. It is important to be able to reflect along the (creative) way, alerting students to their own inner perceptions, and sharing these strengths with their peers.

T: I like the way you began the second line like the first—you've started a feeling of melodic form. I also liked the way you slowed down on "through the sky," which gave the bird time to fly. Nice. Can we sing the song so far, starting with "I wish I were a feather," with the group echoing the last part of the line? [Group sings.] There is one more thought in C. T.'s poem: "I wish I was a tree swiftly shaking in the wind." Are there any ideas for a melody?

S: Why don't we do the third line like the other two?

T: Can you sing your idea?

S: No—but like starting *I wish* from low to high like you did before.

T: Like this? [T. sings:]

I   wish . . .

S: That's it.

T: Can someone complete this idea?

S:

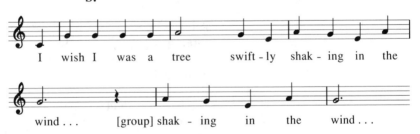

T: So far our form has been AA′A″—the first three phrases have been very similar. This is fine. It would be good to have the last line contrast these three lines by being different, however, making our form AA′A″B, another possible song form. There are different possibilities for the last note of this piece: If you want it to sound final, the ending note should be C, or 1, or *do*. If you want an unfinished feeling, you can end on the third tone or the fifth (E or G) and make your music walk off into the sunset, so to speak. C. T.—do you prefer a wispy or final-sounding ending?

C. T.: Wispy.

Rather than let students inadvertently drift into less than satisfactory musical experiences, the teacher should feel free to alert them to a better solution—in this case, the need for contrast so the form will be interesting and convincing.

T: Then will someone volunteer a melody for the words "But I am me" and *not* end on C? Will the class be ready to echo the line?

S:

But   I . . .   am . . .   me [group echos]

T: Get ready to try the whole poem while I find some blank space on this tape. As we are taping your performance, consider anything else you might imagine doing with C. T.'s work, and be ready to share your ideas with the class. [Entire poem with melody and group echo is taped.]

S: In my mind I saw movement, on the words *feather, bird,* and *tree shaking.*

S: I heard other sounds: like the mark tree Jason made from house keys that jingle during the part where the tree is shaking.

S: I heard just one sound being blown on a bottle throughout the whole poem . . . maybe C . . . or two people on bottles so you could breathe and not have it heard.

T: All very good ideas. I would like you to divide up into three groups—sound effects, movement, and bottle sounds—and take five minutes to polish your ideas. Your group will share its ideas with the class, and from these we will decide on a final version of this poem. Harry, will you be the leader of the movement group over there, bottles to that corner, and sound effects stay here. Walk to the group in which you are most interested and we'll come back together in five minutes.

SUMMARY: MELODY ————————————————————————————

Here, we've considered melody from its simplest level: that of vocal inflection and nuance, moving into more complex melody through sustained vowels, through sung conversation (recitative), and through elemental four- and five-note scales. We looked at melodic form and contour, and we touched on melodic canons.

The ideas offered are appropriate for students of all ages, and provide many levels of experimentation for teachers with much or minimum experience. It is hoped that the suggestions will encourage boldness in an area which can bring music to the students' poems, and to the general classroom. As Langston Hughes said,

To make words sing,
Is a wonderful, wonderful, wonderful thing,
Because, in a song . . .
They last so long . . .[2]

————

[2]*The First Book of Rhythms,* Langston Hughes, Franklin Watts, 1954. Reprinted by permission of Harold Ober Associates Incorporated. Copyright 1954 by Franklin Watts Inc. Copyright renewed 1982 by George Houston Bass.

chapter 4

*the
when-i-fall-asleep
poem*

POETIC FORM AND REVISION TECHNIQUES:
THE WHEN-I-FALL-ASLEEP POEM

Our aim in these introductory poetry sessions has been to initiate experimentation with language. In an uninhibited, nonjudgmental environment, we explored individual creative responses to a variety of subjects. The emphasis has been on language skills and word play rather than poetic form. However, at this point, having inspired our students to be creatively adventurous, we need to map the boundaries of their adventure by defining the structure of free verse poetry. How does a poem look on the page? In what ways does it differ from the story? What is a line? A stanza? In what ways do they differ from the sentence and the paragraph? Many of our students are already aware that there is a difference between the poem and the story and that what they have been writing is, in fact, different from most routine classroom writing experiences.

Using, once again, a fantasy-inspired writing task, we introduce editing techniques, requiring that each student approach the poem with an eye toward tightening and enhancing it. By providing some simple guidelines that will help to clarify the intent of poetry, we also provide the tools each student will need to critique his or her own work and identify those elements which are essential to poetry and those which are superfluous. Since, in most cases, students tend to overwrite, much of their editing will take the form of shortening. This shortening, or tightening, process emphasizes the fundamental goals of poetry: to be compact and have sensory impact; or, more simply stated, to say the most, in the best possible way, using the least amount of words. It is these precise poetic requirements that are most beneficial to the student in all aspects of language application. By learning to choose between what is important and what is not, we learn to be selective. We learn, as well, to think in terms of the impression what we are writing (or saying) will have on our audience. We begin to understand the importance of weighing the meaning of our words and their dramatic effect.

Ultimately, in this writing, rewriting, and editing process we learn to take responsibility for what we have written, to accept that our words are an extension of ourselves.

A poem rich in imagery (''Hands'') was selected by the teacher/poet in the poetry sample lesson. She felt that this poem would provide fertile soil for the students' imagination, allowing them to reach daringly beyond themselves for the unique and extraordinary.

SAMPLE LESSON: POETRY

T: I'd like to begin today's lesson by reading a poem. The poem deals with a fantasy experience. Listen very carefully to what the poem says and for those poetic tools we've been learning to use.

HANDS

I

When I fall asleep
my hands leave me.

They pick up pens
and draw creatures
with five feathers
on each wing.

The creatures multiply.
They say; ''We are large
like your father's
hands.''

They say; ''We have
your mother's
knuckles.''

I speak to them:
''If you are hands,
why don't you
touch?''

And the wings beat
the air, clapping.
They fly

high above elbows
and wrists.
They open windows
and leave.

They perch in treetops
and hide under bushes
biting
their nails. "Hands,"
I call them.
But it is fall

and all creatures
with wings prepare to fly
South.

        II
When I sleep
the shadows of my hands
come to me.

They are softer than feathers
and warm as creatures
who have been close
to the sun.

They say; "We are the giver,"
and tell of oranges
growing on trees.

They say; "We are the vessel,"
and tell of journeys
through water.

They say; "We are the cup."

And I stir in my sleep.
Hands pull triggers
and cut trees. But

the shadows of my hands
tuck their heads
under wings

waiting
for morning,
when I will wake
braiding
three strands of hair
into one.

                    Siv Cedering
                Cup of Cold Water, 1973

T: That masterwork poem was filled with some lovely images. Would someone tell us a little about one of the images they particularly liked? Barbara?

S: I liked the way the poet compared hands to birds.

T: I liked that, too. Why is that an effective image?

S: Because hands are a little bit like birds.

T: In what way?

S: Sometimes they move like birds do.

T: How do birds move?

S: Slowly.

S: Gracefully.

S: Birds don't move slowly. They move a lot and very quickly.

T: What's a good word for the quick movements that birds and hands make?

S: Fluttering?

T: Excellent. Can anyone think of another?

S: Darting?

T: That also works very well and describes perfectly the movement of birds and hands. Anybody else have an image or a line from the poem that they particularly liked?

S: I liked the way the poet said that the hands bit their nails. It's silly, but I liked it.

T: It does bring an amusing picture to mind; hands biting their own nails. Perhaps this tells us that the poet has a sense of humor. Another image or line that you liked? John?

S: The poet compared hands to vessels and cups. I liked that.

The teacher is directing the students (through pointed questions and responses) toward deeper understanding of the masterwork poem, while at the

T: I see those images work for you. Good. Are you able to picture them?

S: Yes. I think so.

T: Explain how you see them in your imagination.

S: Well, hands can hold things just like a cup. I guess that's the way I see them.

same time encouraging them to create their own imagery. She offers a great deal of affirmative input, and keeps the pace of the discussion propelled in the direction of a pre-planned goal—that of student understanding of and appreciation for the masterwork poem, and discovering inspiration within the masterwork poem which will initiate written student work.

The line between what is real and what is not becomes blurred in the context of the masterwork poem. The teacher (acting as a director) is letting the students discover for themselves the extent of the fantasy, and the extent to which the poet is able to make the unreal seem real and believable. This helps to enforce the concept that language used with the skill of a poet is capable of great accomplishments. Further, the teacher-led discussion is drawing a parallel between the

T: What did the poet mean by *vessel?*

S: I think *vessel* meant a boat because the *vessel* tells of a journey through water.

T: You were really listening very carefully. Does the image work for you? Can you picture it?

S: I can, but it doesn't seem to be as good an image as hands being cups. I liked that one better because it's easier to picture. But hands can swim through water.

T: You thought that through very well. Some other images, please. Perhaps some that will let us know that the poet was using the five senses.

S: The poem talks about water and oranges.

S: The poet also says that the hands are softer than feathers and that they are warm.

T: That's the way to listen to a poem. And, by the way, you've chosen some of my favorite lines from the poem. "They are softer than feathers and warm as creatures who have been close to the sun." Does anyone else have a favorite line or lines?

S: The poem says the hands tuck their heads beneath their wings. I really liked that.

T: It's interesting, isn't it, that we can accept these fantasy images so easily? Somehow, we can picture hands becoming birds tucking their heads beneath their wings. It requires a leap of imagination, but we all seem to be able to do it. Poetry gives us the freedom to be outrageous; to paint an impossible picture with words and make it seem possible. Why do you think poetry can do that?

S: Because everyone knows that poems don't have to be real.

S: Also, because it's your imagination and you can imagine anything you want.

T: That's true. What makes us believe the unbelievable? What makes it so real that we can see it, hear it, taste it, touch it, smell it?

S: Using the five senses.

T: Absolutely. What else?

S: Using adjectives and images.

skills being learned in the classroom and their actual application in a published poem by a master poet. The work ends with an image that is real—and revealing—about the poet, once again reinforcing the power of putting oneself into one's poem.

T: Using adjectives and images *effectively*. The poem works when we use *language* that makes it work. How does the poet end the poem?

S: By saying, "I will wake up."

T: Does that bring us back to reality?

S: Yes.

T: What is the very *real* thing that the poet's hands do upon waking?

S: Braid hair.

T: Exactly. A very real and even ordinary thing to be doing. Not a fantasy thing at all. And because it ends the fantasy, it becomes even more meaningful. Perhaps it even tells us something personal about the poet.

S: That the poet has long hair.

T: Yes, and wears it braided. Remember, we've talked often about the importance of putting ourselves into our poems. The poem needs to belong to you. Like your signature or your fingerprint, it needs to identify you even if the subject is a fantasy. Let's try to come up with some images for a when-I-fall-asleep fantasy poem. It doesn't have to be about your hands. Let's try to come up with images that tell us what your feet or eyes or voice or all of you may do when you fall asleep. An image, please.

S: When I fall asleep my eyes roll out of my body like stones.

T: Excellent. Can you take it a bit farther and tell us what those stones do?

S: They roll down a mountain and fall into a lake.

T: Nicely done and easy to picture, I think. Another image, please.

S: When I fall asleep my bed becomes a river and I become a mermaid and swim my way to morning.

T: I love that one, Jessica. Someone else?

S: My feet become frogs and hop all over the place.

T: Tell me a little about those frogs. Color, size . . . are they muddy?

S: They are fat, squishy, bright green frogs.

T: That's the way to use adjectives. Another image, please.

S: My voice becomes thunder and crashes down on sleeping cities.

T: You have the beginnings of alliteration there. Sleeping . . . cities . . . hear the same sound? Expand on that, please. Give us some more alliteration for that line.

S: Sad, sleeping cities.

T: More.

S: Sad, silent, shadowy, sleeping cities.

T: Well done. It's fun to try and come up with words that have the same sound and still add meaning to our poems. May I hear another image for our poem?

S: When I fall asleep my body rolls into a ball and bounces down Broadway.

T: That's a fun one. Let's have one that deals with the sense of taste.

S: When I fall asleep I become a pepperoni pizza at a party.

S: When I fall asleep my fingers twist into pretzels.

T: How about one for the sense of smell?

S: When I fall asleep my ears blossom into fragrant flowers.

T: Ears do have a flowery look to them, so I'm really able to picture that quite clearly. An image for the sense of touch?

S: My skin turns hard and brown as the bark on trees.

T: Excellent. I remember that we already have an image for the sense of hearing. Does anyone remember what it was?

S: The one about thunder.

At this point in the lesson the teacher gives cues to the students to help them fashion their responses. Even if

T: Right. I think we now have an image for each of the five senses. How about an image that has to do with an emotion? Is anyone able to think of one?

S: That's a lot harder.

T: Perhaps it is. Let's see if we can come up with

levity was not the direction the teacher had preplanned, the students have, in exuberant fashion, taken control by providing humorous (but nonetheless well developed) imagery. The teacher now follows their lead, praising the richness of their images and going with the flow.

something together. When we fall asleep might something turn into laughter or tears?

S: How about my eyelashes turning into tears?

T: That works. Remember, we decided that in poetry it's all right to be outrageous.

S: When I fall asleep my hair starts to giggle.

S: And my eyebrows become caterpillars and tickle me till I laugh out loud and wake myself up.

T: Delightful, happy images. Let's take all the images that I've written on the board and look at them as a whole when-I-fall-asleep group fantasy poem.

When-I-Fall-Asleep Group Fantasy Poem

When I fall asleep my eyes roll out of my body
like stones and roll down a mountain and fall into
a lake. When I fall asleep my bed becomes a river
and I become a mermaid and swim my way to
morning. My feet become fat, bright, green
squishy frogs and hop all over the place. My voice
becomes thunder and crashes down on sad,
silent, shadowy, sleeping cities. When I fall asleep
my body rolls into a ball and bounces down
Broadway. When I fall asleep I become a
pepperoni pizza at a party. When I fall asleep my
fingers twist into pretzels. When I fall asleep my
ears blossom into fragrant flowers. My skin turns
hard and brown as the bark on trees. My
eyelashes turn into tears. When I fall asleep my
hair starts to giggle. My eyebrows become
caterpillars and tickle me till I laugh out loud and
wake myself up.

The teacher is now preparing to superimpose form over the group student

T: Do you like your poem? Do you like your images?

Class: Yes!

T: I like it, too. But I'm wondering if your poem *looks* and *sounds* like a poem. What do you think?

poem. Using their own (group) creation as the clay, together with class input, she begins to mold the unwieldy imagery through editing techniques, into the precisely elegant language of poetry. The teacher is also using a simple visual device to reinforce the definition of poetic form. Whenever possible, appealing to students on more than one sensory level is a helpful and memorable teaching technique.

S: It doesn't look like one the way you've written it on the board.

T: No, it doesn't. Why not?

S: Poems look shorter and they don't go all the way across the page.

T: True. Poems do have a shorter look to them and the words do not usually go all the way across the page the way they do in a story. Can you point out some other differences you've noticed between a poem and a story?

S: Poems don't always have periods at the end of a sentence.

S: Sometimes the first letter in each line is capitalized.

T: In certain types of poetry that is quite true. I think we all agree that poems really don't look much at all like stories. They tend to be shorter. They don't stretch across the page from margin to margin, and sometimes the punctuation seems a bit creative. The truth is that poems are really *very* different from stories. They are meant to be. If you will all look at my hands [teacher raises hands over head extending wide the fingers on one hand and tightening the other hand into a fist], you will notice that one of my hands is wide open while the other is curled into a fist. If one of my hands represents a poem and one a story, which hand do you think is the poem?

S: I think the hand curled into a fist is the poem, because poems look shorter than stories and use less words.

T: You are absolutely right. A poem is meant to be tight, compact, and powerful . . . just like this fist. A story, which can be told in a leisurely fashion, is represented by my relaxed, wide-open hand. Stories take their time. Let me give you an example. First, I will describe, in story form, a walk in the woods on a summer day. [Write story on board.]

> It was a beautiful day. The sun was shining overhead in a clear blue sky. Many birds were singing in the trees. There were robins and blue

jays and sparrows and other birds I did not know
by name. There were flowers everywhere;
daffodils, jonquils, lillies, daisies and wild roses.
Those lovely, colorful flowers filled the air with the
most wonderful and delicate fragrance.

T: Look at the story written on the board. I think we can
all agree that we are very comfortable with its form.
We see that form in books and write in that form
ourselves, all the time. It's familiar to us. Let's take
this story and turn it into poetry. [Write poem on
board next to story.]

The sun shone
like a giant eye, out
of the cloudless depths
of a summer sky; the air
was filled with a chorus
of birds, there was a rainbow
at my feet and the air
was perfume sweet.

T: There are some very obvious differences between the
sound and the look of these two versions of the same
walk in the woods on a summer day. Let's go back
over the poem and find some of the things left out and
some of the changes that were made. Begin, John, by
finding some missing words.

S: You left out the names of the different kinds of birds
and the names of the different kinds of flowers. And
you also had a rhyme.

T: Yes, true enough. Actually, the poem has a couple of
rhymes. Even though we are not writing rhyming
poetry, we are, in free verse, free to use rhyme on

occasion if we feel it will enhance the poem or the flow of words—the rhythm.[1]

T: What other differences are there between the poem and the story?

S: You used words like *chorus* and *rainbow* and *perfume* instead of saying that the birds were singing or that there were lots of different kinds of flowers and that they had a great smell.

T: Good for you for noticing all that. You hit on the key to writing poetry: always to look for the one word or combination of words that will create the image, rather than giving a lengthy explanation. I want to point out to you, at this time, that we are dealing (in poetry) with *lines* and *stanzas,* not sentences and

---

[1]Menke Katz, "A Word or Two Against Rhyme," *Aspects of Modern Poetry, Poet Lore,* © Menke Katz, *A Chair for Elijah,* The Smith, 1985.

Poet brother, let your word roll unrhymed
as thunder, let it flash like free lightening
through the fog: over a parched field, the
eager harbinger of rain. The poem in rhyme
bends like a captured foe under the arched yoke.

Poems sit in rhyme like men, birds, beasts
in cages. I saw Samson, with fist in the teeth of
a lion, forced to his knees under the load of rhyme.

A chased deer in the panic of the forest does
not race in rhyme.
A grieved stone does not mourn in rhyme.
The rhyme, patted and rounded by the file of crystal verse,
cuts into the flesh of a word like a wound.
If like thirst, stream, sun, storm is the eternal poem,
lock not the storm in the cell of rhyme.

Give the word the fresh scent of ripe corn
swaying in the wind of a hopeful field,
tasty as the rare bread of my hungry childhood.

O let the word ride endlessly, fantastic
speak face to face, heart to heart
with your neighbor of the farthest century.

Poet brother, wars do not kill in rhyme.
A plummeting airplane, like a wounded eagle
does not fall in rhyme.
A hurricane does not uproot trees in rhyme.
The stormy sea, in full scorn, is an endless rhymeless call
for a day without lock or rhyme.

Menke Katz

paragraphs. It is the line, in particular, that I want to emphasize. Unlike the sentence, which begins and concludes a thought, the line may want to leave the thought unfinished, and in so doing create a moment of drama or suspense. Where a line (or lines) ends may drastically change the meaning of the poem. Where a line ends is often of vital importance to the musical flow and dramatic effect of the poem. Leaving an unanswered question at the end of a line will serve to coax the reader's eye on to the next line. Let's look at our summer walk again, line by line, and see if we can figure out why the lines ended where they did and how they affect the meaning and flow of the poem. First line, "The sun shone"—is there an unanswered question there?

S: Yes, I think so. How did the sun shine, or maybe, where did the sun shine?

T: Right. Next line—"like a giant eye, out . . . "

S: Out of what?

T: Next line—"of the cloudless depths . . . "

S: Depths of what?

T: "of a summer sky, the air . . . "

S: The air what?

T: "was filled with a chorus . . . "

S: A chorus of what?

T: "of birds, there was . . . "

S: There was what?

T: "a rainbow . . . "

S: Where?

T: "at my feet and the air was . . . "

S: Was what?

T: "perfume sweet." In this instance, each line *did* end with a question. We don't always have to do that. Sometimes we will end a line where we would naturally take a breath if we were speaking the lines out loud. Sometimes we want to make a line seem more important, and we can do this by leaving a key word or image all by itself on the line, and sometimes we end (or break) a line for the visual impact it will have on the reader. In any event, we now understand clearly that the poem does not look or sound at all like our story. The story combines sentences into paragraphs. Each sentence offers us a complete thought, and each paragraph offers us those sentences that have something in common. We end a paragraph and begin a new one when there is a break in the idea or a move to a new idea. In free verse poetry, we deal with lines and stanzas (instead of sentences and paragraphs). We've already done some experimenting with poetic line. The poetic stanza (in free verse) may contain one line or twenty or more. We end the stanza when we choose to create a break or a pause in the flow of our poem. Some poems have no stanza breaks and some have many.

Let's work now with our group poem. We have agreed that it does not look like a poem, and if it does not look like a poem it will not read (or sound) like one. Using what we now know about lines and stanzas, let's rewrite and diagram (on the board) our when-I-fall-asleep group poem.

WHEN-I-FALL-ASLEEP GROUP POEM
REVISION PROCESS

remove/capitalize   M   *remove*
| When I fall asleep | my eyes roll out of my body / like stones, | and | roll / down a
                                                        line break   *line break*

        remove   *comma, remove*   *remove*
mountain, | and | fall / into a lake⊙, | When I fall asleep | my bed becomes / a river, | and |
                line break   *line break*

                        remove   *new stanza*
I / become a mermaid / | and | swim my way / to morning. / / My feet become fat, /
line break   *line break*   *line break*   *line break*

                                                comma, small m
bright green, squishy / frogs and hop all / over the place⊙, My voice becomes /
                line break   *line break*   *line break*

remove, add comma   *remove*   *new stanza, remove*
thunder⊙ | and | crashes down / on | sad | silent, shadowy, / sleeping cities. / / | When |
                                line break   *line break*

remove,   *M capitalize*
| I fall asleep | ḿy body rolls into / a ball and bounces down / Broadway. | When I |
   line break   *line break*

remove   *comma, remove*
| fall asleep | I become / a pepperoni pizza / at a party⊙, | When I fall asleep | my
   line break   *line break*

comma, remove
fingers twist / into pretzels⊙, | When I fall asleep | my ears / blossom into
   line break   *line break*

comma, small m m   *stanza break*
fragrant flowers⊙, My skin turns / hard and brown as / the bark on trees. / / My
   line break   *line break*   *line break*

comma   *remove*   *comma, small m* m
eyelashes turn / into tears⊙, | When I fall asleep | my hair / starts to giggle⊙, My
   line break   *line break*

eyebrows / become caterpillars and tickle / me till I laugh out loud and wake /
   line break   *line break*   *line break*

myself up.

T: The title of our poem, "When I Fall Asleep," tells the reader what the poem is going to be about. It is, therefore, unnecessary to use that line in our poem. You will notice, from the diagram, that we have removed it each time it appeared. This tightens our poem and heightens and intensifies the rhythm of the poem. We can also tighten our poem by removing words like *and* and *sad*. We remove *and* because it doesn't add anything to the meaning or flow of the poem. We remove *sad* because, while alliteration is an effective poetic device, we don't want to overuse it. I chose to remove the word *sad*. You might have chosen to edit out a different *s* word. Removing a word or words from a poem gives us the opportunity to exercise value judgments as to which words express our ideas most clearly and add to the drama of the piece. We discover that we can end or break a line in odd and unusual places; right in the very middle of the idea. We can often remove a period and put in a comma instead. This exchange provides an interesting pause but does not interfere with the flow of the lines. We can choose to end a stanza and begin another at a point we feel will add to the impact of the poem. By ending a stanza, we give additional dramatic weight to both the stanza that has just ended and the one about to begin. It is as though we are advising the reader that he or she has come to a corner and is about to turn in a slightly (or dramatically) different direction.

[*Note:* The following changes and revisions should be accomplished through group discussion and experimentation. There is more than one way for the poem to happen. During the revisionary process, the lines should be read aloud repeatedly, by the teacher and by the students, noting how different people place the emphasis on different words and breath phrasing. Let each student decide for himself or herself which phrasing works best, which seems to capture the rhythmic and musical flow of words into poetry. How a poem *sounds* should be a significant factor in how the words, lines, and stanzas ultimately arrange themselves on the page.]

WHEN I FALL ASLEEP

My eyes roll out of my body
like stones, roll
down a mountain, fall
into a lake, my bed becomes
a river, I
become a mermaid
swim my way
to morning.

My feet become fat
bright green, squishy
frogs and hop all
over the place, my voice becomes
thunder, crashes down
on silent, shadowy
sleeping cities.

My body rolls into
a ball and bounces down
Broadway, I become
a pepperoni pizza
at a party, my fingers twist
into pretzels, my ears
blossom into fragrant
flowers, my skin turns
hard and brown as
the bark on trees.

My eyelashes turn
into tears, my hair
starts to giggle, my eyebrows
become caterpillars and tickle
me till I laugh out loud and wake
myself up.

T: Does the poem look and sound more like a poem now?

S: Yes. A lot more. But sometimes the lines look and sound funny.

T: Give me an example of a line, in our group poem, that you think looks or sounds funny.

S: When the poem says: "roll down a mountain, fall into a lake." I think it would sound better if you left in the word *and*.

T: I see what you mean. I also understand why it sounds strange to you. We have to get used to the idea that we are not writing prose (stories). Poems have different requirements and, as we have already mentioned, are shaped by different rhythmical considerations. You *could* use the word *and* but you don't *have* to use it. It's a choice that, as a poet, each one of you has to make privately in the editing process. You may choose to leave the word in, but if you do, you need to have a good reason. It needs to add to the poem in some important way. If it doesn't, then it probably needs to be edited out. Sometimes, when we are rewriting our poems, we will choose to *change* a word because we find a better, more emphatic, way of saying something. In editing our group poem today, most of our editing took the form of removing words and groups of words, but we might just as easily have been called on to add words or change words. Each revision that you do is unique and will place different demands on you as a poet. With all this in mind, I'd like for each of you to begin writing a first draft of a poem entitled, "When I Fall Asleep." First draft means that I will expect you to revise, or edit, your poems at a later time.

student poems

Note: Some of the following revisions were done with the help and advice of the teacher. Some were done by the teacher to use as classroom examples, and some were done by the students with little or no help.

MY FANTASY (FIRST DRAFT)

When I am asleep my spirit leaves me, it travels over land and the sea and comes to the Nile where pyramids used to be. I plunge into the Nile depths and there I travel back through time to the time of the Pharaohs. I am an Egyptian Queen and I rule over all the land, when they fan me it feels like I am flying through the air again. I feel the soft feathers there like silk or like a cat, then when morning starts coming I smile at my husband, the Pharaoh. This is the day I died I went to the tower and I fell and fell and plunged deep into the Nile, but what a sorrowful death I hurry home to join my body in my bed.

MY FANTASY
(REVISED VERSION)

When I am asleep my spirit
leaves me, it travels
over land and sea and comes
to the Nile where Pyramids
used to be, I plunge deep
into the Nile's depths
traveling back through time.

I am an Egyptian Queen ruling
the land, they fan me
and it feels like I am flying
through the air again, I feel
the soft feathers like silk
or like a cat, when morning
comes I smile.

The day I died I went
to a tower and fell
and fell and plunged deep
into the Nile to a sorrowful
death, then I hurried home
to join my body
in my bed.

K. R., 6th grade

WHAT HAPPENS TO ME OVERNIGHT
(FIRST DRAFT)

When I fall asleep I feel myself changing
   I grow and I shrink.
You can hear my raging voice
   I sound like this: RRRRR
You can see me turn all shapes and sizes.
   I grow and I shrink.
I even stretch.

WHAT HAPPENS TO ME OVERNIGHT
(REVISED VERSION)

I feel myself changing
   I grow
   I shrink
my voice rages
   I sound like
   this, RRRRR
I turn all shapes
   all sizes
I grow
   I shrink
I even stretch

               K. L., 4th grade

MY FANTASY
(FIRST DRAFT)

When I go to sleep my mind
drifts away, it goes far away to
fantasyland and dreams of my closet
full of gold and my downstairs a giant
gameroom. My front lawn has a tree as
high as the stars that I can climb and
my house is a mansion that is
12 stories high and with a chimney
made of silver.
I dream of no school and there's summer
four years straight and then winter for two years, then
I feel the seaweed that came from the ocean. I feel
the soft sand, but when I wake up it's all over.
All I see is the sun shining through my window
onto my bed.

MY FANTASY
(REVISED VERSION)

When I go to sleep my mind
drifts away to a
fantasyland, dreaming
of my closet full
of gold, my downstairs is
a giant gameroom, my front lawn
has a tree as high
as the stars that
I can climb.

My house is a mansion
12 stories high, the chimney
is silver, I dream
of no school, there's
summer for four years
straight then winter
for two years, I feel
soft squishy seaweed that comes
from the ocean, I feel
soft sand, I wake
and see the sun shining
like a lightbulb
through my window
onto my bed.

               J. L., 5th grade

MY FANTASY
(FIRST DRAFT)

When I dream my body leaves me, and I fly
just like a bird or a kite
I have no doors around me, I just fly high.
Soaring hundreds of feet above.
I zoom here and there and everywhere.

MY FANTASY
(REVISED VERSION)

When I dream my body
leaves me, I fly just like
a bird or kite.

I have no doors
around me, I fly
high above.

I zoom
here
there
everywhere.

> L. T., 5th grade

MY FANTASY
(FIRST DRAFT)

When I am
sleeping my eyes
get up and I
see the world
I see the beautiful
water of the ocean, I hear
the roar of the waves,
when they splash.
I smell the beautiful air by the sea. I feel
the feathers of a seagull.

MY FANTASY
(REVISED VERSION)

When I sleep
my eyes get up, I see
the world, I see
the beautiful waters
of the ocean, I hear
the raging, roaring
of the waves
as they splash, I smell
the fragrant air
by the sea, I feel
the fluffy feathers
of a seagull.

> J. K., 5th grade

MY FANTASY
(FIRST DRAFT)

When I am asleep I
think of my feet. My
feet do a lot of work.

They run as fast as
a locomotive and they are strong
as a big football players
legs.

And I feel the hot sand
when I walk on the beach
and when I go swimming
I feel the cold water
on my feet.

This is my dream.

MY FANTASY
(REVISED VERSION)

When I am asleep I think
of my feet, they do
a lot of work.

They run fast
as a locomotive, are strong
as a big football player's
legs.

I feel the hot
soft sand when I
walk on the beach, when
I swim, I feel
the cold clear water
on my feet.

This
is
my
dream.

B. W., 3rd grade

SUMMARY: POETRY _____

These revised poems represent the students' attempt to critique their own work. In an effort to explore the rhythms and responsibilities of poetry, they have tried to experiment with the unknown. Often, their own poems sound strange to their ears. The lines seem somehow incomplete without the *ands* and *buts* and *therefores*. The students are, however, beginning to acknowledge that language is workable and, like stone or clay, merely awaits the artist's hand to mold it into form, shape it into meaning. In today's lesson students have begun to realize that creative writing (poetry) is a form of "word art," and the material they have to work with is the rich ore of their own vocabularies and imaginations.

DISCOVERING FOUND SOUNDS IN THE CLASSROOM: THE WHEN-I-FALL-ASLEEP POEM _____

Thus far, those sounds used as a backdrop for poetry have largely come from the body: the voice (in vocalization, sound effect, and providing the melody), finger clicks, stamps, claps, and leg slaps (patsches). In addition, the classroom offers a repository of imaginative and useful sounds with which to play as poem enhancements. Locating and categorizing these sounds for use throughout the year is a delightful lesson unto itself.

In general, sounds can be grouped in the categories of loud/soft; sustained/short; emanating from metal, paper, plastic, or wood sources. Sounds can have pitch or be nonspecific. Considering first those objects which are breakable/scratchable, having the students "play the room" is a good way to experience the musical potential of a classroom.

SAMPLE LESSON: FOUND SOUNDS

A good stop-and-start structure is important here, as is moving from cacaphony to an organized sound framework within that structure.

Pacing this lesson to group similar sounds quickly is also important. Students must respect others' found sounds as they are demonstrated (by controlling their own).

In any sequence of wholesale experimentation, the goal is to move from the general, to the somewhat specific, to the specific. Jumping a step results in not utilizing the full range of found sounds in creative ways.

T: Our room is like a "symphony waiting to be played." It is full of sound possibilities which may not usually be used for that purpose. We may find that some sounds will be useful accompaniments to your original poetry. Will each of you look around the room, and with an object (such as the eraser end of a pencil, or unsharpened pencil, or ruler, or your hand) demonstrate your chosen sound with a short rhythm, one person at a time? Something like

or invent your own. I'll give you a minute to look around, and a minute to try out your sound softly. [Children scatter and experiment.] I've put some categories on the board. When each of you has demonstrated your sound, the class will find the best category for each. They are [reads from board] metal sounds, wooden, paper, plastic, and miscellaneous. Play your rhythm softly one time and one time loudly. [The class calls out category after each plays, and T writes on board.]

Some possible sounds found in a general classroom:

METAL SOUNDS

1. Ruler tapped on the bottom of a metal can from school kitchen
2. Teacher's bell
3. Pencil or ruler run along spiral of notebook
4. Metal leg tapping floor
5. Metal edge of ruler tapping metal cabinet
6. Magic markers tapped together

MISCELLANEOUS

1. Sound of pencil sharpener
2. Paper clips shook in box
3. Globe thumped with hand
4. Chair/desk drummed with hand
5. Hardcover books opened and closed abruptly
6. Chalkboard tapped
7. Venetian blinds played

WOODEN SOUNDS

1. Wooden ruler or pencil tapped on desk
2. Pencils tapped on pencils
3. Rulers tapped on rulers
4. Unsharpened pencils tapped on wooden desks, chair, table

PLASTIC SOUNDS

1. Plastic ruler against ruler

PAPER SOUNDS

1. Notebook fanned
2. Notebook paper crinkled
3. Newspaper wadded
4. Newspaper folded and whacked against a chair
5. Phone book on rug struck with mallet (can actually get different pitches by opening the book to different sections)

At another time these sounds should be considered in new groupings, such as those sounds which have a mysterious quality, those dynamically energetic, those milder, sounds which continue, sounds which decay quickly, funny sounds, scary sounds, etc.

FIRST USES OF FOUND SOUNDS

As the first use of the classroom as a symphony of sounds, students might together create a "rondo rap" using these sounds to frame room or school rules (or spelling rules, etc.). A student-created chant is as follows:

Chant:
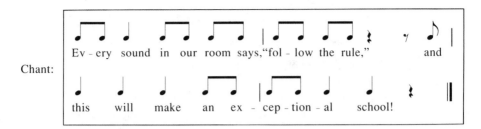

Ev - ery sound in our room says,"fol - low the rule," and
this will make an ex - cep - tion - al school!

Contrasting section played by wooden sounds, one at a time. ‖: [pencils] ♩ ♩ ♩ 𝄽 𝄽 | [rulers] ♩ ♩ ♩ 𝄽 𝄽 :‖ etc.
(fol-low the rule)   (fol-low the rule)

Chant: Every sound in our room says, "follow the rule," and this will make an exceptional school!

Contrasting section played by metal sounds, ‖: [T.'s bell] ♩ ♩ ♩ 𝄽 𝄽 | [pencil on metal cabinet] ♩ ♩ ♩ 𝄽 𝄽 :‖ etc.
(fol-low the rule)   (fol-low the rule)

Chant: Every sound in our room says, "follow the rule," and this will make an exceptional school!

Contrasting section played by plastic/miscellaneous ‖: [newspaper roll struck] ♩ ♩ ♩ 𝄽 𝄽 | [velcro sneaker] ♩ ♩ ♩ 𝄽 𝄽 :‖ etc.
(fol-low the rule)   (fol-low the rule)

Chant: Every sound in our room says, "follow the rule," and this will make an exceptional school!

The students will have performed a rondo in ABACA form and will have a new awareness of the infinite variety of objects which make sound, along with the chance to savor those qualities.

Other Easy, Inexpensive Sound Sources

The Body

Some applications not yet used are "mouthed" whistles (front pucker, side to side) humming, lip pops, buzzing, mouth percussion called "eefen and oafen" used to accompany folk music (particularly from Appalachia) and opening velcro fasteners on sneakers.

The following is an example of "eefen" which provides a wonderful rhythmic accompaniment if you don't hyperventilate:

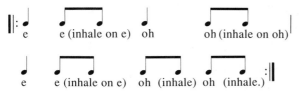

The Home

Aluminum skillet lids make effective sustained gong sounds; soup spoons held as indicated make a wonderful rhythm. Pot lids can serve as cymbals, and assorted

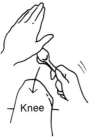

Spoons are struck on right leg and palm of left hand.

Spoons are raked over the stiffly held fingers of the left hand for a fast-note effect.

kitchen implements—wire whisks, etc.—struck together make a host of sounds. Bottles when blown across the top produce organ-like tones and can be tuned by varying the water levels within them. Likewise, a dampened finger run over the ridge of a thin wine glass produces a glorious eerie sound and can also be tuned by water level. Inverted pans struck with wooden, rubber, or metal implements create interesting sounds.

Sounds Found in Nature

Rocks in varying sizes and densities create high and low sounds when struck together. Sticks in varying lengths struck together create pitch. A combination of sticks laid (or nailed) across wood creates a crude xylophone with varied pitches (see following section for mallets).

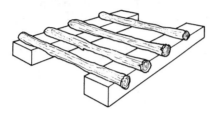

Simple Sounds to Create in the Classroom

Claves—dowel sticks cut to 8 or 9″ lengths; bamboo fishing poles sawed at joints where the bamboo grows

Woodblocks—cast-off lumber from lumberyard (ends) or from child's block set

Drums—metal cans from school kitchen hit with hand or mallet; cylindrically shaped oatmeal containers hit with hands or mallets; coffee cans with plastic tops

Mallets—superball, made by drilling small hole three quarters of the way through a superball (1/4″ hole); a 1/8″ dowel stick is inserted cut to a 10″ length, held in place with Elmer's glue

Reed pipes—paper soda straws, flattened, trimmed at each corner and blown produce different pitches.

Straw

Straw—snipped at corners and pinched together. It works on the same principle as the double reed in double-reed instruments of an orchestra such as oboe, bassoon, etc.

Maracas—small frozen orange juice cans can be filled with different-sized objects to create different sounds: rice, beans, pebbles, etc. Plaster of Paris gauze (found in art stores) dampened and wound around a blown-up balloon creates the container for the pebbles. A 3/4″ dowel cut to approximately 8 inches is inserted for the handle and taped into place. The classroom maracas is ready to be decorated (tempera paint).

Balloon

Playing with the Possibilities Before Applying Them to Poetry

A certain amount of organized experimentation is necessary to learn the characteristics of sounds available in a classroom. Loosely structured assignments using these sounds can steer students into a variety of combinations and experiences, while at the same time giving them a measure of freedom of choice. These sounds are then mentally filed away by the students for later use with poetry.

Here are some possible assignments to promote experimentation, and some student solutions. (The students are working in groups of three or four.)

1. Create a nonrhythmical, sinister piece using sounds of paper clips being shaken in their box, scraped spiral notebook, and voices on different pitches singing, "oooooo."

SOLUTION:

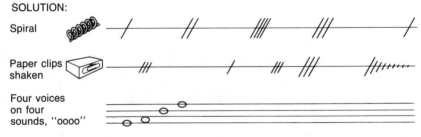

2. Make a humorous rhythm pattern using double-reed straws, mouth pops, and "eefen and oafen."

SOLUTION:

3. Find four metal sounds which are pitched from low to high. Some should be sustained.

SOLUTION:

Teacher's bell

Ruler striking metal cabinet

Kitchen can played on bottom

Frying pan lid

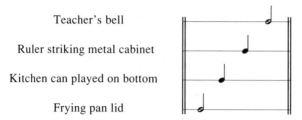

4. Combining wood/metal and miscellaneous timbres, find three contrasting sounds from low to high and play this pattern.

SOLUTION:

Book cover slammed

Coffee-can drum

Globe thumped

5. Create a soundscape with one instrument continuously playing and others entering in an improvisatory way.

SOLUTION:

Pencil improvisation
on desk

Newspaper
rolled and whacked

Chalk turned on side
making continuous line
on blackboard

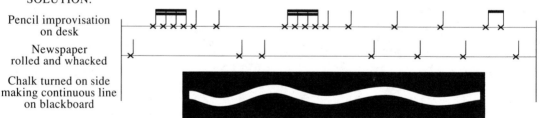

6. Invent a pattern using only contrasting wooden sounds.

SOLUTION:

Pencils tapped together

Pencils tapped on desk top

Wooden ruler tapping chair

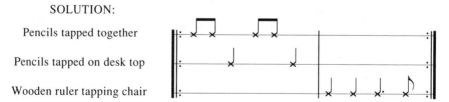

FOUND SOUNDS APPLIED TO STUDENT POETRY

Next should come transitional tasks which will bring the students closer to the goal of using these found sounds to enhance their written work. Word imagery becomes the impetus for finding the right sound, and the students are asked for their ideas. There will always be more than one solution for a task, and the variations should be honored.

SAMPLE LESSON: CONTINUED

T: Find a way to enhance these lines I've taken from your poetry, using our new found sounds. "I grow."

S: We could begin with one person tapping with a ruler, and one by one add our sounds onto it.

T: You mean like a ruler crescendo?

S: Yes.

T: Let's hear it. You start, and as I move my hand across the room, each person will add his or her ruler tap sound. Begin.

Rulers
Tapping:

Sometimes, stepping delicately around a suggestion which was not particularly successful, without hurting the feelings of the student who offered it, requires diplomacy and artful dodging. In this example, the class

S: I think we should do it with our voices, too.

T: At the same time as the rulers?

S: Yes.

T: Demonstrate how you want the voices to go.

S: [Sings an upward, continuous siren.]

T: Class, ready to try? Rulers and voices [they try again]. Raise your hand if you liked the addition of voices . . . only a few. Those who didn't vote, can you explain why?

did not like the siren sound, and was able to express why. Keeping a neutral stance, the teacher intentionally did not dismiss nor adapt the sound, but urged the class to "keep the sound in mind" while moving on to the next consideration and keeping the student's ego in tact.

S: I thought it got too thick.

S: I thought it sounded comic, and that maybe we didn't want it to be funny.

T: Keep that sound effect and those comments in mind, and try a new one. "I shrink." You are going to want a contrasting sound.

S: What about the paper clip boxes—all coming in and then dropping off one by one?

T: We have four boxes. Try it. [They do.]

S: It sounded too much like the ruler tapping texture.

S: I hear just one sound . . . like your desk bell or something that keeps ringing . . . and I see someone moving to the sound . . . growing very slowly and gradually, then shrinking quickly to the bell sound.

T: Let's do it. Rulers ready? Author, will you read, please?

S: Author: "I grow." [Rulers begin tapping as author moves up from the floor into a wide shape. They stop when she is fully grown.] "I shrink." [Bell is played as author moves quickly to a small shape.]

T: Are you satisfied with that, author?

S: Yes.

T: This is from K. L.'s poem, "What Happens to Me Overnight." Could we try saying that line in a three-part canon—group 1, group 2, group 3?

Group 1: What hap-pens to me overnight. What happens to me overnight.

Group 2: What happens to me overnight. What happens to me overnight.

Group 3: What happens to me overnight. What happens to me overnight.

T: Interesting. What might happen in the next line: "My voice rages . . . I sound like this . . . RRRRR."

K.L.: I just hear many people doing the RRRRR sound.

T: All right . . . but the next part lends itself to expansion. You say, "I turn all shapes . . . all sizes . . . Class, name a shape."

S: A wide shape . . . open.

T: Try it. Does anyone hear a sound for that shape?

S: I hear a continuing sound . . . like that great frying pan lid someone brought to school. It rang for a long time when we hit it with a mallet.

T: Do it, and let's see the class move from a small shape to a wide one. [They try.] What's another shape?

S: Pointed . . . elbows out, fingers spikey.

T: Angular! Can you go into those shapes suddenly? I hear a sound every day in this room that might be used . . . your velcro sneakers? Anyone have a pair on? Let's try four people, rip it open and close it, and as you do, we'll make dab, flick movements to correlate. At last, a use for that sound. Name another shape.

S: Round.

T: Let's see you all go into various round shapes; I see some doing it with arms only. Harriet is using her whole body to make a roundness; Andrew has made a round shape on the floor. What's a round sound?

S: Someone thumping the globe.

S: No, someone thumping the metal can.

S: Try both. [They do.]

T: Can you all practice being round with the globe and metal can sounds? Fine. The poem might use one more shape.

S: What about hooking up more than one person together?

T: OK. For sound, let's bring the shakers back in with their paper clip boxes and Tic Tac candies. Can you "play" the moving group into groups of three as they copy your shaking in movement? Make it visually interesting by using your space well—high, low, as we've tried before. [They try it.]

T: There is one more line in the poem to figure out. We need a sound for "I even stretch."

S: That's easy. [Makes the aaahhh sound one makes when stretching until it feels good.]

T: Fine. A universal sound. Could we end as we began, with the "What happens to me overnight" in canon? Let me put a map on the board of what we are doing:

Group of movers:

(moving in a wave)

What happens to me overnight . . .

What happens to me overnight . . .

What happens to me overnight . . .
(freeze with body in
small, tight shape)

K. L.: I grow . . . (movers growing, ruler sound) I shrink . . . (bell, movers instantly shrink)

T: My voice sounds like this: (movers adding to RRRRRR and moving gruffly)
I turn all shapes—all sizes.
1. Pan lid: movers, wide
2. Velcro sneakers: movers, angular—dabs/pointed movements
3. Globe thump/metal can: movers, round shapes, changing to new rounds with the instrument sounds
4. Shaker paper clips: movers, shaking into groups of three—hooking together in some way to make group cohesive
I grow . . . (reprise of rulers)
I shrink . . . (reprise of bell)
I even . . . stretch. (movers stretch languidly with vocal Aaaaaaahhas.)

Movers:

What happens to me overnight . . .

What happens to me overnight . . .

What happens to me overnight . . .

T: So we have created a piece from K. L.'s poem for voice, movement, globe, paper clip shaker, bell and pan lid. Well done! Let's look at B. W.'s revised "Fantasy." Could someone suggest two contrasting sounds with which we could make an ongoing pattern, an ostinato?

S: You mean two sounds that are not the same at all?

T: Right.

S: How about magic markers tapped together, and pencils tapped together?

T: Let's hear the markers. [They tap.] Now play the pencils. Class, are those sounds different? [Class agrees they contrast in their metal and woodness.] Good. Come up with a pattern for those two sounds. [Class experiments. Teacher looks for two groups which have come up with something usable, and showcases those students.] Here's a simple and interesting one—Barbara and Jimmy, share yours, please.

S:

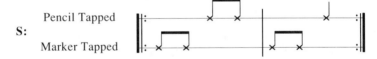

T: It strikes me that in B. N.'s poem his choice of words lend themselves to a strong rhythm. Could one of you please read his first verse while the rest of the class keeps a heartbeat going on our legs?

T: Interesting. The first part works very well, and the very last; but do you notice how the word *of* gets a big accent, coming on the first beat as it does? *Of* is not an important word, and so should not be highlighted by getting an accent. Do you understand that principle? Can anyone use some of the previous ideas, and get *of* off the first beat?

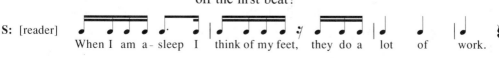

T: That works well. Poet, would you like this to be said only once, or since it is brief, repeated?

S: I think twice, but I would like to hear it first.

T: Surely. After we try it out, you still have the final say. Class, can you keep the pencil/marker pattern going under the words, "they run fast as a locomotive"?

Poem:

Pencils:

Markers:

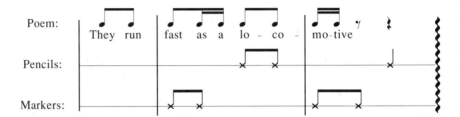

T: And what sounds would you like to hear following that line?

S: What about the obvious—just feet running helter-skelter?

T: Fine. And following the line,

S: This may sound funny, but I hear four grunts . . . like the sounds they make sometimes when they are warming up.

T: Four grunts it is. May I hear the class try only four? Let's let the pencil/marker ostinato continue underneath.

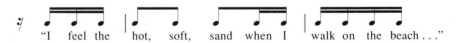

Suggestions for hot, soft sand sounds from our room assortment?

S: What about the sound your finger makes running around the rim of a glass . . . just one tone?

T: Demonstrate, please. Author, OK? Class satisfied? If that is the hot sound, what will the cold sound be?

S: Let's blow into the bottles with more than one person and make a foghorn sound.

T: All right. We have three bottles. Fill them with different levels of water and let's hear them blown together. [They accidentally get a chord, three sounds stacked up at the interval of a third.]

Bottles:

T: Are you satisfied with those three sounds?

S: I would like to hear it colder . . . it sounds too sweet. I'll dump some of my water.

[They try again.]

Bottles, second try:

S: That's more like what I think cold water sounds like.

T: Let's work those sounds into the poem. Be ready to blow your bottles together after this next line is read. Pencil/marker ostinato, start please.

CLASS:

(Introduction)

Pencils:

Markers:

When I swim I feel the cold wa-ter on my feet

T: Bottle Sounds:　　　　and again

Poet: [states alone in conclusion] "This is my dream."

T: How do you feel about repeating the first verse now?

S: (Poet) I would like to only do it once, but do it again at the very end, after "This is my dream."

T: Is the class in agreement with the poet? Fine. Before we try the whole poem, let me help you by putting an abbreviated map on the board. The key for the map will read like this:

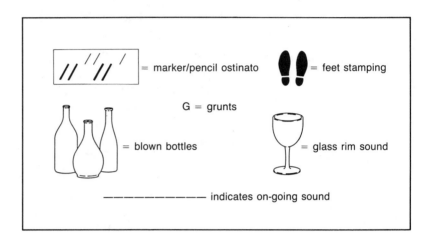

Let's talk through it once from the map to have it well in mind before trying:

GRAPHIC MAP of "When I Am Asleep"

Introduction:

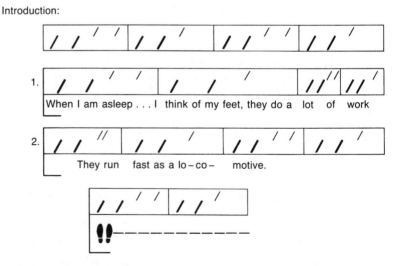

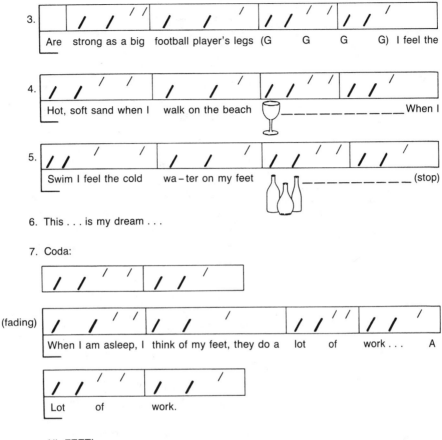

3. Are strong as a big football player's legs (G   G   G   G) I feel the

4. Hot, soft sand when I walk on the beach _____ When I

5. Swim I feel the cold wa-ter on my feet _____ (stop)

6. This . . . is my dream . . .

7. Coda:

(fading) When I am asleep, I think of my feet, they do a lot of work . . . A

Lot of work.

All: FEET!

A TASK OF INTERMEDIATE DIFFICULTY

As groups experience facilitated lessons like the preceding one, they become ready to try lessons reaching the next level of difficulty, which is an intermediary step between the supportive type of lesson, and the one where there is little teacher intervention. In this medium-difficulty task, students (approximately ten years old and up) are given the margins of the assignment, along with the freedom to interact with their peers, working in small groups. There they will experience the social dynamic of that group, argue, agree, build up, tear down, attempt, succeed, and semisucceed . . . all the possible events along the creative way. Sometimes groups will take the task beyond or in a new direction away from the teacher's design, and this is a good sign that they are stretching, and almost ready to be *totally* independent and free of teacher intervention. Here's an example of an intermediary-type sample lesson assignment.

SAMPLE LESSON:
CONTINUED

T: Today, instead of working with the whole class, I am going to assign small groups a part of the poem you wrote together, "When I Fall Asleep." I will suggest two or three sounds, but *how to use them—when and where* will be totally up to your group. You may also use any of the elements we've explored in the past: movement, form, body percussion, texture, canon. Here are the five students I've picked to be group leaders—you can bounce your ideas off of them, and they will help keep the group on the right track. Jane, John, Emily, Ben, and Ruth—here are the excerpts written out. Please scatter around the room, and the rest of you join up with the group you prefer—no more than four to a group.

Group 1: Sounds to include: rocks, vocal; think about movement.

My eyes roll out of my body
like stones, roll
down a mountain, fall
into a lake, my bed becomes
a river, I
become a mermaid
swim my way
to morning.

Group 2: Sounds: Use vocal effects, melody, both melodic and modernistic or all over the place (disjunct melody). May also use movement.

My feet become fat
bright green, squishy
frogs and hop all
over the place, my voice becomes
thunder, crashes down
on silent, shadowy
sleeping cities.

Group 3: Sounds: A rubber ball bouncing. Play with fragments of the poem, using the rhythm of one set of words under another word phrase (i.e., "pepperoni pizza" under "my body," etc.).

My body rolls into
a ball and bounces down
Broadway, I become
A pepperoni pizza
at a party, my fingers twist
into pretzels, my ears
blossom into fragrant
flowers, my skin turns
hard and brown as the
bark on trees.

Group 4: Invent a sad, slow melody for the first thought. Use spiral sounds by scraping a notebook spine; use class-made shakers, and use the dynamic of crescendo in some way.

My eyelashes turn
into tears, my hair
starts to giggle, my eyebrows
become caterpillars and tickle
me till I laugh out loud and wake
myself up.

After ten minutes of brainstorming, each group would share what they had developed so far—it's expected most groups would not be through. They would constructively critique the ideas in progress, and could add a wish to further help the small groups. After those suggestions were absorbed, the groups would reconvene and finish. The poem would then be performed in tandem, with no discussion in between: a classroom performance. Final critiquing would react to the work as a total piece—inquiring if it held together, if there was enough contrast, too much, etc.

If the group is afforded these preliminary exercises, one day it will be ready to move upward and experience the open assignment. This ideally means turning over a departure poem to small groups with little or no suggestions from the teacher. A fifth-grade class might have come up independently with these artistic solutions to K. R.'s poem (see p. 128):

The elements which would stay constant in this piece would be the drum/spiral ostinato and the two vocal ostinatos. Each time the soloist sang the improvisation, it would vary from performance to performance. The teacher's input in this piece would consist of tonal preparation for the improvisation (through singing examples, through small keyboard demonstration, recorder, xylophone, etc.; see Chapter 5). The scale used in K. R.'s setting is the minor *la* pentatonic again, but starting on tone D:

In this older-student, independent setting, the students chose melody, two vocal ostinatos, can-drum/spiral-edge ostinato, cymbal pan lid, and teacher's bell as their way to realize K. L.'s fantasy. Such efforts as these make wonderful pieces to share in programs for other classes, and for events to which parents and the public are invited.

SUMMARY: FOUND SOUNDS

This chapter will hopefully dispel the idea that general classrooms are not equipped with instruments. The found sounds may not officially be instruments but can be attractive, interesting, clever, resourceful and consummately usable sound sources for the creative process, nonetheless. Even music specialists should not overlook sounds available in all classrooms, readily accessible, unique, and often sounding as good as official nonpitched percussion instruments!

We've seen how children can collect such sounds over a period of time, working with the teacher in loosely structured assignments designed to get them acquainted with the properties of these sounds. The progression moved from discovery of sounds, to categorization, to simple tasks created by the teacher using these sounds, to the teacher facilitating a group piece, to the small group where the tasks were still fairly specific, to group work where there was tremendous room for student input and experimentation. By varying the amount of text used, length of text, and complexity of expectations, the sequence can be adapted and applied with equal success to both younger and older age groups.

chapter 5

the how-i-see-myself/ how-others-see-me poem

PERSONALIZING THE POEM:
THE HOW-I-SEE-MYSELF/HOW-OTHERS-SEE-ME POEM

Up to this point, our assignments have emphasized creative thinking and experimentation with poetic techniques. Students have written about colors, feelings, wishes, daydreams, and fantasies. In a way, writing these types of poems provided the students with a degree of anonymity by promoting the illusion that what was said in the poem was somehow removed from them personally. The emphasis was on the pleasure of words, the beauty of imagery, and the intensity of feeling, without ever requiring the students to place themselves (in the form of *I*) directly into the poems. This detachment made it easier to concentrate on creative expression. The poems were written more in a spirit of fun and with less of a sense of accountability for being right or wrong, good or bad. This poetic benefit allowed the imagination to soar, and the students to approach their writing feeling delightfully uninhibited. At some point, however, it becomes important for students to see their poems as reflections of themselves. They need to understand that what they say in their poems is the mirror image of who they are and how they feel about themselves and the world around them.

The following lesson is an attempt to personalize the poems, bringing students directly into the images and intention of the poem. In this lesson we require students to write from the *I* point of view, focusing on themselves as the subject and expanding outward to explore "how I see myself and how (I think) others see me."

| SAMPLE LESSON: |
| POETRY |

This lesson is designed to bring the student directly into the poem, as the subject. In asking the student to recall previous written assignments, the teacher reveals that each poem was really a personal statement of self. Drawing on these past experiences, the teacher hopes to explore self-perception in some detail and to inspire written work which will be both poetically rich in language and style,

T: The subject of today's writing assignment is the most important subject in the whole world. Today, we are going to be writing about ourselves! In reality, all of the poems we have written so far have been about ourselves. When you wrote about a color, you were really writing about how *you* saw that color. When you wrote about a feeling, you were really writing about how *you* felt about that feeling. And when you wrote about fantasies, they were *your* fantasies and said something very special about you. And because each of us sees things differently, we used different images, different experiences and memories to enrich our poems and personalize them.

For the purpose of today's lesson, I want you to think of the world as a wheel. Let me draw it on the board. Look at it carefully. John, come on up and place an X where you think you are on that wheel . . . where you are in the world, not geographically, but personally.

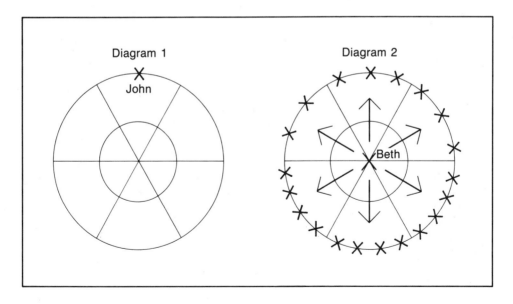

Diagram 1

John

Diagram 2

Beth

and intense and revealing on a personal level.

T: Beth, do you see yourself in the same place that John is?

S: No, I don't think so. I see myself right in the center.

T: That's great. Right in the center. Who else sees themselves as being right in the center of the wheel? Lots of hands are up. I think that we are all, probably, right in the center of our own worlds (wheel). We look at the world from our point of view, and in the *world*, John may be exactly where he placed himself (on the wheel), but there would be a circle around John that places him in the center of his perception of the world. All of our individual circles overlap, as in the following diagram:

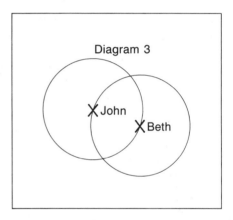

We all think of everything in the world as if it were revolving around us. Do you think that everyone (as indicated by the X's around the wheel in Diagram 2) sees things exactly as you do? In fact, more to the point, do you think that everyone in *your* world sees *you* the way you do?

Here the teacher is a bit aggressive and fast paced, attempting to move the discussion along quickly in the hope that this may alleviate some of the self-consciousness accompanying self-revelation. She

S: No, probably not. I think most people see you in different ways than you see yourself.

T: Give me an example of someone in your life who may see you differently than you see yourself.

S: My mother sees me differently.

T: Someone else?

S: Teachers and friends.

T: Yes. Someone else?

purposely does not dwell on responses, but rather acknowledges them and moves on.

When necessary (later in the lesson) she provides some modeling in the form of an excerpt from a (former) student poem, but mostly this lesson is designed to carry itself along. The hope is that the students will be motivated by their own, and one another's, insights.

S: Brothers and sisters and relatives.

S: Pets.

T: Absolutely. But let's concentrate on people. Do these people who see us differently than we see ourselves always see us in a good way?

S: No. Sometimes my mother thinks I'm pretty terrific and sometimes she thinks I'm awful.

T: I think that's probably true of everyone in our lives. Certainly, when we think of other people, there are times when we think of them in a very good, very positive way and then there are times when we think of them in not such a good way. Will someone give me an example of how their mother sees them? Laura?

S: I don't know how she sees me.

T: I don't expect you to *know* how she sees you, I want you to tell us how you *think* she sees you.

S: Like a good girl.

T: "Like a good girl." That answers the question, but does not answer it poetically. We don't want to forget that we are looking at ourselves, today, through poetry. Our answers need to be images—word pictures—so that all of us will be able to experience them through our senses. Remember all that you know about poetry: images, metaphor, and simile; adjectives, feelings, experiences, and memories; alliteration, onomatopoeia, and, of course, the five senses. Let me give you an example of exactly what I mean.

My mother sees me as if
I were a house with a hundred
rooms and every day she
has to clean every room
on her hands and knees.

My father hears me as if
I were a nail scraping
across a blackboard.

I see myself as if I were
a feather floating
on the wind forever.

Those are some lines from a student poem, and *they* use imagery, the five senses, and intense feelings to describe how this student *thinks* his mother and father see him and how he sees himself. Laura, do you think, now, you could create an image for your mother seeing you as a good girl?

S: Maybe she sees me as if I were as good as a newborn kitten.

T: That's much better. Still, I would like for you to look deep inside yourself for those images that will become your poem. When you're looking for images, try to remember the things that you and the person you are writing about like to do together. If you're writing about your mother and you think she sees you in a good way, create your images out of those things that your mother enjoys or the things that you enjoy doing or sharing together. For example, do you and your mom like to shop together? Might she see you as a gigantic sale at her favorite department store? Does she like to cook? Might she see you as a hot chocolate chip cookie straight from the oven? Would someone like to try an image about how they think their mother sees them? Nat?

S: My mother sees me like homemade apple pie with vanilla ice cream.

T: That's the idea. Another image, please.

S: My mother sees me like a red silk dress and long gold earrings.

In this dialogue, it appears as if the student may be aiming for the laugh, providing a bit of comic relief. The teacher does not attempt to negate the response, but acting as a shield to block class reaction moves the student (through suggestion) toward a more serious contemplation of the assignment. Having elicited a more serious

T: Excellent. How about an image for how your father sees you?

S: My dad sees me like the winning touchdown in the Super Bowl.

S: My dad sees me as a three-foot fish on the end of his line.

S: My dad sees me as a trash can that's too full.

T: Those are picturesque images. David came up with one that was not a "good" feeling. Do you think you can come up with a "good" feeling image, David?

S: Well, my dad thinks I'm the messiest kid in the world.

T: I think we realized that from your descriptive image. Are there some things that you and your dad like to do together?

response, the teacher is quick to praise.

S: We ski.

T: Great. Can you come up with a "good" feeling image using your skiing together as the inspiration?

S: My dad sees me as a ski slope covered with two feet of fresh powder.

T: That's the idea, exactly. Good image. Someone give me an image, good feelings or not such good feelings, for the way your teacher sees you.

S: My teacher sees me as a very smart kid.

T: I like the idea, but I'm wondering if it is an image. What do you think?

S: I don't think it is.

T: Would you turn it into one for me?

S: Smart as a library filled with books.

T: Fine. That works much better. Someone else.

S: My teacher sees me as an unsharpened pencil.

T: I like that one. Another.

S: My teacher sees me as if I were a broken record, talking all the time.

T: Those are all strong images. You explored, with humor and in a serious way, the feelings you think other people have about you, and in doing so, you really explored feelings you have about yourself. Let's take that a step further and ask ourselves, directly, how we see ourselves. Ronni, would you please give me an image for how you see yourself?

S: I see myself in lots of different ways.

T: I'm sure you do. We all see ourselves in lots of different ways, depending on what we feel, what's going on around us, what kind of mood we're in. But right this very minute, Ronni, how do you see yourself?

S: Maybe like the sun being blocked out by the clouds.

T: Oh, that's a very powerful image. It says so much and gives us so much to think about. I think an image is even more effective if it leaves some of the interpretation up to the reader. Your image, Ronni, certainly does that. Let's have some more images for how we see ourselves, please.

Whenever the opportunity presents itself, the teacher highlights poetic skills being used effectively. She is also choreographing an interplay between students, requiring them to listen and respond interpretively to the imagery of their classmates. Being asked for their opinions affords students a sense of self-importance and involvement. It may also provide the added benefit of students taking their own images more seriously, knowing that their ideas will be put to the group for reaction.

S: I see myself like an empty refrigerator, *hungry!*

S: I am a mouse being chased by a cat.

T: Nice metaphor, nice images, creative and thoughtful. By describing yourselves through imagery, you give us, the reader/listener, an opportunity to get involved in the poem. We bring ourselves into the poem through our interpretations of your images. For example, what do you, Robert, think Henry's cat/mouse image means?

S: That he feels scared like a mouse does when it's being chased by a cat.

T: Maybe. What else might it mean?

S: That he feels small?

T: Very possibly. You see what I mean about the reader/listener getting involved and becoming part of the poetic experience? We put *our* (reader/listener) feelings into *your* (poet) images and come up with something that is doubly meaningful for us. Good poetry always provides room for interpretation.

Right now, I would like for us to put a list on the board of all the people in our lives that we might want to include in our poem. Please help me.

Mother Father Sisters Brothers Friends Neighbors
Teachers Principal Aunts Uncles Cousins
Grandmother Grandfather Pets Enemies

T: That looks like a pretty complete list to me. What I'd like for you to do now is to select three to five people from that list and write a poem, using *all* that you know about poetry. Please end the poem by describing how you see yourself. You may, if you like, give us two views (a positive one and a negative one) for each person you write about and for yourself. For example: Sometimes my mother sees me as if I were a flower blooming in her garden and sometimes she sees me as if I were a bee about to sting her.

Please take a moment to think about who you really want to include in your poem and please take the time, as well, to explore your feelings honestly and present them through the poetry of meaningful, visual images.

student poems

I THINK OF ME AS ME

My sister always calls me dumb
But I don't think I am.
My mother laughs at me when I start
To grow
And wear jewelry and fancy clothes
Like my big sister.
But I think I'm old enough to.
My father is sometimes what I want
And sometimes what I don't want.
It depends on what my mood is.
If I feel like skiing down a big mountain
I'll let him fool around with me
And let him pinch me.
He never knows when I'm in bad moods
And don't want to be treated like
A baby.
Sometimes he doesn't
And makes me feel like a grown-up.
Still no one knows about me
As well as I do.
I'm quiet at other people's houses
But noisy in school.
I hate being sick at home
But love being sick at school.
Everyone knows me as someone else
But I know me as me.

C. C., 3rd grade

HOW OTHERS SEE ME

My father sees me happy
and my mother sees me happy
too but my brother sees me
funny but my friends see me
good like a nice
summer afternoon but I
see myself like the
color blue like the
morning sky.

T. O., 2nd grade

ALL ABOUT ME

I think I am as tall
as a tree.
I have eyes
like brown shoe polish.
I am as thin
as my pinky.
My arms
are like steel.
My legs are faster
than a Cheetah's legs.
My hair is fluffy
as a dog's hair.

L. K., 2nd grade

ME, MYSELF, AND I

My mom sees me as a
sweet cottage, all tidy
and neat, a place to relax,
sometimes, she also sees
me as a skyscraper and she
has to wash and vacuum me
everyday.

My dad sees me as a
book that he has to read
all of his life. Sometimes
putting me away in the closet
is a most enjoyable sport for
him.

My grandma sees me as a
tree in the yard and she
is ready to tend me everyday.

My brother sees me as
a toy
all new and waiting
to be played with.

My grandpa sees me as
a child's toy which he has
no use for.

But I see myself as
a leaf falling off a
tree floating far away
from everyone else.

                    A. G., 5th grade

MYSELF

I like me
I am as pretty
as a star
in the sky!

              Y., 2nd
                grade

ME

I think my mother
Sees me
As pretty
As a rainbow
After a wet day.
And like the sunset
Just before Halloween day.

I think my father
Sees me as
A warm cup of coffee
After shoveling
The outside walk.

I think my brother
Sees me as
A little piece of paper
Not valuable, good for anything, or nice.

I think my grandmother
Sees me as a flow of sunshine
Coming through her window
In the morning.
And as a refreshing swim
After sitting in the hot sun.

I think my best friend
Sees me the way I see myself.

I see myself
As a burst of rain
After a hot summer drought:
Cool and refreshing,
Not caring how I look
Just caring
About how I see myself.

                    A. S., 5th grade

HOW I SEE MYSELF
AND HOW OTHERS SEE ME

My brother sees me as
a crazy monkey
who's bad
at self defense.

My teacher sees me
as an automatic pencil
happily doing
all my paperwork.

My mother sees me
as a motorized shopping cart
huffing and puffing
down the aisles
retrieving items.

My grandpa thinks I'm
as SPECIAL
as the only mint
"UPSIDE DOWN AIRPLANE STAMP."

My gym teacher sees me
as a miniature Lawrence Taylor
   d
    i
     v
    i
     n
      g
for a touchdown.

I think of myself
as a wise owl
swiftly scaring away
the hunters
on a cold winter night.

              B. K., 6th grade

WHAT I SEE MYSELF AS

I see myself as
a little baby
coming into the world.
I see myself as
pink flower
petals
among all blue
flower petals.
I sometimes feel
as pretty
as a rainbow.

         B. C., 6th grade

THE REAL ME

I see me as a closed book
with no pages
I was never opened.

My mother sees me
as someone who can't
control his temper.

I am a burning house
with flames rising
higher and higher.

I am stubborn
if there was a brick wall
in my way
I'd try to walk right through it.

To me I have to be
  PERFECT
through and through.

Deep inside of me
in the hollow that is filled
with thoughts
I know
I am not.

         P. N., 5th grade

HOW I SEE MYSELF
AND HOW OTHERS SEE ME

My mother sees me like a
twinkling star bouncing up and
down because I take Irish
Step dancing.
My father sees me as a bunny
hopping up and down in the breeze
like a cute grasshopper.
My brother sees me like a parrot
who always has time to play.
My other brother sees me as a
gentle lamb who always cuddles
him.
Jodi sees me like a giant
snowflake falling like a fluffy
cloud.
And I see myself as water
trickling down over smooth, shiny
rocks.

C. R., 6th grade

HOW I SEE MYSELF

My mom sees me
as a dirty laundry mat.
My father sees
me as a
waiter that gets him
his gushy ice cream.
My grandma sees me
as a toy crusher.
My uncle sees me
as a sports magazine
that tells him
the score.
I see myself
as a boy
that counts the green
leaves in a tree.

M. A., 5th grade

HOW OTHERS SEE ME

My mother sees me
as a heart with an
arrow through it
that is shiny and
"brite" a gold necklace,
brand new.

My father sees me
as a glass of sparkling
white wine, a ball being
caught by a mitt.

My two brothers see me
as a volcano being erupted, a
miserable thundery night, my
being a garbage can.

My grandma thinks of me
as a tomato being pinched
on the cheeks.

My aunt thinks of me
as a pair of lips
being smudged by
lipstick.

I think I am a
"brite" star as
"brite" as the sun in
the early morning.

P. S., 5th grade

SUMMARY: POETRY ———————————————————

This fifth poetry session completes the first section (introductory stage) of the poetry program. We have introduced poetic techniques, experimented with poetic form, and become somewhat more comfortable with the concept of words as tools. Students are daring to use metaphor and simile, alliteration and onomatopeoia, and the five senses with a bit more flair and confidence. Their poems have begun to flow more easily, and they are using language in a somewhat less self-conscious manner than when our sessions began. We need, however, to continue to stress the need for poetic language skills; to rely on repetition to keep the poetry recipe, rainbow of adjectives, sensory awareness, etc., alive and flourishing in our students' writing.

The creative tree has always borne the most fruitful harvests when nourished by a healthy combination of praise and reward. It is for this reason that one needs to accept student work, particularly in the first draft stage, in a positive and openly receptive way. Great emphasis, however, must be placed on the need for editing and revision. It is during the editing stage that teacher input can redirect the student toward application of heightened sensory awareness, clarification of ideas, and inclusion of the essential elements of poetry.

Armed with a variety of language techniques, students are ready to explore new music and movement possibilities and, shortly, begin applying their newly acquired skills to daily classroom activities.

SYNTHESIS OF ALL LEARNED MOVEMENT AND MUSIC TECHNIQUES: THE HOW-I-SEE-MYSELF/HOW-OTHERS-SEE-ME POEM ———————————

So far, this book has shown diverse developments of movement and music, focusing on specific areas. We saw how movement could be used to tell the poem's story in spacial terms; melody to shape it in sung terms; body percussion and vocal sounds to accompany and enrich; and form to re-create and enhance.

Now we are going to synthesize these areas, using all the newly recognized creative skills. This chapter recognizes and assumes the exploration that has gone before to enable the student to function within the most casual of structures, and acknowledges that music and movement skills have been used and reused to keep the possibilities alive and flowing.

SAMPLE LESSON:
SYNTHESIS

[The following group setting of "Me, Myself, and I" by A. G. reflects previous experience in music and movement. In this example, the teacher remains totally open to the group's ideas of what should accompany the poem (if anything) and whether the poem lends itself to rhythmical treatment, or to being accompanied by vocal or body percussion sounds; if it will work with melody; and what form the poem will take. Thus, the teacher's questions are purposely open, giving the group ample opportunity to initiate ideas based on their earlier experiences from more structured lessons.]

John is asked to justify his selection of the tapping sound and rethink his original rhythm choice, as it relates to the rhythmic qualities of the poem. His suggestion is refined by this kind of teacher questioning.

T: You all have copies of the fine poem written by A. G. Would everyone please silently read this poem?

—Having heard the words in your mind's ear, do any ideas come to you for where we might take this poem?

—You see movement in the first verse. Do you see it throughout the poem?

—Would someone please read it aloud that we might hear how the word rhythm sounds to you?

—Having heard A. G.'s idea of the word rhythm, does anyone else envision something in addition going on?

The teacher includes the group in the assessment process. This group input provides John with peer backup.

—John, you hear a pencil tap echoing the word rhythm. Do you hear this tap idea throughout the poem, or in special places?

—Class, would you read the first stanza using A. G.'s word rhythm suggestion, and let John try his pencil-tap idea?

—Class, how do you feel about that arrangement thus far? Then let's hang onto those ideas and continue.

By becoming personally involved in the selection process, the teacher retains the right to express an

—Betty said earlier that there might be movement. Can you demonstrate what you had in mind, Betty? Would three students volunteer to join her to see what the movement looks like as a group pattern?

opinion while giving some of the decision-making power to the group.

The lesson is then synthesized into a series of group exercises utilizing all learned skills.

Do you feel the words chosen to move were effective?

—Group, what words do *you* feel are the key ones for the movement people to focus on? *Tidy and neat?* What others? Yes, I would agree with your ideas of *skyscraper, wash and vacuum, book, tree, in the yard, toy, leaf.* Movement people, are you hearing the class's preference for words to be moved? Try again.

Notice in this questioning, the teacher is *not* steering where the focus is to be, as was the earlier case where there were desired and specific areas to explore (i.e., discovering form, body percussion, and the implications of that to accompaniment, movement qualities, etc.). In this facilitator role, the teacher takes the ideas offered by students and becomes the traffic director, suggesting where firmed ideas should be tried, and encouraging more input where group jelling has not yet taken place. The teacher is also the interest thermometer, sensing how long to pace the activity: when to divert, where a log jam of ideas is not bearing results, and where the group is really for an idea and willing to make it permanent.

The following group settings are results of this more open kind of questioning, backed by assumed explorations done in movement and music throughout the year. As you read through these culminations, it would be good to observe the creative elements used in the pieces, just as you would if you wished to reflect later on the piece you helped facilitate. The following is the fifth-grade example of the results of working the word with A. G.'s poem.

"Me Myself and I," by A. G. (Group Results)

MOVEMENT

(Ostinato group of five)
Step right on word *me.*
Touch ankle with left foot on *self.*
Step left on *I.*
Touch ankle with right foot on the rest (silence). Continue through next part.

POEM AND ACCOMPANIMENT

(Ostinato with group of ten.)

Introduction:

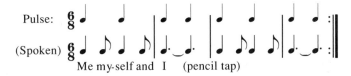

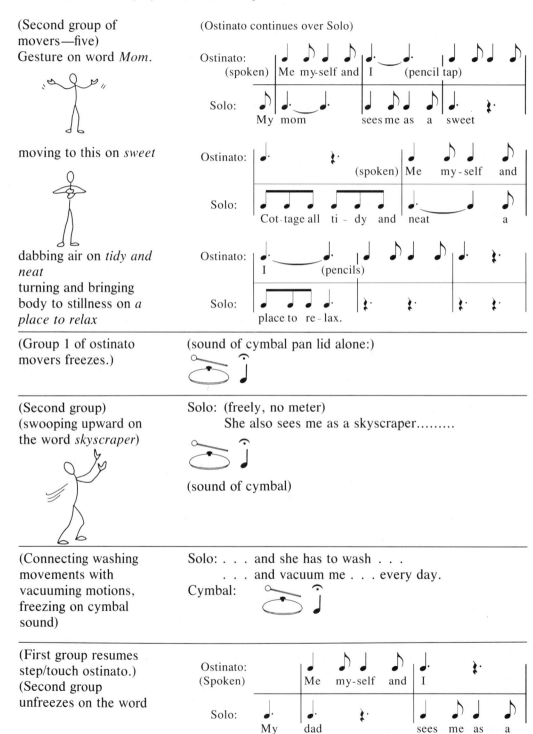

(Second group of movers—five)
Gesture on word *Mom*.

moving to this on *sweet*

dabbing air on *tidy and neat*
turning and bringing body to stillness on *a place to relax*

(Group 1 of ostinato movers freezes.)

(Second group)
(swooping upward on the word *skyscraper*)

(Connecting washing movements with vacuuming motions, freezing on cymbal sound)

(First group resumes step/touch ostinato.)
(Second group unfreezes on the word

(Ostinato continues over Solo)

Ostinato:
(spoken) Me my-self and | I   (pencil tap)

Solo:
My mom   sees me as a   sweet

Ostinato:
(spoken) Me my-self and

Solo:
Cot-tage all ti - dy and neat   a

Ostinato:
I   (pencils)

Solo:
place to re - lax.

(sound of cymbal pan lid alone:)

Solo: (freely, no meter)
She also sees me as a skyscraper.........

(sound of cymbal)

Solo: . . . and she has to wash . . .
. . . and vacuum me . . . every day.
Cymbal:

Ostinato:
(Spoken)   Me my-self and | I

Solo:
My   dad   sees me as a

book, opening hands
and sweeping air with
rainbow shaped arc,
while turning on *all of
his life.*)

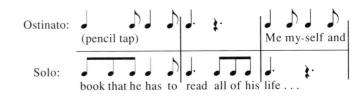

Ostinato:

(pencil tap)

Me my-self and

Solo:

book that he has to read all of his life . . .

Ostinato:

I,

(pencils)

Solo:

(ostinato stops)

(First ostinato stops.)
(Second group freezes
with hands on hips on
sometimes, then mimes
a solid door with hands
outward and stiff on
most, joy of *enjoyable,*
and *sport,* dabbing
three places in space.)

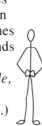

Solo: (freely) Sometimes . . . putting me away in the
    closet . . .
    is a <u>most</u> . . . en<u>joy</u>able . . . <u>sport</u> . . . for him
    . . .

(Group 1 of movers
resumes ostinato.)

(Ostinato resumes with movers, one time, then
  continues under poem:)

(Spoken)

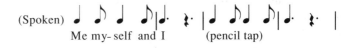

Me my-self and I   (pencil tap)

(Group 1 resumes.)
(Group 2 moves in an
unbroken motion from
grandma shape to tree.)

Ostinato:
(Spoken)

Me   my - self   and

Solo:

My   grand - ma

Ostinato:

I   (pencils)

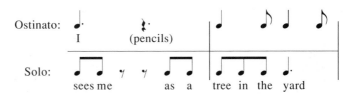

Solo:

sees me   as a   tree in the yard

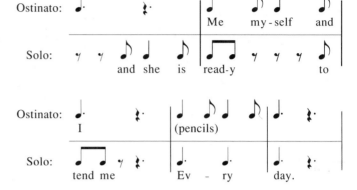

(Group 1: On *play with
a toy*, students skip in
own circle. They stop
and clap the second
measure facing the
audience. Repeated
through next section.)

(New ostinato for voice and clapping)

Solo:
(Spoken)   Play with a   toy   (clap)

(Group 1 moves new
ostinato.)

(Group 2, on *brother*,
indicates height of
child. On the word *toy*,
group begins to build
an interlocking body
toy, moving one at a
time to the pulse. Toy
moves on the words
played with in a
rhythmical way.)

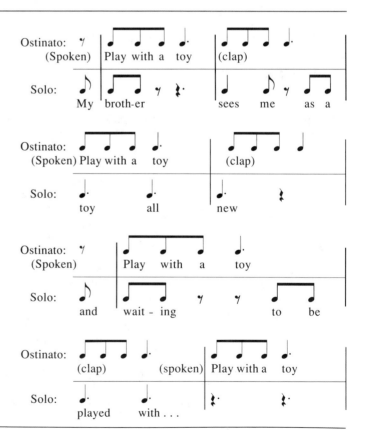

(Group 1 stops.)
(Group 2 unlocks toy one person at a time, and walks apart sadly on lines *Grandpa sees me as a child's toy . . . which he has no use for.*)

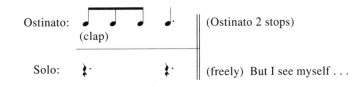

Ostinato: (clap) | (Ostinato 2 stops)

Solo: | (freely) But I see myself . . .

Both groups walk to right making individual circles. *But I see myself,* arms somewhat raised.
(Groups 1 and 2 turn one time and press arms even higher, looking upward at hands on *I see myself.*)

(sound of cymbal)

Solo: (more intensely) I SEE MYSELF . . .

(repeat cymbal)

(Group 1 freezes with hands up.)
(Group 2 begins descending movement scallops with accompanying vocal sounds on *falling off a tree.* They float away from each other on *floating far away from everyone else.*)

Solo: As a leaf . . . falling off a tree . . . floating far away . . . from everyone else.

Group 1 unfreezes to do coda with voice and step-touch-step, holding on last *I* with arms upraised.

Coda:

Group 1:

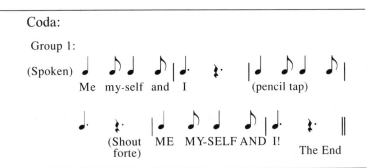

(Spoken) Me my-self and I   (pencil tap)

(Shout forte) ME MY-SELF AND I!   The End

Reflecting on all the creative elements used within ''Me, Myself, and I,'' we observe a rich assortment:

— movement; speech ostinato accompaniment with movement; found-sound ostinato accompaniment; introduction; coda; expansion of form through insertions of ostinatos between stanzas; use of dynamics; use of speech tempo change from rhythmical in 6/8 to free meter.

Taking the time to reflect on the strengths and weaknesses (if there were any) of finished pieces develops the power of group critiquing. It gives students (and the teacher) the chance to have wishes—pondering on what might have happened *if*. This type of evaluation is documented in learning taxonomies as the most significant and demanding to keep creative growth spiraling. In psychologist Bloom's dissertation on the taxonomy of learning, he puts this kind of critiquing on the sixth, and highest, step of his taxonomy after knowledge, comprehension, application, analysis, and synthesis.

Even younger groups can function in this more open kind of creative framework, provided previous isolation of those elements of speech, movement, form, etc. have been sampled. The next example deals with such a poem from T. O. in second grade. Here, all the teacher's good intentions in helping facilitate the group's responses were for naught, and the class remained polarized, half wanting the poem sung, and the other wanting a rhythmical/body percussion setting. The solution was to create *two* settings.

**Spoken Version With Body Percussion
Of "My Father Sees Me Happy "**

T. O., 2nd Grade

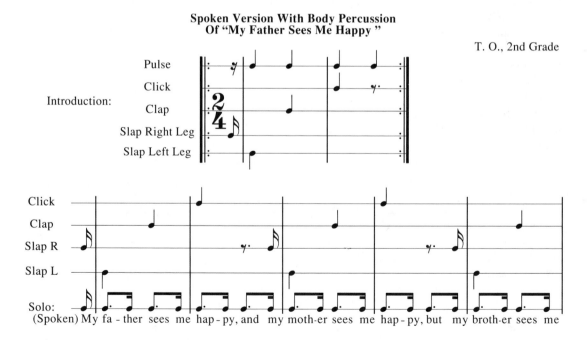

Click
Clap
Slap R
Slap L
Solo:
fun-ny, but my friends see me good, like a nice... sum-mer... aft-er-noon!!

(Ostinato stops)

Solo:
But I ... see my-self like the col-or blue
like the morn-ing sky

Adding Half the Class:
Like the col-or blue like the morn-ing sky

Adding the Full Class and slowing:
LIKE THE COL-OR BLUE LIKE THE MORN-ING SKY!

Melodic Version of "My Father Sees Me Happy"

Do Pentatonic on G

Clapping Group:
Sung Ostinato:
All a-bout me Hap-py hap-py hap-py
1.   2.

Solo:
My

Clapping:
Sung Ostinato:
All a-bout me Hap-py hap-py All a-bout

Solo:
fath-er sees me hap-py and my moth-er sees me hap-py but my broth-er sees me

(Group repeats introduction
as coda, pianissimo)

Both versions were convincing to the group. Both had integrity and gave the text its due. Important to note is that neither setting was written down. Once the parts were decided, it was the job of a student conductor to remind the group when to stop and where to continue, as prescribed by the group. The sung ostinato was learned by rote and graphed on the board as a reminder of the pitches:

<u>All</u>

  <u>a-</u>

    <u>bout</u>

      <u>me</u>

The sounds of the pentatonic scale were initially sung by the teacher to get the students' ears into that particular mode (and the scale could have been demonstrated as easily on a recorder, or small pitched percussion instrument as mentioned in earlier chapters).

The following "How I See Myself" by M. A., fifth grade, became a stick puppet show in the hands of the students. The class decided on the important words, and these, when drawn, became the stick puppets. A make-shift curtain was stretched between two students, each holding an end, and the poem with fairly literal sound effects and graphics supplied by the class began.

STICK PUPPET	FOUND SOUND EFFECTS	POEM SPOKEN AS PUPPETS APPEARED
	Improvisation for scraped chairs and tapped tin can following the poem's first line	"My mom sees me as a dirty laundry mat." (Sounds and puppet emerging from behind curtain)
	Improvisation on teacher's bell and delicious mouth sounds	"My father sees me as a waiter that gets him gushy ice cream." (Sounds and puppet)
	Many people making *Mmmmm* contented sounds on many different pitches	"My grandmother sees me as a blanket waiting to be cuddled almost every weekend." (Sounds and puppet)
	Soda cans being stepped on	"My grandpa sees me as a toy crusher."
	Vocal improvisation of baseball announcer calling a homerun with the crowd roaring	"My uncle sees me as a sports magazine that tells him the score."
	Teacher's bell	"I see myself"
(tree slowly rising with other hand slowly showing to count the leaves . . .)	Mark tree made from hanging keys (made by suspending many discarded keys on plastic fishing line. A magical sound occurs when you run your finger along it, and the keys strike each other.) Final ding on bell at end.	"I see myself" "I see myself as a boy . . . who counts the green leaves in a tree."

"How I See Myself" For Solo/Group Voice and Movement

There can be great beauty in simple settings, as in this one, based on B. K.'s "How I See Myself and Others See Me" poem. The group decided basically on using only speech and movement, the spoken part getting its contrast from solo/group and the movement people taking their ideas from the essence of each line. When someone came up with the idea of doubling the voices and repeating them, another simple but lovely nuance was added. The movement group also had to devise ways to connect movement ideas, one to the next, to avoid looking sporadic.

MOVEMENT	SOLO VOICE	GROUP VOICES
(Four or more people) (Monkey gestures four steps right, four left)	My brother sees me	as a crazy monkey who's bad
	at self defense.	
Multipeople interlocking machine with moveable parts.	My teachers see me	(automatic voices) as an automatic pencil happily doing
	all my paperwork.	
In partners, one pushes and the other is the wheelbarrow.	My mother sees me	as a motorized shopping cart
	Huffing and puffing	Huffing and puffing down the aisles.
	(Retrieving items.)	
Many watching one who is pantomiming licking stamps into an invisible album, feigning interest in the airplane stamp.	My grandpa thinks I'm as special	as the only mint "upside down airplane stamp."

MOVEMENT	SOLO VOICE	GROUP VOICES

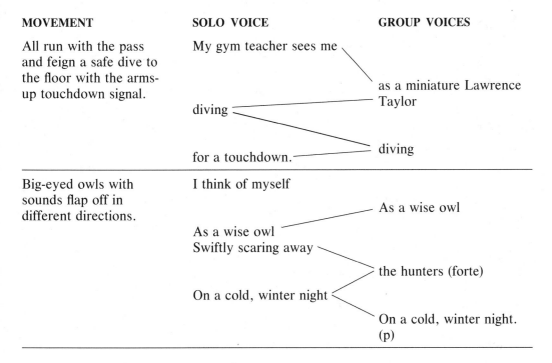

MOVEMENT	SOLO VOICE	GROUP VOICES
All run with the pass and feign a safe dive to the floor with the arms-up touchdown signal.	My gym teacher sees me	as a miniature Lawrence Taylor
	diving	
	for a touchdown.	diving
Big-eyed owls with sounds flap off in different directions.	I think of myself	As a wise owl
	As a wise owl Swiftly scaring away	the hunters (forte)
	On a cold, winter night	On a cold, winter night. (p)

"I Like Me," 2nd Grade, ABA Form With Found Sounds

For this next poem, the second grade decided they would need star-like sounds that twinkled, so the search began for beautiful, ringing found sounds in the room: fingers around glass rims, glasses struck lightly with rubber erasers, the mark tree made from hanging keys. To lengthen the poem, the group brainstormed all the constellations they knew to add to the center section and also decided to repeat the first part. An ABA form was created.

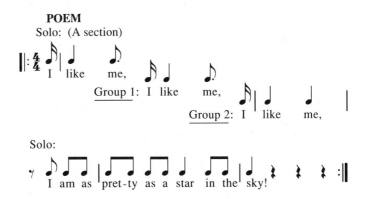

FOUND SOUNDS	POEM

(Low-pitched glass with finger on rim begins and continues.)

Group: (B section)
   Orion! (low glass)

(Middle-pitched glass with finger on rim enters and continues.)

Group: Pleiades! (middle glass sound)

(High sound enters and continues.)

Group: Draco!
   (high-pitched sound)

Teacher's bell:

Group: The North Star!

Mark tree of keys

Group: The Milky Way!

A section is repeated with final ping on triangle or bell after the word *sky.*

"All About Me" For Bottles, Movement, Improvisation, and Group Refrain (Expansion)

In the next example, "All About Me" uses the minor pentatonic cited in Chapter 3, with the teacher having helped the students enter the mode by conversing in those tones in recitative:

The group decided to have two bottles pitched to the low D so that the breathing could be staggered, making the tone appear to be sustained. This tone also helped the soloist find the home tone or key center (D), which was useful while improvising. Four people were the movers, and the rest of the class sang the ostinato in between the soloist, who was improvising.

MOVEMENT

(Turn) (arms (point
     out) to
 ↓ ↓ self)
            ↓
"all about me"
Four dancers growing
in tree line:

Repeat "all about me"
as above.
Hands to eyes, then
shining the sky with
invisible rag

(Turn) (arms (self)
     out)
"All about me"

Moving from wide to
thin shape

Repeat as before.

Regarding arms,
floating them upward,
then flexing with force
on *steel*

Repeat as before.

POEM

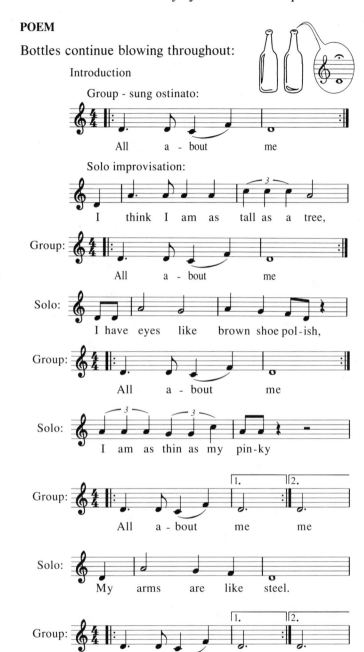

Bottles continue blowing throughout:

Introduction

Group - sung ostinato:

All a - bout me

Solo improvisation:

I think I am as tall as a tree,

Group:

All a - bout me

Solo:

I have eyes like brown shoe pol-ish,

Group:

All a - bout me

Solo:

I am as thin as my pin-ky

Group:

All a - bout me me

Solo:

My arms are like steel.

Group:

All a - bout me me

MOVEMENT   **POEM**

Movers run in place.   Solo: My legs are fast-er than a chee-tah's legs,

As before   Group: All a-bout me | me

Movers dab hair with beat.   Solo: My hair is fluf-fy as a dog's hair,

(turn) (arms out) (self)
"All about me"   Group: All a-bout me,

Repeat above.   Group: All a-bout me, (diminish)

Repeat with smaller motion.   Group: *(pp)* All a-bout me.

For purposes of sharing, a melody has been written—fixed—on the page through notation; but the reader should remember that this is an *improvised* melody and therefore not written down at its creation, nor will it ever be the same way twice. The only thing that would remain constant would be the chosen mode of *la* pentatonic. Different soloists would create different melodies within this mode.

SUMMARY: SYNTHESIS

All the poetic inspirations in the first part of this book began as words on a page, or words in the mouth; and then through the music and movement experience became rhythmical—took on additional emphasis through group or solo interpretation, musical and movement enhancement. The poems changed, taking on new forms and new shapes. Like a tree, the poem is a creative miracle in and of itself.

Even in winter the tree is an elegant linear statement; and then it blossoms, flowers, bears fruit, and changes color—each layering a metamorphosis of the original creative statement.

We've discovered that the poet's tools, plus movement and music, can be used to explore anything: colors, feelings, fantasies, ourselves. And it is through language (words) that we are taught math, history, art, social studies, science, etc. Words, therefore, are the common tool in all learning environments, thus affording access to the math-oriented student in language arts as well as the history-oriented buff in the math classroom. Subjects are different and unique; however, they are taught and comprehended through the grace of language. We have now begun to learn how to make words work for us, and how, ultimately, to use them to expand teaching arenas and open all of the interdisciplinary doors to learning.

SECTION ONE: CONCLUSION

Teaching is an imperfect art and science, and occasionally things don't work out in the classroom as planned. Responses from groups and from individual group members are often not forthcoming, unexpected, or inappropriate. This is the nature of the teaching environment. Many variables are possible when introducing a new subject or trying a new approach. Students may misinterpret the intent of a lesson and head off in a wrong direction; or greet it with silence; or one student may dominate the discussion, leaving other students behind, or bored. There are any number of divergent factors which can and do influence the effectiveness of a lesson. At this time we address some of the hazards of these variables and offer suggestions (embracing our experiences) we believe may prove helpful in overcoming teaching troublespots.

It is important to accept the premise that every student response, even those which are *problematical* or singular, can expand the lesson into new, creative shapes. Thus, the teacher becomes a *filter* through which ideas are refined and released—not judged or discarded. For example, the student who responded to a lesson on color poems by offering the image "Blue is the color of wonders" (p. 198) ignited a spark which burned for days. The original classroom reaction was one of silence. Students seemed unsure of what was meant by *wonders,* how the word fit the assignment (of finding an image using the five senses for the color blue). They were also unsure of what the teacher's reaction was going to be; and for a moment the lesson stalled. The teacher rejoined enthusiastically, praising the originality of such an idea, and seeking from the classroom as a whole a definition for the word *wonder.* "What are wonders?" The reaction was "wonders are wishes, dreams, fantasies, possibilities, things that lack reality"; and the teacher began to list student-suggested wonders on the blackboard. Fog was a wonder, rainbows, lightning, snowflakes, spider webs, flower petals, bird songs, etc. The discussion was animated and intense. It became inspirational. This is the kind of "miraculous" student-initiated response that one cannot plan for but should be ready to seize. Thus, color poems were unceremoniously abandoned in favor of discovering the nature of wonders. To have ignored this student gift of serendipity, by redirecting the class back to a discussion of colors, would have been to ignore the myriad offering of what *wonders* connote.

This type of unplanned experience suggests that in all classroom situations teachers must retain an ample degree of flexibility, receptivity, and adventurousness. They need to approach lessons with a sense of humor, wonder, and abandonment. We cannot stress enough the importance of *embracing* student offerings, whether they seem appropriate or not; and being willing to accept the outrageous, and perhaps even be a little outrageous ourselves. This sometimes requires heading north when the original destination was south.

As teachers, we constantly encourage students to take risks and to allow themselves to be vulnerable. *We* can do no less. Regardless of an individual's teaching comfort zone (we all have areas of comfort, and those more alien to our particular teaching styles), nothing is lost by remaining accessible to possibility. Whether material is taken and used directly from this book, or interpreted and applied with a personal touch, or garnered from other sources, a subjective viewpoint is the essential ingredient to any creative lesson. Troubleshooting from this approach promises the greatest chance of reclaiming and renewing the lesson which seems to be going astray.

Suggested solutions will sometimes be presented for poetry, sometimes for music and movement. However, it is important to note that the solutions are not limited to one classroom area, but may be applied across the spectrum of the curriculum.

Troubleshooting and Teacher/Student Dynamics

Situation

Silence: little or no group response to teacher invitation to task.

Possible Problems and Suggested Solutions

1. Unclear Teacher Presentation

This manifests itself in a recognizable puzzled silence. Questions elicit little or no response, and through attempted application, it becomes clear that students are unsure of what is being asked of them. One must avoid the temptation to interpret this kind of silence as student inattentiveness or blatant unwillingness to participate. Indeed, one must be willing, on the spot, to evaluate the effectiveness of teacher presentation. If unclear presentation appears to be the problem, the teacher should indicate this to the class: "Perhaps I didn't present this clearly . . . let me explain it again." At this time it may be helpful to present the lesson in a number of different ways, watching carefully for student signs of understanding and enthusiasm.

Example: Having presented a set-up lesson designed to stimulate a writing experience about the sea, the teacher encounters blank looks and silence. He or she re-presents the lesson, coming at it from a number of different vantage points, and asks the following questions and presents examples: "The sea is as green as a frog's back . . . the sea is white with foam . . . the sea is rough . . ." "Which of these, if any, is an image?" "How can we turn those that are not images, into images?" "Should they be similes or metaphors?" "The sea is as rough as *what?* . . . sandpaper? a cat's tongue? a hurricane? thunder?" The silence usually gives way to a discussion of imagery (a subject with which students are familiar). At this point, it might be helpful for the teacher to be recording (blackboard or paper) the students' images as they are suggested. It can later be pointed out to the students that they have, in fact, been verbally "writing" the poem they were confused about, and discussing the poem (through imagery) they thought they couldn't discuss. Very often, their delight in the beauty and clarity of their own images stimulates further discussion.

Thus, in dealing with the kind of silence resulting from unclear teacher presentation, it is imperative *not* to reproach students but rather to come at them from new and varied directions. Here, a strong but vulnerable teacher voice is important: "I think . . . (in the teacher's voice) the sea is as gentle as my granddaughter's eyes." Through personalization, the teacher offers images from his or her own experiences, and the lesson is clarified. Students now have viable examples and a promising point of departure.

2. Inadequate Teacher Modeling

Since the problems encountered in the classroom often overlap, it follows that the solutions will overlap as well. Some of the solutions for unclear teacher presentation may be equally applicable here. Examples of modeling occur in most areas of this text. Using a movement lesson as our canvas, we discover that the teacher should be ready to illustrate *verbal* instructions with clear and easily interpreted *movement examples,* while leaving room for student exploration. Likewise, in any melodic work the teacher should be prepared to demonstrate examples in the sets of tones (keys) in which the students will be working. *Seeding* any initial lesson with teacher-given examples can ensure a number of things: that students will see the teacher as a willing participant, ready to join in the risk taking (an important aspect mentioned before); and that there is opportunity for students to enter the inception stages of a task, moving toward the revelation of a sequenced and nonthreatening progression.

An example of teacher modeling leading to student imitation (which avoids the silent response syndrome) may be found on pages 22–24. Through this process, a sense of security is initially established. Succinctly, the progression is "watch me" (observe); "you do it" (copy/echo/imitate); "try your own ideas" (create); copy a peer's idea (reinforcement); "co-join ideas" (create longer forms); "describe what you did" (analyze); "use movement terms" (upgrade language); "put it all together" (synthesize).

It is generally the case that student *discovery* is a more powerful teaching technique than information feeding. Note first in the beginning of this lesson (pp. 22–23) that the teacher illustrated the mystery color through a movement demonstration, inviting students to use their observation powers to bridge the gap between a color and a movement. At the same time, students were discovering the new language of movement ("watch me"). In the question framed by the teacher, there was margin for interpretation, leaving the students free to choose from many right answers. When the students were asked to copy or echo the teacher movement ("you do it"), they could respond within a safety zone, because they were merely following the teacher's lead. The invitation to try another motion of a student design (create/reinforcement) added weight to the amount of investment and thought demanded from students, and encouraged them to bring the motion into space (which is another level of difficulty—from static movement into a larger area). Discussing the results of their movements from a subjective point of view provided students with a movement-quality reference criteria (analyzing). Labeling these movement qualities (using the Rudolph Laban terminology) offered students a richer vocabulary (upgrading) with which to evaluate their efforts.

Page 90 illustrates a music lesson where the modeling of tones is accomplished through musical conversation before being used in student improvisations. Further, a masterwork used as a model for a parallel poetry writing session may be found on pages 113–14.

3. Fear of Ridicule From Peers

The types of problems that arise in a classroom as a result of poor group dynamics are legion and almost always lead to a problematical interaction. In the scripting section of the book, we have chosen to present good group dynamic situations to portray optimum lesson flow. Teachers are aware that the ideal lesson is very seldom the case.

One of the most inhibiting and potentially destructive elements in the classroom is student fear of ridicule, or a negative reaction from peers (i.e., derisive comments/laughter). This type of student negative brew serves up a silent response and muted enthusiasm for those creative lessons which require verbal interaction and input.

First, all teachers must analyze the group persona to determine if there is a poor dynamic which is the result of peer fear. Having made that diagnosis, and realizing that at the presentation of a lesson there will not be a rich array of *verbal* responses, the following suggestions may help to nurture and tap the temporarily blocked creative energy:

— In a language lesson, have older students *write* their responses to the initial presentation and then exchange with a fellow student and read each other's works aloud. (This may alleviate some of the pressure of sharing one's own work with the entire class. It may also give students an opportunity to get more deeply involved in one another's work, and by so doing develop a more empathetic stance.)

— Younger students, lacking a sophistication of writing skills, have a different problem. The teacher might suggest that students respond by *drawing* a picture of the image that comes to mind. This means of expression is appealing to students on this level, and thus betters the chance for an uninhibited response.

— Assess and deal with the negative feelings that may arise:

1. Openly explore student feelings:

   — Make it a classroom rule that all students will share their work. Keeping a tight teacher control, allow students to respond (even in a negative or derogatory fashion), but *immediately* turn the discussion into an analysis of how these negative responses make one feel, and make the group feel as a whole. The following is a possible script:

T: Mary, how did it make you feel when John laughed at your comment?

Mary: It made me feel very bad.

T: Did it make you feel anything else?

Mary: Angry.

T: John, how do you think it would make *you* feel if someone laughed at *your* comment?

John: Not too good, I guess.

T: Can we all discuss the feelings that we have about speaking aloud in class? Does it make you feel good to get up and share your thoughts with the group? Does it make you feel proud? Does it make you feel frightened? Please write down on a piece of paper three feelings you get when asked to share aloud your ideas with the rest of the class.

After the students write their feelings, the teacher requires each class member to read what they have written aloud. Three responses might be:

ANGRY   FRIGHTENED   NERVOUS

The teacher then turns the lesson toward a positive language experience by asking the following questions:

— Angry as *what?*

— Frightened as *what?*

— Nervous as *what?*

The students are then required to take their feelings and turn them into images (the beginning of a poem):

— angry as *a charging bull*

— frightened as *a mouse being chased by a cat*

— nervous as *a tooth about to be pulled*

In an actual writing experience, responding to negative classroom feedback, the poem, "The Nag" was written (see p. 43).

The teacher can then extend the lesson into an ongoing poem/discussion about negative feelings; and poetry becomes a cathartic experience for the class as a whole. This lesson then becomes a point of reference should the behavior reappear.

2. Establish class atmosphere by direct teacher intervention:

T: [reacting to derisive laughter] John, in this class, we want to feel free to try new things, and to express ourselves without being afraid to make a mistake. When you laugh at someone's response, you no longer allow this to happen. Exploration in our classroom is one of the most important things we do. I'm going to ask that all of you, from this point on, greet the efforts of your classmates with *positive* comments only.

There is perhaps no more stifling type of behavior than aggressive and negative response, and it must be dealt with in combination (i.e., teacher/student input) or by quick and decisive teacher intervention.

4. Lack of Student Leadership

It is not uncommon to have a group with no clear student leadership. Most groups do best verbally when there is a lead to follow (i.e., one student will respond to a teacher modeling, giving not only an example to the rest of the class, but perhaps needed courage as well). When no leadership is evident, the following suggestions may help to spark participation:

— In language, give assignments prior to the presentation of a lesson.

T: Joseph, I'm going to be talking today about colors. Before I begin, let me remind you of our discussions in the past about using your five senses when writing poetry. When I finish talking to you about colors, I want you to be ready to write down [or articulate] three responses to the colors using the sense of touch. Mary, I want you to have three responses to the colors, using the sense of hearing (etc.). I will then ask you to share them with the class. [Through this advanced-assignment task, it is assured that there will be a verbal lead to follow.]

— In movement, set up tasks in small groups, assigning leaders, thus giving students the opportunity to flex their leadership qualities in a controlled, comfortable, and nonthreatening environment.

T: We've been exploring verbs and what these words can prompt us to do in movement. I have demonstrated some of these verbs for you. Take any from the board which I have *not* moved, and (in groups of four) be prepared to present these words in movement to the class. I will assign a leader for each group, and you can bounce your ideas off of that leader. [This manageable, pre-assigned group activity results in mosaics which, when combined, become the focus for a larger class piece.]

— In music, when no leadership propels the class in a forward direction, the teacher must assume fully the role of leader. The teacher must give numerous examples, pad instruction, use repetition, and provide positive stroking for student effort. When the teacher feels reticent or lacks musical skills, the call to a music specialist may be appropriate and desirable.

Situation

Too much, too fast: The group dynamic here consists of an overly zealous atmosphere where a significant number of students wish to lead the class and have their suggestions adopted.

Possible Problems and Suggested Solutions

1. Battling Verbal Traffic: General

This type of classroom can get chaotic and confused. Good ideas may get pulled under and lost in the tide of enthusiasm. It can also lead to squabbling and negative feelings, which are actually born of a positive outflow of ideas.

Classes of this type need a strong teacher presence and a clear outline of how the class will function. The teacher becomes, in effect, a skilled and sensitive facilitator of verbal traffic. He or she must point out that ideas need soil in which to be nurtured, and that the soil is the attention of fellow classmates. It is important to establish the realization that listening is not a passive role, and that the listener is contributing by digesting, analyzing, and reshaping what is being said.

2. Battling Verbal Traffic: Specifics

Specifically, creative control of this type of group may be accomplished by one or more of the following:

— Break group into individual units of two, allowing them to share aloud their ideas, enjoying the immediacy of a response while not interfering with class flow. Once the initial need to share has been sated, the entire group can be reformed and ideas shared in a more relaxed format.

— Make sure that pacing is considered when clearing space for individual ideas (i.e., allot time frames for opening discussion, for quiet thought, for class group input, for teacher reflection and redirection, and for selection of ideas through a variety of methods):

  — Tell students, "Vote for the idea (the melody, the movement) which you think will propel the piece the most successfully."

  — Trial and error: Teacher selects, at random, ideas on which to act as a group, and the group then ultimately decides which were the most effective.

  — If the pacing needs quickening, the teacher can simply arbitrarily select (having allowed for widespread student input) those ideas/melodies/movements which will best satisfy the goals of the lesson.

3. Battling High Volatility: "Sound Carpets"

While it is delightful for a teacher to have an enthusiastic, responsive group, it is important to remember that creativity comes in a variety of forms and sounds. The too-quiet classroom can be stifling, but so can the too-loud classroom. What is needed is a variety of "sound carpets" on which to create: the quiet hum of students sharing in small groups; the absolute silence of individual contemplation; the hypnotic timbre of a single voice expressing a view or in dialogue with a teacher; the explosive joy of laughter, enthusiasm, and sheer reaction; and, sometimes (but not always or for too long) the cacophony of too much, too fast.

Situation

The unfocused group: sporadic/nonproductive kinds of responses or those totally out of context.

Possible Problems and Suggested Solutions

1. Dealing With an Overcrowded, Distracting Curriculum

The obvious problem here is that it becomes very difficult for the teacher to maintain a flow of ideas that are pertinent to the topic at hand. The characteristic of the group is of a splayed and fractured nature, and seems to be going off in all directions at once. This is not uncommon and is due, in large part, to the nature of today's curriculum, which takes students from place to place at a rather harried pace. This is one of the problems this book is trying to address by offering interrelated and cross-curriculum teaching, providing an environment which fosters a more cohesive and bonding approach.

2. Dealing With Unfocused Behavior Due to Tension: Bridge Breaks

Tension, both physical and mental, is not uncommon even on the elementary level. It is essential to have receptive minds and relaxed bodies if a lesson is to blossom to its full potential. Reducing tension may be accomplished by providing students with an opportunity to physically unwind: a stretch, a deep breath that is let out without a sound; or it may be helpful to suggest focusing on an image (e.g., "As you silently exhale, think of a starry sky with a million dots of light. Focus on one star. Block everything else out. Mentally touch the star. Listen to the sound of its silence. Use your five senses to explore the darkness and the light."). This may be a lead-in to a lesson, or it may simply be a deep mental breath, an opportunity to clear the mind and prepare a clean, fresh mental sheet on which to create. Gentle exercises which stretch the body and bring the breath into play, as well as colorful teacher imagery, are beneficial in helping children of all ages to relax and focus.

3. Dealing With Student Needs: Going With the Flow

If a group appears to be completely caught up with a previous activity (volatile baseball game, hatching chickens, emotional dispute between two class members, a film which captivated, etc.), the teacher may have to change direction and move with the class in the wake of their enthusiasm, despair, innervation, exaltation, or preoccupation. The teacher is a receiver as well as a giver and has to be able to assimilate the mood and disposition of the class and allow this input to shape the moment. This invokes the joy and the challenge—and the *artistry*—of teaching.

4. Dealing With the Exigent Moment: Preplanning

The class that is unfocused because it meets between an outdoor gym class and school dismissal time is not terribly open or motivated to a language/music/movement lesson; but often the teacher is faced with this exact situation. One of the solutions that seems to work is to seed the lesson in *advance* with the students, so that they enter the room in an anticipatory and excited mood. For example, as the class is leaving for lunch, the teacher might suggest to them that at their language arts class, scheduled for later that afternoon (between gym and dismissal), "we will be using as our focus for writing the most important subject in the world." Invariably, the students say, "What is that?" The answer is: "You'll find out as soon as you arrive from gym today." This seed setting almost always provides the advantage of at least a few of the students coming in with the question on their lips, "What *is* the most important subject in the world?", and the focus has begun to set.

Anticipating the possibility (from previous experience) that the class will have a difficult time focusing on the lesson, it might be helpful to instruct them prior to lunch break to bring something back with them to the classroom—a nature sound they heard while out on the playground; a movement they witnessed in nature (trees waving in the wind, cloud movement, birds, etc.); or any other number of things which could prove to be the focus of the day's lesson.

Individual Dynamic

Situation

Inappropriate response: For a variety of reasons, a student intentionally or unintentionally misconstrues teacher directives.

Possible Problems and Suggested Solutions

1. Student Deliberately Misunderstands Assignment/Teacher Cue, Etc.

Often in this instance the student is going for the laugh. The important thing for the teacher to remember is that even this type of response can be dealt with in a positive way, thereby reducing its disruptive effect.

For example: In the course of a preliminary edging in for poems dealing with the topic "The People of My World," Brad was called on to volunteer what he had brainstormed about this subject. He had chosen to talk about his neighbors. As he began, it became clear he was extemporizing beyond his original notes. It also became clear that he was heading in a direction designed to provide a bit of unscheduled humor. He included a wealth of salient details about his neighbors' reactions to his dog's visits to their lawn. He spared no verbage. The class began to follow his lead. At this moment the session could be either won or lost, depending on teacher reaction. To acknowledge that what Brad said was inappropriate was to negatively reinforce his aberrant intention. To divert the trend or try to find pertinent worth in what was said, in effect, would take the wind out of his sails and add substance to the classroom discussion. Thus, the teacher took a deep breath and reflectively said, "We have learned a lot about you, today Brad; we've learned that you are a person who keenly observes the behavior of your pet and of your neighbors; and that you are very much aware of their likes and dislikes. It takes a sensitive person to be that observant. In poetry we need to develop just those types of skills."

In these situations, the teacher, in essence, acts as a shield to deflect the remark that may destroy the direction, mood, and intent of the discussion. It must be dealt with quickly and gracefully, so as not to deflate the misguided student who is contributing (in his or her fashion) to the discussion, nor add fuel to the fire.

2. Student Offers a Rambling Response

In a situation where the teacher presents the topic for discussion and a student, in responding to that topic, hits the *periphery* of the idea, getting caught up in his or her narrative, a number of possibilities present themselves. On pages 187–88, we addressed the viability of going with the flow; there are times, however, when this may not be the solution of choice. The teacher, in this case, may elect to subtly insist on a return to topic.

T: Could anyone, using imagery, express the nature of sadness? Jim?

S: Once my brother got the measles, and we were supposed to go on vacation, and he got all the attention, and we didn't get to go, and everyone sent him presents, and my mother said I couldn't watch TV because it was noisy, and I couldn't have any friends come over to play and . . .

T: [gently interjecting] How did all these events make you feel? Did they make you feel sad?

S: [thinking] I guess I was more mad than sad.

T: Does anybody in the class see sadness in Jim's story? Is it sad not to go on vacation when you're all excited about it and ready to go? Is disappointment the same as sadness?

Here the teacher has attempted to find *elements* within Jim's fairly unfocused account which will keep the class concentrating on task. It is germane to point out that this type of rambling story usually inspires fellow classmates to volunteer *their* stories about vacations, siblings, illness, and a myriad of other nontask focuses. Without seeming disinterested in their offerings, the teacher must set time limits and attempt to refocus the group:

T: We've heard Jim's story, and a number of others, and there are still hands in the air: but today our goal is to explore feelings, in particular, sadness, and to write poetry about this feeling. I'm encouraged by the fact that you are calling on personal experiences to stimulate a flow of emotion; however, at this point we need to focus not on the stimulus, but on the emotion itself. So take a quiet moment to reflect on those stories which best illustrate the feeling or emotion of sadness, and then please tell us why you've chosen that story.

---

3. Student Offers the Innocent Nonsequitur

Often a student response made with the best of intentions derails the group focus. The class may react to the unorthodox response with disruptive laughter, derisive comments, or puzzled silence. The teacher must immediately interject a sense of balance to offset the tilting class equilibrium. He or she may choose to address the nonsequitur head on, and in so doing move the lesson back on track; or the teacher may choose to appeal to the student's evaluative powers for self-help, or the analytical powers of the group for peer advice. Another possibility may be that the teacher can use this nonsequitur as a contrasting springboard to widen the scope of the lesson.

T: As I say the verbs you have helped me list on the board, I would like you to put those action words somewhere in your body, and try to show me the verb in movement:
    OOZE

Class: [All but one child are slowly moving arms, torsos, legs in a weighted motion, in all directions. Tom, the exception, is slashing the air wildly.]

T: And relax. Tom, I wonder if you're silently saying the word *ooze* in your own mind as you were moving . . . did you notice how much quicker your motions were than the rest of the class? What sorts of things ooze? Do birds ooze as they fly? Does a fire engine ooze out of the firehouse? [Appealing to the child for self-help]

Tom: [silence, indicating he is unsure of the word's meaning]

T: I think perhaps we need to define the meaning of the word *ooze*. Can someone give Tom an example of an element which oozes? [Appealing to the group for peer advice]

Student: Catsup oozes.

Student: Honey.

Student: Toothpaste.

T: Tom—turn your arm into that toothpaste and show me an oozing motion. *That* was a convincing demonstration of that verb.

Using Tom's original movement to widen the scope of the lesson, the teacher might wish to point out that Tom's motion was antithetical to the original verb, and in so doing develop other contrasting motions using opposites. This might ostensibly lead to a deepening of the moving-a-verb lesson.

In a poetry writing session, this type of unrelated response is not uncommon, and, in fact, needs to be anticipated.

T: Since school is just beginning, and we are in the process of getting to know one another, it might be helpful and fun to concentrate today on poems which help us discover things about ourselves. We often see ourselves, I think, in ways quite different from others around us, particularly those who are closest to us. I'd like to begin the lesson by listing on the board people in our lives who may see us differently than we see ourselves. John, do you have a suggestion for someone in your life who may see you differently than you see yourself?

John: My aunt was over at the house yesterday with her new baby boy.

Student: [calling out] My mother has a new baby!

Student: [joining in] My cat had kittens! And Ginny's Mom is going to have a baby.

The teacher becomes painfully aware that somehow he or she has lost the lesson threads, and the plan for the poem is rapidly unraveling.

> T: John, I'm sure your aunt is *very* excited about her new baby—and wasn't it wonderful that she brought the baby over to meet his cousin? When your cousin grows up, he may be someone in your life who sees you differently then you see yourself. He's too young now, but your *aunt* has known you since you were born. How do you think she sees you? Sometimes in a good way, sometimes in a bad way?

Again, linking in with one element, the teacher leads the class back through the front door.

4. Student Who Gets Left Behind

Each child moves at his or her own pace, and there are as many tempi as there are students in a class. But at any given time, or any given lesson, a single student may (for any number of reasons) get left out or left behind. It may be for lack of interest on the student's part—lack of understanding, lack of self-confidence or skills and abilities. It may be just a bad day for that student. Whatever the reason, it behooves the teacher to try to enfold this student, and help him or her to benefit from the day's lesson. This may include simply encouraging the child by feeding responses from which he or she can work:

> T: [addressing "lost" child] Barry, I haven't heard you offer an image for any of the colors we've been discussing today. Do you have a favorite color? Red? Blue?
>
> Barry: Red's nice.
>
> T: Do you have anything at home that's red? A toy? A favorite shirt? Something in nature that's red you particularly like?
>
> Barry: [picking up in interest and energy] I like fire engines.

The singling out in a positive way has allowed Barry to feel that his views will contribute something to the group discussion. The teacher has provided him with a means of responding that is nonthreatening and that gives him center stage and promises good results for him and the class.

If the student resists being drawn out into the group, offering a special task that may be presented at a later time could propel him or her into a more comfortable situation without relieving the student of all responsibility to the group.

> **T:** Beth, you've indicated that you have no wishes, dreams, or fantasies to contribute today to our discussion. Perhaps you might like to sit quietly over by the window where there's a lovely view of the beech tree, and imagine yourself living under that tree—like an elf, or a wood nymph. Take a piece of paper and pencil with you and jot down ideas as they come. The class will look forward to you sharing your ideas with them later.

Sometimes *nothing* seems to work, and the student simply refuses to be a part in any form of the day's activity. In teaching, sometimes the reality is not pleasant and *no* solution presents itself. Experience, however, teaches us that "hope is the thing with feathers,"[1] and that tomorrow is another day.

5. Student Who Is Obstreperous, Noncooperative, and Uses Energy in a Misdirected Way

Every teacher has had to deal with this type student. The problem presents itself on all grade levels, in all group dynamics, across the board. It is a classroom phenomenon and is never easy to address. The reasons for this type of behavior will not be categorized in this text due to the unwieldly number of possibilities. Recognizing that generalities may not be applicable, here are some attempts to retrieve this type of child and restore him or her to the lesson.

— Channel negative energy into positive outlets (e.g., observe certain repetitive motions and invent a way to *use* these motions as a movement piece—pencil tapping nervously on desk, knee bouncing, finger fidgeting—or as a rhythm behind student texts). Motions might also be used as image stimuli for motions found in nature (e.g., what taps? what has a quick, repetitive motion? etc.).

— Place a noncooperative student with a cooperative one long enough for peer influence to have a possible effect, short enough not to frustrate the better-focused student. The hope here is that by having the "better" student react to the noncooperative student's work, there will be a positive fallout and a degree of motivation provided.

— Find ways to use the student's misguided energy as a motivation for class activities (e.g., the student who seems unable to sit still, continually

[1]Emily Dickinson, "The Complete Poems of Emily Dickinson," Little, Brown & Co., p. 116, 1960.

balancing his chair on two legs, rocking, moving things about on the desk's surface may be used as an image for the restlessness of nature—the movement of leaves on trees, the swaying of branches in a storm, the ocean's tide depositing treasures on the beach, and then removing them). We may, in fact, ask this student to be the demonstrator, while the rest of the class observes and tries to draw parallels which may later become the images used in writing poetry. There is the risk, of course, that by highlighting this behavior we may be encouraging its continuance. On the other hand, there is the hopeful possibility that the student will flourish by this attention, and that positive attention may be the very element he or she is seeking.

6. Student Who "Hogs" the Floor (Exceptional Student)

This student presents a unique and difficult problem, because more often than not the student who dominates the classroom discussion is a student with much to offer. He or she is usually self-confident, excited by the lesson—and eager to make his or her opinions known to the class as a whole. The thin line the teacher has to walk is how to contain this child's enthusiasm without dampening it, and restore a sense of equality to the various members of the group. Teacher and students alike need to be able to delight in the contributions made by the overzealous student. Two possible troubling repercussions might be:

a. Fostering jealousy on the part of the other students because of *deserved* teacher recognition and praise; and

b. Group self-denigration because of feelings of not being able to rise to the perceived level of excellence.

It is essential to recognize that these problems may surface, and to try and head them off before they do. Note the temperature of the group, the other students' reactions to the overzealous student's contributions, and to your reactions as a teacher. Know when to strike a better balance, and when the largest number of students will be best served by playing down the individual's role. This is the key to utilizing the strengths of this special student without adversely affecting the group dynamic. These suggestions are by necessity subjective because there is no panacea or simple solution for dealing with group interactions. We do, however, offer the following somewhat more concrete suggestions:

— Instill a sense of discrimination in the overzealous student by suggesting that more is not necessarily better, and that we need mentally to edit our class contributions before presenting them.

S: [raising hand for fifth time in five minutes, in response to the teacher's call for adjectives that describe the sun] Round—and yellow—and smooth—and hot—pretty—bright . . .

T: [gently interrupting] Thank you for *all* those appropriate and visual adjectives which help us to picture the sun. What I would like you to do now is to select two of the many adjectives you've offered, and silently form *full* images in your mind. Choose only those two adjectives which will best describe the sun. Please take your time. Can someone else please suggest new and colorful adjectives?

In offering this overzealous student the opportunity to extend two adjectives into full images (i.e., "the sun is *yellow* as a dandelion . . . the sun is *bright* as a gold coin"), he or she has been presented with an advanced assignment, acknowledging his or her abilities and the fact that he or she is moving at a faster pace than the rest of the group. By separating his or her activity from the rest of the group's, we have tactfully excluded him or her from further vocalization at this time. This gives the rest of the group the opportunity to catch up as well.

— Emphasize, to the "exceptional student," the essential role that listening plays in a classroom. Assign this student the task of *listening* as an analytical observer, so that he or she may, later in the discussion, offer reaction, criticism, praise, thus becoming a valuable peer resource. Example:

T: What is *your* opinion as to which of the suggested adjectives are the most vivid? Which do *you* think best describes the sun?

— Reassure the "exceptional student" that their fears of having their silences misinterpreted as ignorance are unfounded: that the teacher *knows* they know. Example:

T: You have provided us with a feast of adjectives this morning, and I'm sure you still have others you would like to share. However, I would like to hear your full images now, and then have other students share full images for their adjectives.

7. The Selectively Blocked Student

It is frustrating to both teacher and student when a response is not forthcoming. Sometimes the cause is simply that a child cannot respond in the learning mode that is being used at that moment. For example, every teacher has had a student who is vocal and vibrant during a class discussion, and immobilized by the command to write. This is perhaps the most commonly encountered blockage; however, some students suffer from the reverse dilemma, contributing nothing to the class discussion, but producing an outstanding piece of written work. Still others who can do neither find the abstract language of movement and music welcome realms in which to be creative.

In particular, these types of students who have a strong penchant for one learning style/mode or another may benefit greatly from working the word through many mediums. Success in one area may provide the student with the courage and curiosity to explore those heretofore inaccessible learning arenas.

We have attempted to address those problems which seem to arise most frequently. There are dozens of other troubling snags which may thwart the flow and effectiveness of a lesson; but conversely, there are just as many wondrous, spontaneous moments when the words, the movement, and the music "like stars, turn the classroom bright."

section two
word-working implementation

WORKING THE WORD

At first the word
was just a word, long
and flat like a shadow cast
across the page and then
your eyes rounded
on a thought,
the word
stirred, shifted, filled
with a deep breath
of imagination;
became
sky
storm
sunset
dreams as big as laughter
spilled off the page and ran
like a river around the room
and the word became
words; turning, tumbling
towards completion
of a thought and carried us
along a flood
of sight
and sound
and smell

and taste
and texture pressed
like love against the mind; then
like the rivers restless
rhythm the words moved
musically in space, in time, became
the rush of voices and the flow
of song and that one
flat word fattened into more
than memory alone could hold; reached
through us to embrace
the soul.
So do not clench the words
like sunshine in your fist
and miss the magic
of their light; LET GO,
LET THEM FLOW . . . until
like stars they turn
the darkness bright.

Susan A. Katz,
written for Upper Nyack
Elementary students,
March, 1990

197

INTRODUCTION:
APPLICATION OF TECHNIQUES
THROUGHOUT THE CURRICULUM _____

In the first half of this book, we've examined evocative techniques in the areas of language, movement, and music. Our goal has been to make them a part of the everyday fabric of learning. Each isolated technique presented in the first section is, by itself, relatively easy to assimilate and apply. Synthesizing these techniques is challenging because one must be sensitive to the following:

— The group temperament and dynamic—its unique possibilities and background.

— The individual imprint within the group, and the importance that the individual plays in defining the group.

— What will inspire student poetry and be the applicable elements in the enhancement of the experience; which poems will sing, which will move, which will cry out for rhythmical treatment.

— Which experiences are the most appropriate to the school environment, within the time frame of hour, day, school year.

— Serendipitous opportunities, such as writing about the fragility and interdependence of life on this planet in response to a headline environmental disaster.

— The ongoing possibilities and the individual lesson which may serve as an entree to the larger curriculum concentric.

This, then, represents the ultimate challenge of teaching: the blending of these variables into a cohesive, natural flow. This brand of teaching invites and intrigues both student and teacher alike. It deepens and widens and spirals into an expansive word-working learning experience. This is the orchestration of teaching which never gets easier, nor should it.

Having accepted these fundamentals of creative teaching, one now needs to believe that the process is reciprocal, and that much of what will ultimately contribute to exciting classroom experiences must come from the students as well as the teacher. So the teacher must be willing to relinquish a measure of classroom control. It is a leap of faith that allows the student to generate creative energy that may propel the class in promising directions. As ideas rebound between student and student, student and teacher, the emphasis is on a kind of "creative chaos" where we learn by "going where we have to go."[1] This is an expansive experience for both teacher and student. It has a nurturing impact which provides each student with a sense of self and contributes to his or her feeling of significance. There is *joy* to be found in this type of scholastic adventure.

[1]"The Waking," *The Collected Poems of Theodore Roethke*, Doubleday Anchor Publishers, 1975.

An example of this type of teaching might occur in a science class. In addition to exploring geodes in the traditional teaching style of asking for properties, origin, and geographical location, we might layer the experience; we might suggest to the students to run with the ideas of applying colors, feelings, sensory perceptions, sound, movement, or other techniques previously learned. This may result in a totally new juxtaposition of concepts. The discussion may veer to the "secrets of stones," "smooth as an ice cave," "rough as the bottom of the ocean," "shiny as the inside of the moon." The geode design itself, with its undulating lines, may lead to a many-voiced aleatoric interpretation, or the qualities of the stones may inspire alliteration: "Solid . . . shiny . . . sensuous . . . sinking . . . silent . . . stones" (student poem, M., 3rd grade), which could then be interpreted in movement—heavy, flicking, flowing, floating, falling.

This science lesson has crafted language arts, movement, and music into a layering of learning. *This is the whole point of what this book is suggesting.* Layering curriculum is the most effective and pertinent type of learning experience. Such learning is also memorable in that it is repetitive and requires a larger investment on the part of the student.

In an actual introductory classroom experience (third-grade level), the students were asked to suggest images for colors. One student insisted she was unable to think of an image. The class went through the spectrum of colors with no response from the student. Images were listed on the board such as, "blue is the color of blueberries," "blue is the color of the summer sky," "blue is the color of a robin's egg." Finally, the reluctant student's hand went up, and with some trepidation she offered the image, "Blue is the color of wonders." That offering led the class down a side street of wonders more evocative and exciting than the original course. A far more effective series of lessons followed than had been originally planned. The teacher sometimes has to be willing to say, "I planted tomatoes, I got a watermelon . . . but it's a *great* watermelon!" The kind of teaching presented in this book suggests that ideas can come from anywhere at any time, to implement and enlarge on that which has to be taught.

The first section of this book provided detailed scripting from which a teacher might evoke creative language responses which then generated music and movement activities. This groundwork required the infusion of additional information into the classroom (i.e., poetry recipes, imagery, metaphor, simile, alliteration, how a poem looks on paper, onomatopoeia, diagramming the image, the difference between a poem and a story, line break, exploration of movement qualities, speech and rhythm play, body percussion, form, canon, melody, vocal sounds, found sounds, dynamics, and more).

The aim of the second section is to *use* these elements within the context of the everyday curriculum. There are examples of how this is done within the areas of field trips, math lessons, environmental issues, seasonal focuses, science explorations, etc. Suggestions are offered, based on experience and experimentation; however, each teacher should rely on his or her own creative instincts to make the event *singular*. The hope is that these suggestions will enrich the soil of your thinking and inspire you to plant your own word-working seeds.

chapter 6

extended field trip experience

EXTENSION: FIELD TRIP

A school field trip is an extended learning experience. It reaches out beyond the limits of the classroom to explore new worlds. It suggests, by its inherent qualities, adventure and new discovery. For these reasons we have chosen the extended field trip experience to serve as a laboratory presentation, offering it as an introductory chapter to Section Two, and as an in-depth outline for application of the skills discussed in Section One.

Any school field trip can offer opportunities for richly integrated amalgams. With preresearch done by the teacher and shared with the group (any field trip worth taking is worth researching!), student anticipation and expectation are heightened, making the actual experience multiply valuable. Reflections and projects occurring after a trip bring closure and serve to deepen the total experience. The attention paid by the teacher to inherent possibilities (i.e., movement, speech/song/found-instrument sounds/art/poetry) can change a field trip from a singular happening to a long-remembered event.

The trip which follows was taken to Storm King Art Center in Mountainville, New York, with ten-year-olds from Upper Nyack Elementary School. Rapidly earning the reputation for being one of the finest sculpture parks in the world, Storm King lies approximately two hours north of New York City. It melds megalithic sculptures with the rolling topography of its 400 acres. The sculptures have great appeal, ranging in size from monumental to moderate, by such famous sculptors as Alexander Liberman, Alexander Calder, Louise Nevelson, Henry Moore, David Smith, Isamu Noguchi, Kenneth Snelson, Mark Di Suvero, and Tal Streeter (to name nine of the 200 plus sculptors represented).

The art, classroom, poet-in-the-school, and music teachers collaborated, starting with a reconnaissance photography trip where black and white prints were taken. These were then used as visual motivation in the classroom prior to the trip. Because this was an intracurriculum experience, the goals were many and varied:

— To break through what may have been the children's preconceived notions of what constitutes museums, and also to share abstract and nonobjective art in an outdoor environment.

— To open students' eyes to the monumentality of the creations.

— To be aware of the ambition inherent in creativity: how a person can follow up in reality after his or her initial creative impulse.

— To be aware of the exceptional professional skills in engineering, materials, design, and landscaping brought together in this particular environment.

— To lead the students into a realization of the relationship between visual sculpture and its translation into sound, movement, and language.

— To apply creative language skills (i.e., metaphor, simile, alliteration, onomatopoeia, etc.) to that which has form and substance.

— To select appropriate adjectives which enhance the image, and describe feeling and subject as applicable to the individual sculptures.

— To use the sculptures' creative energy as a stimulus for initiating a new entity.

— To encourage language experimentation (abstraction and permutation of the original creation).

— To experience the impact of the work on a sensory level, to internalize it, and make it uniquely the students'.

— For students to feel the worth of their own contributions.

— To heighten visual accuity through sketching the sculptures, later to be used for interpretive work in the art classroom.

— To use the environment and actual sculptures as departure points for individual art projects, movement compositions, and poetry.

What follows are the specifics which brought us to these goals.

Nine principal sculptors were chosen to be the key ones for recognition of style. These were intentionally chosen because their works were in abundance in the park, and particularly dramatic. Through a quick study of the photographs, the students were soon able to analyze style and apply this new skill in identifying other sculptures by the same artist (e.g., Alexander Liberman predominantly uses large, cylindrical shapes; Kenneth Snelson, a cross-thatching of narrow, metal poles, etc.).

These nine sculptors' names were offered as possible rhythm building blocks. The students individually spoke the sculptor's names in possible rhythms, and together the class figured out the corresponding rhythmic notation:

Tal Streeter

David Smith

Louise Nelson

Mark Di Suvero

Henry Moore

Kenneth Snelson

Alexander Calder

Alexander Liberman

Isamu Noguchi

LESSON IMPLEMENTATION

Combinations of these patterns were explored.

Al – ex – an – der Cal – der, Hen – ry Moore

These combinations translated into body percussion patterns, over which individual students improvised (clapping, hand drum, desk top, metal chair, leg, etc.).

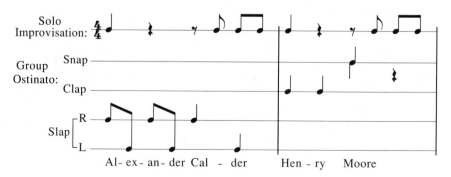

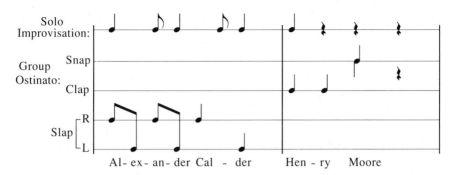

Al- ex- an- der Cal - der   Hen - ry   Moore

Next, they were transferred to small percussion, and also used beneath student improvisations.

The group was then asked to explore a musical order· for *all* the nine sculptors mentioned—an order which would have variety while allowing students to say their names without distorting them. They came up with this:

A ‖: Alexander Liberman, Louise ——— Nevelson,
     Alexander Calder, Hen - ry - Moore :‖

B ‖: Kenneth   Snelson   Isamu Noguchi
      Tal Streeter David Smith   Mark ——— Di Suvero :‖

There was lots of playing around with inflection (for instance, Isamu Noguchi's name seemed to invite it!) and dynamics, with the majority determining the outcome: first time forte (loud), repeat piano (soft), ABA form. It was discovered that this form worked well canonically and so became a speech canon.

This then became the basis for a melodic setting. The task in this instance was to use a mode recently studied, dorian (which occurs when you play from D to D on a piano).

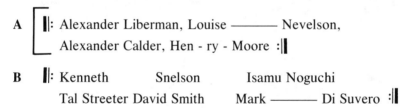

Further, the group-written melody was to work as a canon by constructing the melody so that every strong beat landed on the first, third, and fifth note of the dorian scale, insuring a harmony when sung in canon. The seventh tone was a possibility as well.

1st   3rd   5th   7th

The resulting canon came from a collection of many students' ideas, by trying the ideas out—singing them, playing them on recorder, honing the results.

Layering Through Language

Familiar now with the sculptors' styles, and comfortable with their names from having spoken the speech piece and sung the canon, we began to look deeper into the works using metaphor, simile, and alliteration. Through the application of these poetic skills, we reshaped the strange and wonderful sculptures into words.

In layering the field trip experience through language, we selected a particular sculpture and asked the students to brainstorm aloud (with the teacher listing the words). Students were invited to suggest words that seemed best to capture the spirit, the flow, the movement, and the energy of the piece in question. For example, students responded to this particular sculpture with the following words:

—thin	—spidery	—flowing	—elastic
—wiry	—hard	—floating	—angular
—heavy	—big	—thunderous	—suspended
—light	—broken	—bright	—shiny
—stretching	—smooth	—wistful	—large

Kenneth Snelson, *Free Ride Home* (Collection of Storm King Art Center, Mountainville, NY)

Once the words were listed, students were asked to think of them in two ways: first, as descriptive of the sculpture, and second, as possible images that either described the sculpture or enhanced it. For example:

— Hard as what?

— Floating like . . . ?

— Spidery as . . . ?

Encouraged to remember all of their language skills, students shared images aloud:

— Heavy as a bridge,'' ''a crackle of thunder,'' ''sharp as a prickle,'' ''shiny as a new, black car,'' ''shiny as a crystal mirror,'' ''flowing like hair in the wind''

Some unedited examples follow.

& U.
C.B.

5-14-39
Grade 4 ☆

Poetry

big
tall
hard

It is as big as a brige or a mountins

and as tall as a skyscraper.

It is as hard as a large diamond

Alexander Liberman, *Iliad* (Collection of
Storm King Art Center, Mountainville, NY)

a f
Poetry

May 22,1989
Grade 4 H

words
round
deep

as a ball
as a well

strange
folwing
wigely

as something you saw
for the first time
as a river.
like a worm

Alexander Liberman, *Iliad*, detail (Collection
of Storm King Art Center, Mountainville, NY)

Kenneth Snelson, *Free Ride Home* (Collection of Storm King Art Center, Mountainville, NY)

Kenneth Snelson

It's as tall as a sky scraper.

It's like a wild maze that you have to run into.

It's as cold as ice in the winter.

It's as heavy as a bulldozer

It's as thick as a book on a shelf.

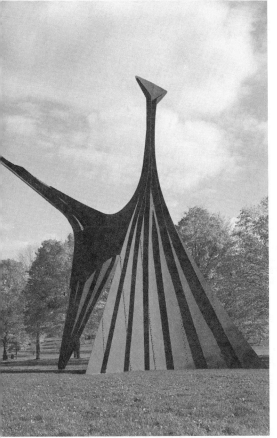

Alexander Calder, *The Arch* (Collection of Storm King Art Center, Mountainville, NY)

Writing
Poetry

May 22, 1989
Grade 4H

1. hard as a rock.
2. heavy as a building.
3. big as a house.
4. wide as a branch
5. climbing as a tree.
6. trapping as a cave
7. tall as a mountain.
8. licking as a ice cream

1 a black knight defending its castelle with a sword

2 a dog guarding the earth.

3 an angel flying in heaven.

4 two people dancing together

5 a tiger trying to reach its destination.

6 a buried tresure from underneath a million years ago
          I.K - 4K

This sharing of ideas and images helped to expand creative possibilities. The sculpture became more than form and substance. Lines moved and interacted, one with the other, through imaginative interpretation.

Each student was then asked to select a single sculpture from an assortment of xeroxed photos. It was suggested that they choose the sculpture with which they felt most comfortable and which seemed to them to offer the widest variety of creative possibilities. They were then asked to list words (adjectives) that defined for them the scope of that particular sculpture. Having listed the words, they were asked to create images; and then extend the images into language sculptures that took on new shape and form. The following are examples of students' unedited works. The typed examples are edited.

Alexander Liberman, *Iliad,* detail (Collection of Storm King Art Center, Mountainville, NY)

L. H.
Poetry

May 22, 1989
Grade 4'H

The tube-shaped sculpture is an everlasting eye, watching the tourists who happened to pass by.

A giants straw which he will be using to slurp a sour soda.

Circles

circles tubes dots move in a circle with you go to me a train as circle tube go to follow and circle

Woodpile

Trunks of straight trees
in a woodpile
They are hollow;
Peer in and
You see stars
in a night sky;
Peer out and
Walk the straight one
A balance beam,
A tightrope;
Be careful or
It will bend and break
Under your weight,
Taller than trees;
But just two
Feet tall.

Adonai

D. B.

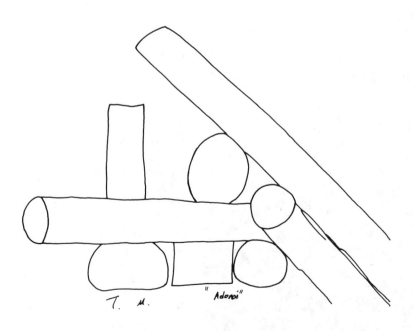

T. M.   "Adonai"

N C
Writing Poetry

May 22, 1989
Grade 4 K

Stranger

A stranger in
the night
standing bold and
strong, cold and
bare, but

still standing
there, as a
guardian over
your tour
helping but free

loving, kind,
not lazy,
not hasty,
but still
a stranger in
the night.

Alexander Liberman, *Adam* (Collection of
Storm King Art Center, Mountainville, NY)

FALLING

Images and dreams once kept alive by
children now left to die as they are
falling to the ground soon to
be alive again inside of children
and then to be left falling . . .
falling to the ground in sorrow
for that is the last
of those dreams and images.

M. K., 4th grade

WOODPILE

Trunks of straight trees
in a woodpile.
They are hollow;
peer in and
You see stars
in a night sky;
peer out and
walk the straight one
a balance beam;
a tightrope;
be careful or
it will bend and break
under your weight.
taller than trees;
but just two
feet tall.

E. O., 4th grade

Alexander Liberman, *Adonai* (Collection of
Storm King Art Center, Mountainville, NY)

The small painter paints on his
    extraordinary triangular canvas.
He is dipping his tiny brush in the
    depth of the sea of sparkling turquoise.
He envisions the finished masterpiece
    in his mind.
His brush pulls across the rough canvas
    making colorful lines and shapes.
He dips it gingerly into the rippling
    crystal water.
With a flourishing stroke he closes
    his imagination's door for a day.

                M. Y., 4th grade

Alexander Liberman, *Adam* (Collection of
Storm King Art Center, Mountainville, NY)

Isamu Noguchi, *Momo Taro* (Collection of
Storm King Art Center, Mountainville, NY)

One-half egg
I am inside it
Its walls are smooth
like plastic on gravel
the shell is shiny
like glaze on pottery
it is bumpy
it's cozy but I hear
a voice
my mother
I depart from my egg.

              E. O., 4th grade

Man holds a statue
with a finger,
yet he never touches it.
It is leaning; falling;
yet it is straight
held in the ground
with cold winds
blowing around it;
whipping;
one more blow, it
will topple over
like a teetering nestling
on the edge of its nest.
Two separate pieces
connected.

E. O., 4th grade

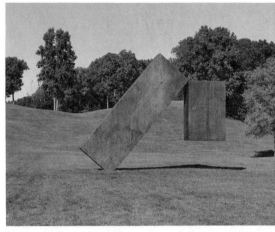

Menashe Kadishman, *Suspended* (Collection of Storm King Art Center, Mountainville, NY)

A swirled
lollypop
a pin in a
crystal ball
that is ready
to destroy
the world.

N. T., 4th
grade

A globe
Shining and spinning
in its own
       queer stillness . . .
Sitting in
   eerie light and feeling,
Inside it,
   a life is growing,
       changing, learning.

G. R., 4th grade

Jerome Kirk, *Orbit* (Collection of Storm King Art Center, Mountainville, NY)

It seems to reach out to the cloudless
bare sky and start to day-dream.

It seems to fold, and flicker up and down
as if there is danger and he must be hidden.

It seems to bounce at the sky to
say "let me come up too."

It seems to smell the wetness of a rain cloud.
It sees the clouds floating and flying around,

It seems to hear the musical chirping of birds,
And feels the fuzzy rabbits
Snuggling it.

G. L., 4th grade

*Throughout this experience,
language elements have
appeared in a natural and
effective manner. Isolating this
particular poem, notice the use
of many of the techniques and
skills addressed in the first part
of this book.*

Tal Streeter, *Endless Column* (Collection of
Storm King Art Center, Mountainville, NY)

Isamu Noguchi, *Momo Taro* (Collection of
Storm King Art Center, Mountainville, NY)

A big, broken coconut | *alliteration*
Sad and lonely | *emotion*
Heavy and warm
Round and standing still | *alliteration*
Like a fat, lazy rock | *simile*
with a beautiful shining color, | *adjectives*
Lying on the hot earth
with a few tree branches
on top of its head.   *imagery*
It's waiting . . .
For a gigantic dog
to lick its head.   *imagery*
It can't move
From left to right.
It's trying to move its head . . .
Scratch . . .
But no hands.
The hot sun is in love | *imagery*
with the broken coconut | *metaphorical*
Trying to move west   *imagery*
so the coconut's juicy water
Won't dry.

B. R., 4th grade

In this example, it is exciting to note that the student poet has stretched the assignment beyond its limits of sculpture, language, field trip—and included something learned in another classroom. In a small but significant way this illustrates the kind of curriculum interaction this book is suggesting.

Here comes the roadrunner, short and lean,
Daniel Boone takes off his hat
   to the big, full moon.

A. A., 4th grade

Isaac Witkin, *Kumo* (Collection of Storm King Art Center, Mountainville, NY)

Here is an especially strong example attempting onomatopoeia and internal rhyme, as well as the more sophisticated use of dialogue within the poem.

Heavy steel tubes,
Crashing to the ground
Tumbling around,
Breaking trees and bushes
Slashing the ground.
They dent each other
As if to play or say,
"Come and play"
"Come and play"
"I'm lonely"
"Come and play"

K. C., 4th grade

Alexander Liberman, *Adonai* (Collection of Storm King Art Center, Mountainville, NY)

Kenneth Snelson, *Free Ride Home* (Collection of Storm King Art Center, Mountainville, NY)

This is a particularly fine example of imagery and the poet's ability to move from image to image and still have the poem maintain its integrity and its emotional impact.

Old oak trees after a storm,
Crumpled up with fear.
A little child's pick-up-sticks
Crashing to the ground.
A first grader's stick figures.
Cowboys and Indians.
Bang bang.

S. H., 4th grade

Grace Knowlton, *Spheres* (Collection of Storm King Art Center, Mountainville, NY)

This poet captures the sculpture in a single, extended metaphor.

These round
eggs sent
from space
awaiting the
time to
awake and
hatch.

S. S., 4th
grade *The extended image in this poem provides a full and satisfying visual word picture.*

Isamu Noguchi, *Momo Taro* (Collection of Storm King Art Center, Mountainville, NY)

One is an egg
    that a baby chick
        has just come out of
To wander around and
    explore the world.
The other is the gravestone
    of a man,
        known by many for his kindness
        and sensitivity to other people.
The two lie there
    looking at the sun in the day
    and moon in the night
    remembering when they were still
Something important.

J. A. S., 4th grade

This is a strong example of carefully chosen words, positioning of words, and contrasts (e.g., ''frozen but soft ground,'' ''still hill,'' ''hard block . . . hot sun'').

A hard block of steel
Waiting to be mended
Under the hot sun . . .
A box for heaven
Stuck in the frozen,
  but soft ground.
A steel block
On the still hill . . .
Watch out!
It's going to fall.

      M. M., 4th grade

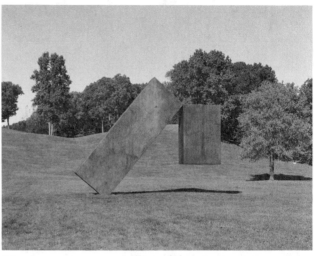

Menashe Kadishman, *Suspended* (Collection of Storm King Art Center, Mountainville, NY)

This poem illustrates the effectiveness of personalizing the image (e.g., ''mother's black hair'').

My mother's black hair
  sticks up like she had a scare . . .
Like a spider web, flying in the air . . .
Like a piece of lightning
  falling by mistake.

      L. S., 4th grade

Tal Streeter, *Endless Column* (Collection of Storm King Art Center, Mountainville, NY)

The classes were inspired melodically by the sculpture as well as verbally. "Endless Column," Tal Streeter's work, led one fourth grade class into sequence, where a melody patterns itself higher or lower. If you follow the contour of the melody, you can see the sculpture ascending, then descending. The task this time was to write a group piece in Aeolian mode, which on E is as follows:

Resulting Melodic Interpretation of Graphics

Endless Column

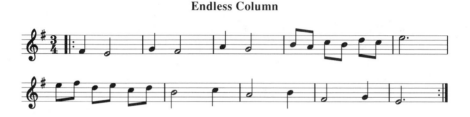

The other class created a halting, disjunct, angular piece for the same sculpture. It also led them into a new written concept of mixed meter (more than one meter).

Vocal Sound Experimentation

Before looking at the sculpture photographs as possible graphics to inspire vocal sound and movement, those sounds which can be made with the mouth were reviewed. (Final products are generally better if the time is taken to play with the elements before creating the finished product.) With the teacher modeling a variety of consonant and vowel sounds for the class to imitate (echo), the students were helped to feel comfortable with extremely high and low sounds, and extremes in dynamics:

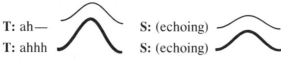

T: ah—   S: (echoing)
T: ahhh   S: (echoing)
T: Puh puh BUH!   S: Puh puh BUH!
T: T-T-Ssssssssssssss   S: (echo)
T: MmmmmmmmmmmmmmmJAH!   S: (echo)
T: ZzzzzzzzzzzzzzzzzKUHmmmmmmmmmm   S: (echo)

The teacher modeled plosive sounds (P, B, T), affricates (T, K), sibilants (S, Z), continuants (M, J, N), and vowels and demonstrated a variety of tempi, high/low sounds, and dynamics.

One good warm-up game was to have the group sit in a circle and, starting with the teacher, each make a hand/arm motion, and accompany that motion with a sound, passing it on to the next person when finished.

At this point it was natural to advance from sound and movement to sound inspired by graphics, the ultimate graphic being the photograph of the sculpture. Presenting simplified graphics for interpretation was a good intermediary step before going to the actual sculptures, which were more sophisticated and thus required more advanced skills. As a group, students made up these graphics on large craft paper, or individually. The graphics could then be performed with one person conducting, time-line fashion with his or her finger slowly moving along the bottom of the graphic to suggest when a sound was to occur; or individuals could interpret their own. The graphics could be read from left to right (or both simultaneously with two groups), or upside down. They could be read backwards (in retrograde). Dots alone were the simplest to interpret, followed by dots and lines, and most difficult, dots, lines, and planes.

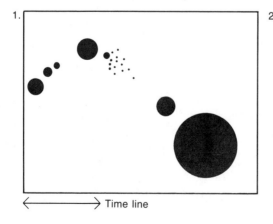

⟵   ⟶ Time line

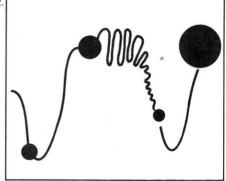

Examples of two graphics for one group's interpretation

3. Dots and lines (for three groups
   of vocalists)

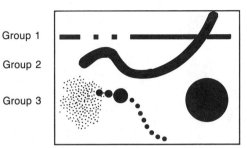

Group 1

Group 2

Group 3

4. The most difficult aspect of this graphic is
   deciding how to create a sound for the plane
   of color on the lower part of the graphic.

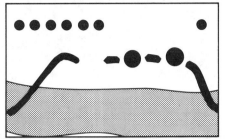

Movement and Sound Games

Before interpreting the simplified graphics in movement and using them as floor patterns, another game which stimulates possibilities is "follow the dancer." Starting with a seated circle and one person in the middle who is the leader, the group is challenged to make a collective sound which best represents the movements of that leader. The leader is encouraged to make large and thereby "loud" gestures, using all of his or her body; likewise, small gestures and angular ones would be made for soft and separated sounds.

Student conducts speech piece comprised of sculptors's names.

Exploring vocal possibilities to ensure interesting and varied results when putting sounds and movement to the sculptures.

Teacher and student demonstrating some circular movement possibilities when working with a partner.

Students exploring circular shapes with partners accompanied by symbol sound.

Preparing to move the form "Nevelson/Liberman/Nevelson" (ABA).

Boys demonstrating movement solutions with angular gestures to the Nevelson sculpture while girls await their turns. Letting students observe each other and make positive suggestions often strengthens the movement task.

The girls then share their circular interpretation of the Liberman sculpture as boys reciprocate.

When the group has the idea, two leaders are placed in the center, and each gets to choose his or her favorite movement: short/sudden/small (dab, flick); sudden and angular (slash/punch); weighted and slow (wring/press); light and continuous (float/glide). (See Chapter 2.) The circle is divided, and each half is to follow its given leader. The two leaders are thus creating the sound piece not only as they improvise it, but as the results which they *hear* are dictating: Sometimes the sounds would call for being together, sometimes separate. With older groups (ten and up) you can involve as many as three or four leaders with assigned followers. The more people in the center, the thicker the texture and thereby more difficult.

With this kind of warming up, the presentation of a sculpture for interpretation in movement is a logical extension for the student; and the results should be rich and satisfying.

T: What kind of motion would this sculpture make? Can you do it with your knee? hip? nose? shoulder? How would you walk this sculpture if it were suddenly a *floor pattern?*

Can you accompany your walk with a sound which tells me the character of this sculpture?

Can you increase your tempo? your dynamics?

Now can you do the pattern with your arms, adding the sound, while you are moving the floor pattern?

Everyone choose a way, or a combination of ways, to move this sculpture and stop when you hear the sound of the cymbal.

Interpreting Sculptures in Sound

T: Look through these photographs with me, and stop me when you see one which is the *opposite* of the Tal Streeter style. I see you picked the Liberman with flowing circles, connected instead of disjunct . . . truly a good example of the opposite. Can you now make a hand motion which represents the shape of this Liberman you chose? Let this motion go into your elbow, head, arms. Take the circles into your space and see how many places you can make them . . . keep going. Can you add a sound which reflects your smooth, continuous, flowing, floating motions? Good . . . breathe when no one else is breathing so your sound is continuous (staggered breathing) . . . listen to the group as you make your sound . . . nice. There is a darker circle in this picture. May I hear that also in your soundscape? Again, can you keep your air pattern going in circular motions but add a circular floor pattern as well? It can be the size of a manhole cover, or the whole room . . . it's your circle . . . notice others as you do your own . . . relate to a circle passing by.

Alexander Liberman, *Iliad,* detail (Collection of Storm King Art Center, Mountainville, NY)

T: Next, could we combine these two graphics, the Streeter and the Liberman, to create a larger movement form, ABA?

Do you want to stay only with vocal sound, or add an additional color from a small percussion instrument or found sound?

S: I hear the cymbal in the B section.

T: A big crash?

S: No, soft and continuous.

T: Fine. Who would like to be the musicians?

Using these techniques, students created a variety of movement forms which were beautiful, focused, abstract, and believable. The integrity of the subject matter and the power the sculptures conveyed were responsible for generating this artistic bonding.

During the trip, students carried clipboards with eight mystery sculptures pictured. They were asked to identify these works by title and sculptor. They were also given paper on which to sketch one favorite sculpture. Earlier we had discovered a little accidental arena at the base of Calder's "Arc," and we used this for a concluding mini-program. Excerpts from the students' poetry were shared, as well as the songs, speech canons, and movement forms created in class. Then, led by one of the classroom teachers, we wound through the sculpture in an exuberant line, much like people did in the twelfth century, when whole villages did "Estampies" through the town. For us, it was across the field, and back to the waiting buses.

SUMMARY: FIELD TRIP

Back in the classroom, subsequent closure involved more poetry writing, reacting to the trip as a whole, as well as the sculptures; and in the art room, it led to junk sculpture (sculptures created from cast-off junk) with a new eye and understanding of balance and integrity of dimensional design.

Putting this into a generic vein, the field trip experience, with all its implications and enrichment possibilities, could as easily have been applied to a trip to the zoo, the botanical garden, a historical village, natural history museum, art museum, etc. It is equally apparent that the age range of students is not a factor—the techniques slide easily through grade levels.

The emphasis in this book is on erasing the lines between curriculum. Consequently, we believe that a field trip—well planned and orchestrated—might easily filter through every aspect of the curriculum. The possibilities for utilizing this kind of experience are as limitless as the individuals who are willing to experiment with them.

chapter 7

extended science experience

EXTENSION: SCIENCE LESSON

Science, which is an arena of discovery, lends itself beautifully to the extension process. We are dealing with ideas that often start in the abstract and are channeled through experimentation into facts and finite notions—the knowledge unfolds slowly. With each unfolding, there is new awareness. Most other subjects begin almost exclusively with fact. For example, in history we can memorize Lincoln's Gettysburg Address and react to it creatively; but the Address remains fixed. When we respond to this factual type of material, we respond emotionally, intellectually; but the original stimulus remains permanent and unchanged. However, in science, the process *is* one of change, and one which brings forth a harvest of remarkably individual perceptions.

This type of creative scrutiny—through imaginative exploration—becomes a new science teaching tool. When children examine a snowflake and say it "bites like a freezing breeze," "sailed . . . like a ballerina," and "lurked like a butler in a mansion," they have embraced a metaphorical way of defining its properties. The snowflake is still a snowflake—but it is now much more. As Aristotle said, "The greatest thing by far is to have command of metaphor. This alone cannot be imparted to another; it is the mark of genius, for to make good metaphors implies an eye for resemblances."

Student Poetry and Music/Movement Extensions: Snow

Grades one through six wrote poems in response to science lessons on snow. Students were instructed to examine snow—during storms, watching it fall, examining its movement in space, letting it settle on the hand, drawing pictures—using all acquired poetry skills and the five senses.

SNOW

Snow is white
When the sun comes out it makes
it sparkle.
And then at night when the sun
goes down the snow is plain as
white.

S. K., 1st grade

Extension Possibilities   Find a
white sound (finger run around
glass rim? many voices sing ah
on different pitches?)

Find a sound that sparkles (a
homemade mark tree made
from dangling keys? a bonafide
bell tree?)

Explore ways of slowing down
the poem through silences or
repetition to create spaces in
which to use the sounds.

COLD WINTER DAYS

The snow is as cold
as the ice below
and the frost
bites like
a freezing
breeze
on my hands.

M. K., 2nd grade

In this poem, which has a
driving rhythm, what body
percussion ostinato could
accompany the words?

After the body percussion is
solidified with the words, try
the poem in canon with the
second group entering at the
ice.

SNOW

The soft six-sided snowflake seldomly
   slid silently.
The snow sailed across the sky like a
   raven, danced like a ballerina.
Slept like a baby,
   jumped from the clouds to the
   house like a kangaroo,
And lurked like a butler in a
   mansion.
The snow was as cold as a cold
   ice cube, fun as camp.
A white polar bear and soft cotton.
The snow sailed spryly-springing
   from side to side.
Swiftly but superfluously the snow
   sneaked down suctioned by gravity.

I. P., 6th grade

Create a slow, soft, sound
ostinato with musical or found
sounds. For example,

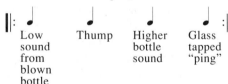

| Low sound from blown bottle | Thump | Higher bottle sound | Glass tapped "ping" |

Add other sounds over that
ostinato for sailing across the
sky, jumped like a kangaroo,
suctioned by gravity.

Student Poetry and Music/Movement Extensions: Egg Hatching

The poetry and music lessons which follow were in response to a science lesson where students observed, in the classroom, the egg-hatching process in an incubator over a period of weeks. Through poetry, music, and movement, students were asked to translate the experience, once again using their five senses, poetry and music skills, and by investing themselves emotionally into the evolving process.

THE EGG

It starts out as a crack.
Then all of a sudden,
The chick pops out!
It comes into the world,
Small, black or yellow.
He's sticky like glue.
He's wet like having been
caught in the rain.
It goes under the light.
There it fluffs up like a
petal on a flower.

J. W., 4th grade

THE SQUISHY DAY

One day I felt squishy.
My egg was too small.
I took my sharp beak
and I pecked,
pecked,
pecked . . .
I broke a piece, I was
almost free.
I rested and pecked,
rested and pecked . . .
I was free!
I was me!

M. D., 4th grade

POSSIBLE MOVEMENT PIECE

T: Can you become the shape of the little chicken inside the egg, round, tightly tucked? Feel the watery fluid around you . . . how it feels to be gently rolled over every now and then so you will grow healthy and well formed . . . see the darkness . . . know when it is time to hatch . . . to come into the world . . . feel the shell against your egg tooth and how much energy it takes to break out of your egg prison . . . peck the shell with all your might . . . then rest . . . peck again until you have a small hole formed . . . rest . . . keep working at getting out of the house which has held you for many weeks . . . your bill is out . . . one wing . . . the top of your body . . . one leg . . . you're free! . . . but very wet, and very weak. You must rest . . . but soon you dare to try to stand . . . you are wobbly . . . you take a few unsure steps . . . you fall . . . you rest . . . you try again . . . the light from your incubator feels warm on your back . . . you look for another chicken . . . there is only another egg . . . but a hole in the shell holds promise! . . . you may have a sister or brother chicken soon . . . you try drinking the water . . . and eating the mash . . . you feel stronger . . . you are able to peep, and hop . . . you are becoming a very fine baby chick!

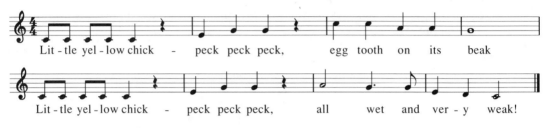

Lit - tle yel - low chick - peck peck peck,   egg tooth on   its   beak

Lit - tle yel - low chick - peck peck peck,   all   wet   and ver - y weak!

Written by Mrs. Palmer's first grade, Upper Nyack Elementary School, with word and melody suggestions by students.

Musical skills:

Form: ABAC

Mode: *Do* pentatonic on C

CHICKENS HATCHING

I look like a ball
of wet yarn.

I'm so skinny
and wet.

When I dry I'm like a
fluffy ball of yarn.

I sound like this—
Peep! Peep! Peep!

K. T., 4th grade

A CHICKEN IS BORN

First you see an egg, white
as vanilla ice cream. Then
it's cracking and cracking
open. Then you see a
little chick wet, not
fluffy yet. You hear
chirping all the time
that sounds as soft
as music. It feels
wet as a towel after
you wash it.
A new born
baby is here!

J. T., 4th grade

A NEW CHICKEN

Then all of a sudden—Brightness.
At last, the New World.
It is one of Nature's many wonders.
It is a dark, lonely world.
He is very wet.

He kicks and sticks his head out.
It is amazing to see new life.
And one day long ago
You were like this kind of operation.
I watched the egg,
From a little hole to Big.
There is only one word
That says it right.
       Incredible!

          D. K., 4th grade

WHAT IT WOULD BE LIKE
TO BE A CHICKEN

I am a chicken
Inside an egg picking
Through the hard egg.
I can see big people
Looking at me. When I
Get out of my egg,
They look like giants
As they look at me.
And when I get fluffy,
They hold me very
Carefully so they don't
Drop me on the ground.

         C. M., 4th grade

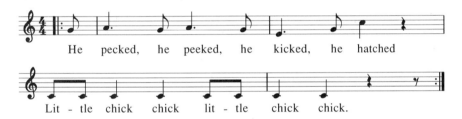

He pecked, he peeked, he kicked, he hatched

Lit - tle chick chick lit - tle chick chick.

Text in response to teacher questioning, "And what happened next?" Order determined by the first grade.

Musical skills:

   Form: Question/answer
   Mode: *Do* pentatonic on C

_____ **student poems** _____

The Natural World

These poems were written in response to a series of science lessons which explored the natural world. Students were asked to creatively interpret elements which sparked their imagination. The focus was on using personification, metaphor, and simile, and experiencing the natural world through the five senses.

SUNLIGHT

The sunlight is sweet candy.
It is as soft and smooth as satin.
If it would never rise neither would I.
The sunlight's rays
scatter showing its strength.
It starts to sing sleepily
while it goes down.
The sunlight hides shadows,
scariness, and sorriness.
It is so successful,
steady
still and strange.
The sunlight is very special and
splendid.
Sunlight reminds me of
spring and summer.

C. P., 5th grade

STARS

The stars are scattered in a swarm,
Like snowflakes falling in a storm,
Like scientific sculptures made of stone,
Steeled in a solar home.

They swim across the nighttime sky,
In search of those of their own kind.
Shuffled in a paper bag,
Trying hard to exit fast.

They look like wild static,
They sound like rattling bones.
They taste like sweet, white sugar,
And smell like pollen from a rose.
And last of all,
they feel like sand
running through your hands.

D. W., 5th grade

SANDS

Sitting alone
Moon making
reflections on the
water.
Water hitting
the shores.
Grass swaying softly
Small sandcrabs
running wild on the sand.

C. M., 5th grade

THE ROCK

I was strolling in a dark, damp forest
and saw a gold, glowing rock.
When I picked it up,
my hand began to shiver with fear
and soon everything I touched
began glowing.

T. S., 3rd grade

FLOWERS

I smell fresh
flowers that have
a strong fragrance.
I hear a whisper in
my ear, the wind is
telling me a secret.
I see lovely flowers
with long, green stems.
I feel delicate petals
and soft leaves
in my hands.
I taste fluffy
pink cotton candy
and it is creamy
and smooth.
A flower feels
love for itself.

A. R., 5th grade

OCEAN

The ocean sparkles like a
glittering, sparkling star,
And glows like a glow-worm in
  the night.
The ocean hops like a hopping
frog.
And freezes like freezing ice.
And beats
like a beating drum.

                    D. K., 5th grade

STORMS

The sandy storm swooped
down on the helpless
city like a hawk swooping
down to catch its prey.

The lightning flashed
in the sky like a
firefly buzzing
around at night.

The roaring rain
splashed onto the
ground like a
lion attacking
a tiger.

The thumping
thunder in the night
is like a stranger
banging on your
door.

A rainbow appears
that is lit up like a boy
who just got
a new toy.

                    S. P., 5th grade

RIVERS

A river creeps like a cat hunting.
A river tumbles like a rock falling
down a hill. A river moves like a
slow turtle walking. A river
skips like a person playing hop scotch.
A river roars like a lion that is mad.

                    D. L., 4th grade

THE MOON

Into the night
Races the moon
Blackness around it
Pre-eminently
Interminable skies
Where she rests,
The monstrous hulk,
Barren and bright
Brazenly stands out
Of the moonlit sky.
Exceeding cosmos,
The universe is
The intense moon
Where man conducted
scientific tests.
Neil Armstrong came,
As the lunar module fell
to the surface
like a feather and
Put down the American flag.

                    N. P., 6th grade

NATURE

Stones are like a turtle in its shell.
Clouds are like people
  sleeping on a soft white pillow.
The moon is like Neal Armstrong
  floating in space.

                    J. I., 5th grade

GRASS

The green, glowing grass
is as glassy as gold.
The glittering grass
is like the sun against glass.
The grass is shiny,
gray and golden
like on a frying pan.

The grass is blowing
like a ghost haunting a house.
The grand old grass is growing.

M. T., 6th grade

EXPLORATIONS OF ROCKS AS MUSICAL INSTRUMENTS

There is a universal appeal to geology. First, we are all "glued" onto the rock part of the earth which provides our fundament. But even more, rocks *feel* good to the touch and may provide cool comfort in a pocket, as with a Chinese worry stone. They are beautiful in texture, shape, and color. Rocks *sound* interesting when struck together, and flat ones skip nicely across the surface of a pond; almost everyone has a favorite rock somewhere in the house. Acknowledging the universal fascination with them, it's a logical progression to enjoy their possibilities through language (i.e., poetry), movement, speech, rhythms, form, improvisation, melodic invention, and instrumental playing.

Rocks as Instruments

When students clap two stones together to determine high or low sound (pitch) they are in the brotherhood of those who played stones in ancient China when Confucius lived. The instrument was called the *pien ching,* stone chimes, and was played with a stick. Confucius was said to have marvelled to hear "dumb stones sing," and mused he probably would never hear anything sweeter in his life.

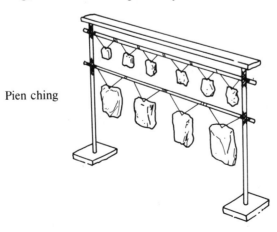

Pien ching

A speech pattern could be invented, framing four rock sounds, high to low, to savor the quality and timbre of the rocks:

A Section

Lis-ten to the rocks lis-ten to the rocks ring: 1   2   3   4

(Four sounds of rocks, low to high)

Con-fu-cius and you heard the si-lent stones sing   1   2   3   4

Add a B section, where each of the four rocks improvises for eight beats. Return to A section.

When students invent a grid piece for their three or four "colors" of sound created by different rocks,[1] they are in the brotherhood of some African, Caribbean, and Polynesian cultures whose music can be conveyed through grids.

	1	2	3	4	5	6	7	8
High sounding rock	X			X			X	X
Medium sounding rock		X	X			X		
Low sounding rock	X			X	X			

Students count to eight and play on the X'ed number.

When students invent rock-passing games with rhythmic speech, they are in the ancient brotherhood of all people who have invented such activities since the beginning of time, and are still doing it.

(Students seated in a circle, each with a palm-sized rock in their right hand)

Group 1:
(chant and
pass)

Rock I pass the rock,   keep a beat   keep a beat
Lift   place   lift   place

(On the word place, students put rock in front of student to the left of them.)

For older children, have more than one rhythm going at the same time:

Group 2:

Rock   I pass the
Lift   place   lift   place

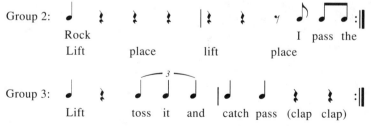

Group 3:

Lift   toss it and   catch pass (clap clap)

[1]Wagner, Betty Jean, *Drama as a Learning Medium,* NEA, 1985, p. 48.

Rocks in Speech Play

Mineral names feel good in the mouth and can be arranged in orders which have an interesting rhythmic feel. Students can be asked to invent these rock-name chains, and can lengthen the form by inserting a rock improvisation in between sections, for a rondo form.

[A] Az-u-rite, do-lo-mite, feld-spar, talc, am-phi-bo-les, ag-ate, gran-ite, baute

[B]   Rhythmic improvisation on stones for same length as above, or twice as long.

[A]   Repeat A above.

[C]   New rhythmic improvisation.

[A]   Repeat A above.

As a way to remember the exotic mineral names, this kind of speech drill could also be transferred to body percussion, taking student suggestions, and could then become a piece based on the mineral names with a rock ostinato accompaniment.

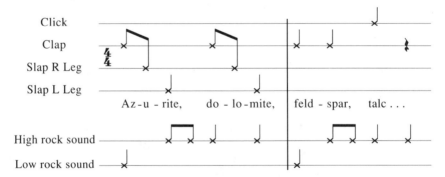

Student uses the "five senses" to experience the properties of a geode.

Learning the geode "by touch."

A Rock Rondo Using Student Poetry

The three main categories of rocks and their properties could be transferred to interesting nonpitched percussion, adding one melodic line. This, in turn, could become the A section of a rondo in which student poems become the contrasting B, C, D, etc. sections:

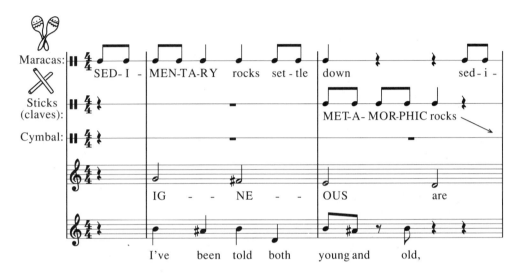

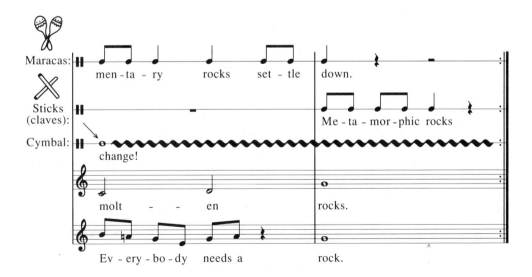

STONES

Stones are as sweet
  as flowers
in my mother's garden,

As perfect
  as a perfectly
carved sculpture.

As bumpy
  as riding
A horse bareback.

SHARP as a piece
  of broken glass
that pricks me
  over and over again.

As sparkling as the sun
    that blinds me
By the second.

Round as a shooting comet
  s - h - o - o - t - i - n - g
across the sky.

As happy as
  watching fireworks
SHOOT OFF
  in the sky
on the fourth of July.

          S. M., 3rd grade

A section repeats:

NEW STUDENT POEM

Stones are as rough as
    a stormy sea,
Some are as three-dimensional
    as a 3-D movie.

They are as hard
    as rock candy
in my mouth,

As loud

as a whistle
    when a strong wind goes by,
as sweet as chocolate.
    They make me happy
        as when I get a present.

        B. J., 3rd grade

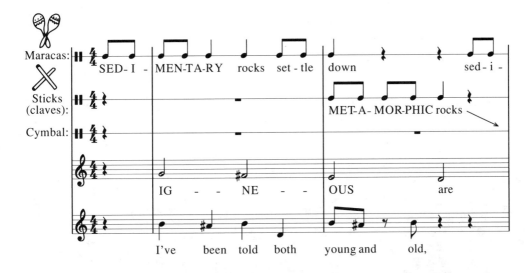

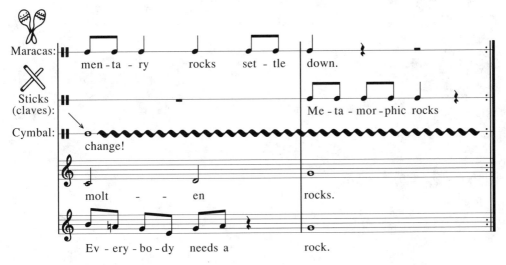

Rocks as Visuals

There are movement forms and stories within the diverse patterns found in geode slices. One such beautiful rock could be

— The departure of a contemporary tale, revolving around the mysterious circles within one geode; or

— The basis for a group sound, which might then serve as a backdrop for a student poem; or

— The basis for a group rhythm, which might serve as a backdrop for relevent vocabulary—eolithic, paleolithic, neolithic, etc.; or

— Grouped to make a movement form—one geode danced, the second vocalized, with the piece concluding as a danced geode.

Rocks and stones hold secrets waiting to be released, not only through scientific avenues but also through those diverse roads found in language arts and music.

Students and teacher exploring rocks and geodes using their five senses.

Student listening to geode.

Student smelling geode.

Students exploring the tactile imagery of geodes.

student poems

"The Secret of Stones"

Stones are like
Dunkin Doughnuts, Munchkins
with diamonds inside.

Stones are as sharp as
the prickers in my
backyard.

Stones are like a light
breeze of wind
at the beach.

Stones are like plain salt
on my dad's steak.

Stones are as sour as
a sour orange that was
outside all day.

Stones make me feel as
happy as everytime I
go to the arcade.

Stones are like
a baseball that a baseball
player was ready to pitch.

K. K., 3rd grade

As sour as a strawberry
    ice-cream at an ice-cream shop,
As bumpy as a tomato
    in a garden,
As colorful as a
    rainbow in the sky,

Like crystals
  wiggling around in a storm,
As fresh as a
  cake in the oven,
As happy as
  having a birthday party.

           M. D., 3rd grade

Stones are as beautiful as a
pretty silver ring
that's just been cleaned.

They are as bumpy
as a mountain, and
as smooth as
a big piece of ice.

Stones are as rough as
a hard piece of wood.
They are as yummy and sweet as
a chocolate chip cookie
that just came out of the oven.

They are as quiet as
a still tree
standing TALL
in my front yard.

Stones are as bright
and beautiful as
a diamond earring
on my mom.

They are as cheerful as
having a new-born baby
in the family,

As beautiful as
a bride
walking down the aisle,

As yummy and sweet as
those cinnamon twists
my aunt brings
whenever we see her,

As bright as a
shining star
in the beautiful sky.

           S. Z., 3rd grade

As fresh as
  my little brother's hair
right after a bath,

As hot as
  a volcano
right after it has erupted,

As sweet as
  homemade chocolate
that has just come out of the oven,

As colorful as
  a rainbow
    glowing
In the mist,

Rough as
  a vulture's spotted egg
in its nest,

Stones are like
  dancing under
    electric stars
in the darkness,

A wolf moaning
  on a mountain peak.

As shiny as
  diamonds
on a clear cold night,

As rich as
  holding a crystal in your hand.

           J. B., 3rd grade

Stones are like crystals
twinkling in the sun
on a warm day in the fall.

They are a bird nest
filled with cute, fluffy,
baby birds.

Stones are rough
armadillo skin.

They are LOUD
  SLAPPING
    POPPING
      CLANKING
        SCREECHING
tires on the road.

They are like a fresh apple pie
sitting on the windowsill
cooling off.

They are as delicious
as eating strawberry cake
topped with whipped cream.

They whistle as loudly as
the fresh wind in a storm.

They are the secrets of
a big shell you find
at the crack of dawn.

They are
  SPLASHING
    SPLATTERING
      STONES.

        Anon., 3rd grade

Stones are as sour
  as cranberry juice
in my mouth,
  like salty sparkling
silver water
  at the beach,
as sparkly as
  a diamond in
the jewelry store,
  as rough as a
turtle's back,
  as cool as a
rainshower in spring,
  as black as pepper
in the jar,
  as strong as
an ocean breeze.

        A. F., 3rd grade

Stones are
  as smooth as
    water in a lake,
as pretty as
  fish jumping out of
    the water,
they are
  a misty
    scent,
they gleam
  as a dime
    in the sunlight,
as fresh
  as fish
    from the sea,
as happy
  as me
    when I am
fishing.

        A. S., 3rd grade

    Stones are a
moon made of
  sparkling crystals.
They are like
  a rough snake,
slithering silently.

    Stones are as sweet as
a lollypop with a tootsie
  roll inside.
They are like an
  ocean stirring silently
in the night.
    They're like a baby kitten
just being born.
    Stones are as loving as
my mother and father
  are to my family.

        M. U., 3rd grade

SUMMARY: SCIENCE LESSON _____

In the process of extending science through language, music, and movement, the natural world becomes real, while taking on surreal qualities. The geode has been explored and explained scientifically in the science lesson; but by extending the focus of the geode beyond the limits of scientific discovery, we are able to visualize the opportunity for a myriad of creative possibilities. There are now sounds in the stones; movement to be interpreted through the crystal formations; and sensory images that extend the geode into the realms of the imagination to be seen as "an ocean stirring silently in the night," "a light breeze of wind at the beach," "rough armadillo skin." The geode becomes "splashing, splattering stones," a "wolf moaning on a mountain peak," "loud slapping, popping, clanking, screeching tires on the road." By exploring the natural world through the heightened and extended imagination, original investigated elements are enlarged, and more memorable learning takes place.

chapter 8

extended endangered species experience

EXTENSION: ENDANGERED SPECIES LESSON _____

All life is dependent on all life, and as such, issues of creature survival are a recurrent theme in almost all subject areas. For example, in American history we study the exploration of the frontier and its negative impact on native wildlife, which in turn drastically affected native human populations. In science we study the cyclical effects of humankind's interference in the natural world (i.e., insecticides, air pollution, acid rain, habitat destruction, etc.), all of which threaten the interdependent chain of life. In language arts, poems, stories, and plays depict the conflict and competition between humans and animals. From the prehistoric walls of caves to the walls of modern museums, we view this struggle. It echoes through the music and myths of the world.

But more recently, and more importantly, we have come to realize that the diminishing world wildlife population diminishes *us* as well. We have come to understand that the link between humans and our fellow creatures is a *mutually* dependent one.

All of these realizations inspire us to use *endangered species* as a focus for extended study. Because these issues arise as an integral part of the curriculum, they present the opportunity to confront and acknowledge these irrevocable survival truths:

1. That the problems and long-range ramifications of ignoring the issues could prove universally fatal.

2. That we are dependent on the survival of *all* creatures of our world, for our own survival.

3. That we are the caretakers of our world, and must accept our role and responsibility in effecting positive global change.

4. That we are not helpless or alone in this effort. There are organizations which strive through legal, informational, and direct affirmative action to reverse negative global trends, and to which we can contribute and lend support.

There is a need to understand the life force that exists in all creatures if we are to become sensitive to their right to exist. By introducing into the classroom the voices of creatures that call beneath the sea and cry in the air, and reverberate from mountaintop to valley, we individualize and personalize them.

There are musicians who are uniting the human and creature worlds by weaving the strands of our divergent lives together, such as Paul Winter, who celebrates self and "creatures from whose song we can learn and take heart" in his record "Common Ground." Poet Gerald Clarke, who celebrates the wolf in his book *Montoya,*[1] reveals his understanding of "the nature of the predator, but not the predatory nature of man." In the field, scientists have collected and documented the haunting whale songs that echo through the oceans of the world. And we learn that a creature who speaks, even in a language we don't understand, communicates the relevancy and essence of its life to us. We begin to comprehend that we share certain finite life qualities, and thus it becomes easier to empathize and identify with our fellow creatures through poems, music, and innovative study.

student poems

Endangered Species

Student involvement in this particular subject matter, whether as a result of a science lesson, social studies, etc., lends itself dramatically to tapping emotional poetic responses. In this writing assignment, we are asking students to empathize with the reality of life for another species. We ask them as well to try and envision the world through its eyes. Some examples might be to write from the point of view of "I am the last whale . . . . I am the last wolf," exploring all the ramifications of that creature's precarious hold on life. Attempting to use any and all poetic tools at their command, students are often intuitively able to reduce the immensity of the situation down to its most basic, most poignant level, exposing a single animal's fears and perceptions.

[1]*Montoya,* Gerald Clarke, The Golden Quill Press, 1987.

THE BIG HUNT

I went deer hunting.
I went in the old wood.
The air held the smell
of sap on the trees . . .
I could taste the sap
on my tongue.

Suddenly I heard a noise.
I picked up my gun
and shot the deer in its side.
The blood like a red rose
dripped like an icicle in the sun.

He dropped to the ground.
I saw all the animals
run to safety.
I picked him up.
His fur was all tattered.
Then I buried him.

I felt like the woods
would miss that deer.

J. R., 5th grade

THE WOLF

I see the fur of the
coat and food, I see the
animals running around
at the sound of guns
shooting.

I hear the sound of
the howling and grass moving
while the animals run away.
I hear the sound of guns
shooting at the animals, I
hear the screaming of the
animals.

I am the taste of meat and
liver and blood on the meat.

S. V., 5th grade

GLEAMING EAGLES

On the shore, white
eagles gleaming plain
white like the moon
shining high
glowing, glowing,
and glowing, in the night
and flying, and the wings like
little winds.
And the eagles sitting in
their nests, making them
like little carpenters
and the hatching of
the little ones, clap, clap, and clap
and the nice breeze flowing
with the eagles.

M. P., 5th grade

WHALES

I am
In the ocean
Waves are coming
like thunder.
I hear something.
It is sad.
It is a whale!
It sounds like
the whale is
crying because
other whales
are being killed.
It is
a mother and
her baby.
They are crying.
They are like
Little children,
the wind.

N. G., 4th grade

WOLF

In the dark woods you see a
white wolf with
sharp teeth.
You hear the
growl loud and clear.
You taste the
fear coming closer.
You touch his fur,
soft and smooth.
You smell his breath,
hot and angry
right near you.

M. F., 5th grade

THE LAST WOLF

I am the last wolf.
I see many men running around the
woods with guns,
I hear the guns shooting, I run,
I taste my saliva sliding down
my throat,
I smell fresh flowers,
I fear the man standing in front of
me with a gun,
I feel the bullet going through
my body,
The last wolf is gone,
No more hunting us.

R. S., 5th grade

BALD EAGLE

I see nothing but a clean desert
and a lonely wilderness.
I hear nothing but the sound
of the wind swooshing through my
black wings.
I taste nothing but the air
in my mouth, making it dry.
I feel nothing but the twig

which I ripped off the earth.
I smell nothing but the smell
of the seaweed on the ocean.
My feelings are loneliness
soaring in the sky.
My emotion of sight is nothing but
rocks and twigs.
I hear the boring sound of my wings
flapping in the wilderness.
And I am . . . lonely.

C. E., 5th grade

KOWALA BEAR

I am the last kowala
bear of my kind I am
light brown with eyes
like the sky I am in a
forest I see trees I'm as
lonely as a cloud in
the sky I feel
furry and lonely I smell
like the fresh air blowing
I taste the milk of a
coconut I am lost
and sad
I'm away . . . but
happy to be free.

R. B., 4th grade

ANIMALS IN THE SEA

Whales are
talking to
one another.
A boat is
coming to
kill them.
Then they
talk like
the sounds of
a Shofar on

New Years Eve.
One whale got
caught
and quickly the other
whale swims away.
A harpoon shoots out
like a thunder bolt
and has poisoned him
and the sound of the dying whale
fades away.
The sailor was
sad because he
killed the whale
and he had a
broken heart.

> J. T., 3rd grade

WHALE

When I went
to an ocean
there were
sounds that made me
scared as a
cat in an
alley.

Now I know
what those
sounds are.
They are
the sounds of
a whale crying like
a child in pain.

Now people hunt
whales which makes me
mad as a wounded
tiger.

> S. G., 4th grade

I AM THE LAST WHALE

I see a black sea.
I hear a whale die.
I taste tears,
I smell hunters,
I touch myself
and feel
sadness.

> M. P., 3rd grade

THE WHALE

As I lay upon
the scratchy sand,
the sun comes down and
the wind hits my face.

I hear a whale cry,
I realize that
some people would think
the sound is ugly;
but I think
it is beautiful.

I also realize
that he is the last
of his kind.

Tears stream down
my face and I
ask myself
what it would be like
to be the last of my kind.

I hear a shot
and a desparate cry
for help.
Suddenly it is silenced.
Then I know
how it would feel.

> T. T., 3rd grade

POLAR BEAR

I am white and
lonely, when I look
around me, all I can
see is ice and water,
no other animals or
people to play with,
and all I have to eat
is ice cold fish.

When I listen, I
hear the waves
splashing, and three
seagulls chirping and
flying away until
I can't see them
anymore.

My fur feels
nice and smooth
like silk, my
nose is like
ice, my tongue
is rough like
sandpaper, my
teeth are like
the points of pins
and needles.

      E. K., 4th grade

DOLPHIN

If the dolphins
were extinct
that would be sad,
If you ever saw
a dolphin with his eyes
like silvery diamonds
and his slick, powder blue
gleaming body,
and hear him splash
against the water
with a soft sound,
you would want to
save them.

      M. R., 4th grade

PANDA

There was a panda
in a tree.
It looked like a
little fluffy
teddy bear.
It smelled like
steam in a steam room.
Its ears were
sticking out of his head.
He was the color of
the midnight sky
with little white stars
and its arms were
wrapped around
the big tree
with his
eyes sparkling.

      M. P., 3rd grade

Will the whales
just disappear
I say over and
over again in my mind.

Their songs
sound like
sad cries
calling for help.

"Save us," they call,
"they're killing us
one by one.

We were once free to
roam the waters
without the fear
of being killed.
Why must we die?"

      J. W., 3rd grade

WHALES

When I was little
I heard the waves
in the wind
and then the whale
got shot
and all the whales
passed on the message
that there were
fisherman around,
so watch out.

We were all suffering
and I was crying
and then there was
silence.

I saw the last
two whales and the
last two fishermen.
When I returned
there was silence.
No whales talking
to teach other . . .
After I saw that,
I left with
tears in my eyes;
I felt so sad
for the whales.

> B. B., 4th grade

WHALES

I can hear the waves
and I can hear the
whales talking
their voices sound
like a rainy day.

I can feel the
wind blowing
it feels like a
blizzard.

I taste saltwater
and smell fish
in the salt water,
and the waves look
plain and dull.

> M. F., 2nd grade

WIND

The wind is talking
to the birds.
The whale is talking
to the sea
and I'm very sad.

> D. K., 2nd grade

THE WHALE POEM

When I was young
I used to be afraid
of the wind and
the whale was so
big it was 100 feet
long and it sings good
when I was a baby
I used to be afraid
of the whale singing
and then when I grew
up it sang so sadly
I almost cried
then I tried to
stop and I did
and the whale was
killed then the
ocean was empty
all was left were
little goldfish
and the sky
was full of
clouds.

> S. W., 3rd grade

Original "Ocean Child" Music and Poetry

These next examples of poetry and original songs were collated into a book which, when sold in the school, became the means to adopt real whales through the "Whale Adoption Project" in Massachusetts.[2] Other animal welfare societies and zoos have also begun such programs, making it possible for students to use their arts to aid our world creatures. The melodies were inspired by Paul Winter's "Ocean Dream" from the record "Common Ground," in which the whale is referred to as an "ocean child," and melodies sung by real humpback whales are woven into the arrangement. The notes used are the first five of a mode called Lydian, which creates a mysterious mood owing to the raised fourth tone: F,G,A,♮ B, C.

P. P., 4th grade

O - cean child   in   the   sea,   Won-der-ing where he   is . . .

I feel myself gliding through the water
Having no care in the world . . .
I see the beautiful sun-filled water
Gleaming on the sand at the bottom . . .
I smell the salt water
and taste the sweet plankton.
I hear the bubbles of scuba diver's air tanks
as I play with them.

W. C., 4th grade

I feel the flow of the water drift by,
I hear the mysterious echo of the waves above.
I see the sapphire, greenish ocean surrounding me.
The ocean tastes like a million tear drops which
   I have shed.
I sing the lonely, ancient song for
I am the world's last whale.

R. B., 4th grade

I am the wonder of the ocean,
I am the ancient song.
I am the wonder of the ocean:
I am form.
I am the wonder of the ocean;
I am the sky,
I am the wonder of the ocean
I am the sand.
I am the ocean child.
Call me home.

B. M., 4th grade

Call me home to the sea,
Ancient song like the ocean I love,
Sea creatures snuggle beside me
   at night . . .

R. L., 4th grade

J. T., 4th grade

[2]Whale Adoption Project, International Wildlife Coalition, 634 North Falmouth Highway, P.O. Box 388, North Falmouth, MA. 02556-0388.

I see the sapphire blue water
Gently pushing against me,
I hear the waves slowly rolling overhead;
And then a lonely cry . . .
I taste the bitter taste of salt water;
I smell the blood of my very good friends . . .
Now I am alone and on my own.

                    J. T., 4th grade

Silken water cradles my enormity,
Takes me down, down all blue and green
Takes me flowing, calling me home
Hear the echoes of my brothers
Ancient voices now still
But I am the child of the ocean
Forever.

            Mrs. T., music teacher

Being a whale smells like having a new scent
of what the water really is.
I feel like being free in a land
where fun and happiness never end.
You listen to the beautiful sounds of the water . . .
It is so graceful in your ears . . .
It is so rejoicing.
It brings everything to life.

                    M. M., 4th grade

A whale is an ocean child
    and it wanders the sea beautifully . . .
When its family and friends are captured,
    they sing an ancient song . . .
They sing, ''Call me home''
When its family and friends die,
the whale is sad and lonely,
And waits to be captured himself . . .

                    A. O., 4th grade

I feel the gentle waves
of the water,
I hear the sounds
of my companions singing,
I see my friends
beside me,
one friend missing.

I taste
some of the fish in the water.
I smell the human's boat
and the harpoon with it.
I hear the ancient voices
calling me home.
In London town I meet my death.
Save the whales.

                    M. C., 4th grade

Ocean child,
sing the song of the sea;
I don't like seeing my
family being killed . . .
It makes me very sad;
My life used to be
so peaceful
when I swam swiftly through
the clear, crystal blue waters;
Please don't kill my family
and friends . . .
We sing the ancient
song of the sea . . .

                    L. N., 4th grade

                    E. K., 4th grade

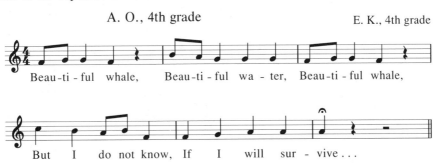

Beau-ti-ful whale, Beau-ti-ful wa-ter, Beau-ti-ful whale,

But I do not know, If I will sur-vive . . .

I, the whale
Taste the salty waters of the sea.
Ancient songs call me home
For I have lost my way.
Call me home . . .
I shall feel the way through my heart,
The foamy waters are soft and deep . . .
Waters, help me from being killed
by harpoons . . .
Foamy waters protect me from
other things that kill my friends.
Ancient songs, call me home
For I am your last
Ocean child.

R. F., 4th grade

The ocean is an ancient song
That the big whales sing softly
  under the blue-aqua water;
I want to be saved.
I don't want to be killed by
mean people with sharp, dangerous
Harpoons.
I am the ocean child;
I used to live in an ocean
  with peaceful sounds,
But now I live in a dangerous place . . .
Please call me home . . .

T. T., 4th grade

Wonder of the sea
My home, my world, my dream . . .
The whale so calm, but not free . . .
Ocean dream.

S. B., 4th grade

I taste the salt
of the ancient seawater
as I drift through
the salty sea . . .

R. G., 4th grade

My skin feels cool
because of the silky waves
which run over me.
The water is beautiful
and like a blanket
keeping me warm in winter.
The water is beautiful
and runover with
sparkling beauty . . .

W. G., 4th grade

A whale is a
blue thing in the sea.
It's as big as 50 ft.
A whale is as cool as an ice cube,
as interesting
as lightning.
A whale is as smart
as the wisest man.

C. H., 4th grade

Marlene

Whales have a right to live, haven't they?

SUMMARY: ENDANGERED SPECIES LESSON _____

As a result of the work dealing with endangered species, students became interested in finding out more about groups which are actively protecting wildlife. The following is a list of some of the organizations which students chose to support through school fund-raisers.

1. Greenpeace, P.O. Box 3720, Washington, DC 20007
2. World Wildlife Fund, 1250 Twenty-Fourth St., N.W., Washington, DC 20037
3. Environmental Defense Fund, 257 Park Ave. South, New York, NY 10010
4. National Parks and Conservation Assn., 1015 Thirty-First St., Washington, DC 20007-4406
5. Defenders of Wildlife, 1244 19th St., N.W., Washington, DC 20036
6. Center for Marine Conservation, 1725 Desales Street, N.W., Washington, DC 20036
7. African Wildlife Foundation, 1717 Massachusetts Avenue, N.W., Washington, DC 20036
8. International Fund for Animal Welfare, P.O. Box 193, Yarmouth Port, MA 02675

The extension process enabled students to tap the intensity of their concerns and feelings for the creatures that share their world and gave them a language (of words and movement) with which to speak their passion.

chapter 9

extended math experience

EXTENSION: MATH LESSON

There is a growing awareness that math is a language which can be spoken in many voices and, like all languages, can be translated. Today, many creative teachers are increasing the use of manipulatives, for example, as a concrete way for the young child to experience math spatially.

Our lesson translates math into the following languages: language arts (poetry), speech/rhythm, and movement. In a sense, these types of activities reflect a desired repetitive teaching approach. The actual learning in the classroom is deepened by this repetition. Also, different students learn differently, and these diverse needs are met by approaching math from many angles.

Numbers take on new life through discovering living things in their shapes, enhancing them through metaphor, letting the body duplicate their forms and angles, savoring the taste of them in the mouth, and listening for the sounds they generate. Math problems leap and glide and become "six slithering snakes in the sand," "ten terrible monsters," "seven seashells on shore," "eight aching ants," and "two terrific turtles tapping tiny toes."

The various approaches explored in this chapter have been used on all elementary school grade levels simply by reducing or increasing response expectations. The techniques themselves do not change. Using alliteration, for example, to lighten and enliven a math problem or a single number is as much fun for a sixth grader working independently as it is for a kindergarten class working as a group.

The whole point of moving math into other disciplines is to enable students to discover that music, movement, and language are a part of math, and math is a part of music, movement, and language. Math can be approached through any door to learning, and in this way, we are not just bringing something to math: We're bringing math into the whole learning arena where ideas flow in and out, back and forth in circular motions.

MOVEMENT AND MATH

With young children, math and number shapes can be used in a kind of joyful experimentation. Numbers can be drawn in the air, learned tactically through sandpaper representations, and put into the whole body through movement games.

Number shapes, large and small, can be moved in the air, starting with any part of the body as "stylus." For example, the nose could draw a small number two, the arms a large eight, the shoulders number ones. Children can be selected to choose the number and the body part as one game possibility.

By adding a sustained musical sound, such as a hand-held cymbal, a variation of the game is developed in which the teacher (or student) not only suggests the number, the body part to move it, but also adds a tempo ("waist, number 0, slowly," "elbow, number 1, quickly"). The sound of the cymbal (sustained for slow, muted for fast) begins the movement. (Vocal sound could also accompany these number movements.) With older children, more complex combinations can be devised, such as, "at the sound of the cymbal, walk a number 8 while drawing in space a zero with your head, slowly." Number combinations can be predetermined, such as "8, 9, 8" with the student making the movement decisions—air space? floor space?

Working in groups of two—then later three and four—students can work together to create numbers. For example, two people solve the problem of creating a number three: Do they lie on the floor, each body cupped to form the number? Do they find a way to draw it together in space? Each group would have its unique solution. "Guess Our Number(s)" is a variation of this game. Two or more groups charade numbers, first telling if the numbers are to be added, multiplied, etc. The class has to solve the math/movement problem. When particular number combinations are pleasing, they could be set aside for later expansion into math dances.

A group-dynamic cooperation game can occur when the class is divided and timed to create the shape of a teacher-suggested number. This type of activity is in keeping with the marching-band formation tradition, although in this case students may choose to lie down and form their numbers on the floor with their bodies. They have as long as the cymbal sound rings to complete the number. This game demands a great deal of group sensitivity, visual skills, and spatial acuity. The group that forms the number first wins that round.

When dealing with older children, it's clear that they do not need these games to familiarize them with number shapes. Instead, math movement provides a healthy release of whole-body energy from the finite focus on the page. It allows them to move physically and mentally through the broader scope of space, and return to the page renewed. These extensions of the math lesson provide new ways of experiencing numbers without actually aspiring to teach math per se—enhancing, rather than enlightening.

Feeling the shapes of numbers.

"Moving" the math lesson outside: Numbers as body shapes and group movement pieces.

"Holding" number shapes.

Finding numbers in "space."

Moving to the rhythm of numbers.

LANGUAGE AND MATH: ALLITERATION _____

Numbers are identified by words; 1 is a number, and it is also a word: *one*. As a word, it has additional implications. It can be rhymed, used to experiment with alliteration; it can become part of a thought or metaphor, and extended into a poem.

TEACHER MATH-POEM EXAMPLES:
ADDITION/ALLITERATION

```
    Four 4's fought ferociously and furiously        10 terrible three-toed toads
+ Two 2's tried tactfully to stop them            +   7 shy, unsuspecting sisters
=        6 stout superheroes saved the day        = 17 seconds of serious shrieking
```

```
       7 seriously sunny days
   + 1 wonderful watering can
   = 8 elegant, fabulously fragile flowers
```

Extending the Poem Into Prose

These first-grade math/poetry experiences could become the reason for a group big book, such as are used in whole learning programs, with illustrations drawn by the children; or used as a second-grade departure to a mini-drama created by small groups; or as the framework for a narrative poem or prose piece with the possibility of dialogue to be fleshed out independently by older students.

```
   55 trees stood trembling
      like terrified soldiers
      in the storm.

×     4 days the dreadful storm
      did its best to destroy
      the dense woods.

  220 days later, the wind swept away
      the wild and wicked clouds
      and the sun watered the
      soil with warmth.
```

This could then become the beginning of a longer story, with characters and dialogue that might ultimately become a class presentation or the libretto for a school operetta. The story might read as follows:

Once upon a time in another place, there was a sack of seeds that was carelessly spilled from the turret of a high castle on a hill. They blew to the North and settled in the rich, black soil on the banks of a sparkling lake. It was said the lake's waters were magical, and so they seemed to be: for the seeds sprouted and grew faster than any forest ever before. And 55 trees soon stood tall and straight as sentinals guarding the castle and all within, until one day a dreadful storm threatened to destroy them. It raged 4 days until . . .

student poems

Alliteration

   7 slithering snakes plus
+ 2 tender turkeys equals
= 9 nibbling newts.

   3 terrific turtles plus
+ 1 wiggling worm equals
= 4 ferocious foxes.

 10 tremendous tortoises minus
− 5 funny frogs equals
= 5 fishy feelings.

M. L., 3d grade

   7 stunned spiders sleeping in the swamp, minus
− 2 terrified tarantulas in a turqoise tree, equals
= 5 frightened frogs falling fairly fast

J. R., 3rd grade

   6 slithering snakes in a swamp, plus
+   4 frightened frogs in a fight with the snakes, equals
= 10 terrible toads in a tangle.

   8 aching ants with pain, plus
+   8 eating ant eaters, equals
= 16 delighted ant eaters.

E. P., 3rd grade

7 slippery, slimy, snakes, snoring, minus
— 6 female snakes sleeping sloppy equals
= 1 lazy group of snakes.

L. K., 3rd grade

4 fumbling falcons, minus
— 2 terribly terrific toads, equals
= 2 terribly terrific gone toads.

Anon., 3rd grade

SIX slimy snakes
  s-l-i-d-i-n-g
    across
      the scratchy sand.
MINUS
  FIVE
    ferocious
      frightening
        fat frogs,
EQUALS
  ONE
    weird and
     w
       a
         c
           k
             y
               worm.

S. L., 3rd grade

Numbers also strike us visually, and as visual stimuli can be re-created through the imagination into poetic forms:

TEACHER MATH POEM:
DEFINING NUMBERS THROUGH SHAPE

Fractions are fractious
half-here
half
there half-way
to somewhere.

Three is a circle longing
to complete itself, broken
it begins again.

Four is the ache
of angles, arms
arranged artfully.

Eight anticipates
itself, slides toward
renewal, ends to begin
again.

Five is alive
with possibilities; it winds
its way through
the sharp world
of angles and slides
into the softness
of circles.

Nine unwinds downward; six
slithers towards
the sky.

S. A. K.

Working in groups of three or four, older students would find this type of poem challenging as a movement piece. Picture students circling into a shape which ultimately becomes the 3 in the second stanza, and the angular movements which would be called into play in "four is the ache of angles." "Eight" could become a floor pattern where the movers are simply gliding in a figure-eight shape; "five" could take time at the start, investigating those "possibilities," and devising a way to "wind" itself into the numerical shape. The last stanza affords a great upward and downward conclusion. The background sounds behind the narration and the movement could be as simple as found sounds, or as detailed as those in the music room. The narration could be spoken or sung, or the experience could simply end with the math poem, which might then resurface during art time, where the numbers can live in color and space.

The decision of how and when to extend a lesson is a selective process which must be decided on by the teacher involved; but the teacher should be aware that the process is not one of subtraction (i.e., nothing is taken away from the lesson by extending it). It is one of multiplication. For example, this lesson might have begun with the teaching of fractions in math time, only to turn toward the poem and language arts, and then become the focus for art/movement or music experimentation.

student poems

Seven is half of a
triangle sitting silly and
saying sorry things.

Two is a terrific turtle
tapping tiny toes.

Nine is a nice nut nesting
neatly in a tree.

Three is some twisted
twigs.

One is a straw in a big
fat glass.

Four is like a fearful house
sitting in a gooey swamp.

Five is a part of a
car laying in the sand.

Six is an upside down
nine hanging
on the tree.

Eight is two heads
hanging by a rope.

Ten is a plate and
a fork on the big fat
table.

      C. B., 3rd grade

1 is a straight line
across the world.
2 is as squiggly as
a piece of purple yarn.
3 is half
of an 8.
4 is as straight as 3
lines connecting.
5 is as curvy
as a hook
with a top.
6 is a blue lake
and a winding stream.
7 is a piece
of a triangle.
8 is two circles
winding together
in the blue sky.
9 is an upside down "b"
10 is a sharp knife
and a round plate
on the table.

      B. J., 3rd grade

One is as straight
as a flag pole
without the flag.
Two is a twisty, turning
worm squirming
in the dirt.
Three is a sideways m.
Four is a broken up one.
Five is a dead
tree
falling
down.
Six is as twirly
as part of my
bannister.
Seven is a broken
flag pole
sitting in the
field.
Eight is two
round tables
pushed together.
Nine is as twisted
as a piece of
red licorice.
Ten is a pancake
with a straight piece
of bacon.

      N. M., 3rd grade

NUMBERS

  1. is as graceful as a ballerina dancing.
  2. is as curvy as a roller coaster.
  3. is a bird flying away.
  4. is as twisty as a pretzel.
  5. is a long lengthy piece of tape.
  6. is as round as a chocolate lollypop.
  7. is as silly as an upside down lollypop.
  8. is two heads bumping each other.
  9. is like an upside down six.
10. is a rocky road ice-cream.

      M. L., 3rd grade

WHAT NUMBERS LOOK LIKE TO ME

1 is as boring
As a stick
Lying across
the world.
2 is like a twisted
Vine stretched across
My house.
3 is as brown
As two bears
Sliding down
a grassy bank.
4 is as sad as
four lonesome kittens
lost at night
in a lonely forest.
5 is a colt
just being born.
6 is as pretty
as a bending
flower

blowing in the breeze.
7 is happy
as a newly born
puppy
trying to stand up.
8 is the strong scent
of cinnamon
sprinkled
on my muffins.
9 is as beautiful
as a slice
of my birthday cake
on my birthday.
10 is the slapping
of the waves
fighting with each other
at the ocean.

S. A., 3rd grade

USING RHYTHMIC SPEECH IN MATH DRILLS

There are many other activities which can be generated in the math room, such as games created by students to facilitate concept drills.

— The teacher asks a student to sing a simple tune for a times table, such as the fives tables:

Student: Five times five is twen-ty five.

The teacher adds a body percussion for the class to copy:

Clap

Slap Legs

Sitting in a circle, the game becomes one of each child keeping the rhythm going with the body percussion while singing the fives tables. Each child sings what the leader first sang, but changes the table—for example, 5 × 6 is 30, 5 × 7 is 35, and on around.

— Addition combinations can be made into audible rhythmic pieces through body percussion games. The students select two contrasting sounds (such as click, clap) and assign one sound to each side of the room. The click is represented by an asterisk, and the clap by a #sign. Creating the number piece requires that the students be aware of the different combinations which can make a number, such as 8:

(Claps begin)	# # # # # # # #	= 8
(Clicks enter on 8)	# # # # # # # *	= 7 + 1
	# # # # # # * *	= 6 + 2
	# # # # # * * *	= 5 + 3
	# # # # * * * *	= 4 + 4
	# # # * * * * *	etc.
	# # * * * * * *	
	# * * * * * * *	
	* * * * * * * *	

— The staccato of words found in the metric sequence (millimeter, decimeter, centimeter, meter, kilometer) once became the reason for a train poem. The students created this poem because they felt the words, spoken quickly, duplicated the sound of a speeding train. The lesson began as a way to help students remember the sequence of metrics from small to large. The lesson was extended by the students into a rap poem, which became the A section of a rondo. Interspersed between the spoken parts of the rondo, students would estimate (using the metric system) the length of the train boxcars that had been drawn on the board by students.

— In language arts, numbers can be used to parallel familiar rhymes such as found in early childhood poems:
    "one two" (instead of "buckle my shoe"), "look what's new"
    "three four, I've learned more," etc.

— Numbers can also be used in the exploration of onomatopoeia, such as:
    "Six is the sound of crackling sticks . . ."
    "Nine is the whine of wind through the vines . . ."
    "Four is the mournful moan of the dove . . ."

— Personification also lends itself to the extension of math into poetry, as in some examples from previous student poems:
    "Two is a terrific turtle tapping tiny toes . . ."
    "Five is a colt, just being born."

Using numbers as a road to other destinations sends positive messages to students about math and its applications in other parts of the curriculum.

SUMMARY: MATH LESSON

Playing with the sounds, shapes, and spatial qualities of numbers broadens students' perceptions of mathematical concepts. It permits them to assimilate the language of math through the language of words, music, and movement, thus allowing for a layering of learning.

chapter 10

extended music-inspired experience

EXTENSION: MUSIC-INSPIRED LESSON _____

In this lesson, students were asked to translate existing masterwork music through sensory perception into *verbal (written)* imagery. Musical pieces were selected from primarily classical compositions that were rich in *sound* imagery:

- *Snowflakes Are Dancing*—Tomita (based on works by Debussy)
- *Missa Gaia*—Paul Winter (music based on natural sounds)
- *In the Spanish Style*—Christopher Parkening (guitar pieces)
- *Strauss's Greatest Hits*—Eugene Ormandy (waltzes)
- *Sleeping Beauty*—Tchaikovsky (highlights from ballet)
- *Sorcerer's Apprentice*—Dukas (dramatic program music)
- *Pastoral Symphony No. 6*—Beethoven (diverse symphonic texture)
- *Deep Breakfast*—Ray Lynch (mood music)

The students were asked to listen with all of their senses, attempting to discover music-inspired images. The music itself was the source from which these images ultimately grew into poems. No emphasis was placed on analyzing musical elements such as were previously considered in student poetry expansion lessons (form, introductions, codas, canons, melodic treatment. These elements were an important part of preceding lessons when student *poems* were the source of inspiration.) In other words, the emphasis came from the opposite direction: *music* into words.

At the onset of this lesson, the teacher turned out the light and instructed the students to close their eyes. She asked them to listen to the music as though they were inside the sounds, as though the music itself was happening all around them.

They were further instructed to respond to the music by using their senses: Did they feel hot or cold? Was the music bright or dull? thick or thin? rounded or sharp edged? menacing or comforting? Did it whisper or scream? Also, they were asked to look for teacher-suggested real images: mountain streams, rainstorms, sunlit meadows, fall days, icicles, and so on.

After having listened to the music once, the lights were turned on and the students were asked to take out paper and pencil and list the myriad of images which appeared during a second hearing. Before turning the music on a second time, the teacher pointed out to the students (what many had already observed) that music was a changeable canvas on which images moved rapidly from warm and comforting to cold and threatening, to joyful and playful, etc. A kaleidoscope of imagery was exactly the unfocused (subject) focus for which this phase of the writing process was geared. At this time, students were merely asked to jot down the images as they appeared to them rather than attempt to craft the poem. This lesson involved a sequence of stimuli which began with the music, moved to the image, and then later (through a process of selectivity and editing) was shaped into a finished poem.

student poems

Listening to Music

The following poems were written while listening to Tomita's *Snowflakes Are Dancing*.

MUSIC IS . . .

Music feels like fire burning
inside my body.
Music looks like axes
flying after you.
It tastes like now and later
melting in your mouth.
It sounds like a gun firing
in your ears.
It feels like a freezing snowball
right in your face.
Music smells like
apple pie baking in the
Oven ready to be eaten.

T. P., 4th grade

MUSIC IS

A whale swimming 20,000
Leagues under the sea.
Music feels like
rough sand paper
rubbing against my hands.
Music looks like the
ocean waves tumbling.
Music smells like
salt water from the ocean.
Music tastes like
blueberries freshly washed.
Music sounds like seagulls
chirping while flying
over the ocean at sunset.

J. M., 3rd grade

MUSIC IS . . .

Whistling
A haunted house
Rain
Bells
The sun
The ice cream man
doves
Stars
Tip-toeing
Rockets
Spring
A wedding
Snow
A cemetery
Space
China
Angels
Winter
Animals
A statue
flags
running
Wind
Whirl-wind
tundra
People all over.

    A. P., 6th grade

MY MUSIC POEM

Snowflakes falling on a cold day,
A windy day in autumn
   with leaves falling,
Floating in space with stars
   and planets around you,
A person running in the dark,
The ocean on a windy night,
Somebody in a field of flowers.

       Z. V., 5th grade

MUSIC

Music is the dancing of a ballet
It is the whistling of great, giant
ghosts.
Music is the tingling of bells on
a sunny silent day.
It is the struggle for survival
in a sticky desert of the Sahara.
Music is like being chased by ghosts
in a haunted house.
It is being deserted in the
midnight of mid-space.
The slow sprouting of plants.
Music is people ice skating on a
frozen, cold lake.
Music is screams from a haunted house
in the hills.
It is the free flying of the Bald
Eagle.
Music is a loud conversation going
on between two actors.
The heavy breathing of a runner about
to cross the finish line.
Music is the sadness of a funeral.
It is like being on top of a high
mountain.
A diver jumping off a cliff and into
a pool of water.
Music is trying to run in a forest
with a pack of dogs chasing you.
Music sounds like an alien craft
landing on earth.
It is the blowing of wind through
trees,
A person whistling while sitting
on a jail bench,
The hooting of an owl on a cold night.
Music is like flying through the
air on a winged horse.

       T. D., 6th grade

Ducks are floating
along a soft, silky, silver
stream.
Airplanes roaring through
the sky with the wind
screaming.
Bells ringing in a church.
Monsters are out to get
you when you're home alone.
A fairy godmother just
came and gave you three
wishes.
The wind is howling
because it is angry at
something.
A ship is drowning,
because the rivers are
scared.
Fluorescent lights are
shining on only one person,
as if you are the only
person in the world.

                    B. R., 6th grade

MUSIC IS

Orange and red colors breezing in
the air
Bells ringing everywhere
Jingling sounds
Banging, slamming, jamming
Soft sweet sounds
Loud harsh sounds
Being at a wedding
Back, forth, up and down sounds
Long and short sounds
Flipping sounds
Approaching sounds
Scary sounds
Fast and slow sounds
Traveling sounds
Alien sounds
Dancing sounds
Whistling sounds
and Fading sounds.

                    J. A., 6th grade

DAY DREAMS

The harp is a singing bird that won't stop
The shattering glass is like snow, so
    pretty and different.
The fantasy ran wild like a young wolf
Running away from civilization like
    leaving your troubles behind.
Voices from far away lands telling you
    life is one, big happy ball.
Warm kittens and dogs fighting with each other
    like love birds.
Monsters haunting a house you love
Being quiet as a mouse.
Love like a cake just coming out of the oven.
Giving away your peace, and faith like
    it never will matter to you.
Motions and motions that come from
    statues and will never stop.
Caterpillars having a new life
    like a baby crying for help.
The sea at ease.
Flowers and leaves blowing in the wind . . .
    free.
A screaming moon will go on forever
    Bells sounding like a kitten purring.

                    M. N., 5th grade

MUSIC IS . . .

like a big
kettle drum
with its big
loud boom.
Music sounds
like an overweight
elephant that stomps
around its cage.
Music feels like
a furry teddy bear
that a baby
likes to cuddle
up with.
Music is as
fast as a
rabbit scurrying

across a lettuce patch.
Music looks
like a clown doing
funny tricks
for little boys
and girls.
Music is as
stern as a
king giving a
command.
Music is as
proud as a
lion's roar.
Music tastes
like hot cocoa
on a cold winter day. *omitted*
Music feels *from*
like a bee *music*
stinging you *piece*
with all its

might.
Music is a fish jumping out
of the water.
Music looks
like a toy
sailboat
making its way
across a lake.
Music looks
like fireworks
lighting up the
sky.
Music is *omitted*
a fish being *from*
caught by a *music*
fisherman. *piece*

B. C., 3rd grade

STUDENT POETRY EXCERPT

A fourth-grade music class chose the lines from B.C.'s poem that they wished to enhance musically, and developed the following ideas in a group setting:

All: MUSIC IS LIKE A BIG KETTLE DRUM . . .

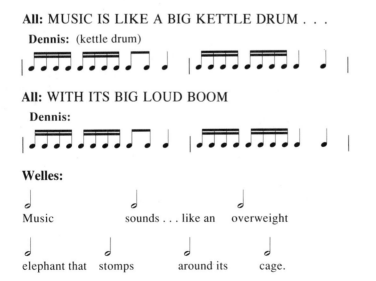

Tammy: (fast) Music is as fast as a rabbit . . .
Scurrying across a lettuce patch . . .
(seven beats of metallophones and glockenspiels playing their keys quickly)

Allana: Music looks . . . like a clown doing funny tricks,
For little boys and girls

(Glockenspiels improvise)

Ralph: Music is as stern as a king, giving a command.

Recorders:

Guiro

Frankie: MUSIC LOOKS . . . LIKE FIREWORKS . . . LIGHTING UP THE SKY . . .

(Cymbal; adding metallophones; adding xylophone; glocks; thicker texture and crescendo; kettle drum joins and crescendo; big cymbal crash at end and hold.)

SUMMARY: MUSIC-INSPIRED LESSON

As a footnote to this lesson, it is important to point out that creativity happens differently in different students. For some, the process of music to image to poem will be comfortable. Others will need to write the whole poem at the onset (crafting as they listen to the music). For this student, the teacher needs to be flexible and allow him or her to come back to the poem and reshape it, enhancing the imagery at a later time. The creative process cannot, for the most part, be controlled and must always be respected.

The student poems in this lesson were rich in imagery and imagination and lent themselves naturally to completing the circle of working the word. At the completion of the student creations, it seemed logical to take these works and explore them for movement and music potential, for speech play and external sound enhancement. There was joy in this process of coming back to where we began and experiencing the reshaping of original (music-inspired) creations through imaginative work.

chapter 11

extended nature and seasonal experiences

EXTENSION: NATURE AND SEASONAL LESSON

Working with nature settings and the changing seasons provides us with a laboratory of possibilities for isolating and fine-tuning our perceptions. It is through intense sensory awareness that we begin to discover how one sense can stimulate another, and how intellectually potent responsive observation can be. So much of our world is lost through inactivity of the senses. When asked to describe their walk to school (the same walk taken every day), students often give a very perfunctory account of trees, buildings, playground, etc. Rewalking those same steps with instructions to isolate their senses—that is, using first the hearing sense (closing their eyes), using the sense of smell (to the exclusion of the other senses), using the tactile sense (skin, fingers)—they are treated to a new and sometimes startling assortment of stimuli.

This sensory approach to nature results in students' recognition of the reality that their world is a whole made up of many parts. The tree, which previously had been seen in its entirety, is now perceived through its component sections: trunk, bark, branches, twigs, leaves, flowers, seeds, etc., and each one of these facets, in turn, has its own taxonomy and set of properties. Different elements appeal to different senses and create new sensory reactions and images: The bark is rough, is scratchy beneath the hand and to the finger, and often reminds students of rocks and stones, of sandpaper, of beach sand. The leaves are soft and pliable and can be crumpled, sniffed, manipulated. They create a kaleidoscope of imagery, including that of "crinkly paper," "mother's perfume," "cotton balls," "animal fur," "mint," etc.

Students are further instructed to think of their senses as antennae capable of receiving *all* of nature's signals. At the same time that they are experiencing the abundance of nature's energy through their *senses,* they are becoming *sensitized* to rhythms, patterns, sounds, and silences—and recapitulation of the changing seasons.

In essence, what each student is asked to remember is this: What we are not focused on will pass us by. The bird may be singing, but unless we are listening, we will not hear it.

In addressing the lesson, it is important to remember that the poetry / music / movement extension using nature and the seasons as stimuli can result from the study of snow, eggs, chrysali, insects, etc. in science; or from bird calls and the nuance of animal movements in music; or from master literary works in language arts such as William Wordsworth's "I wandered lonely as a cloud"[1] and "My heart leaps up when I behold"[2]; or from natural geometric shapes (beehives, ice crystals, etc.) in the math classroom.

Not every classroom is situated in an environment which lends itself to a nature walk or the firsthand observation of a burgeoning spring or crystalline winter, etc. There are environmental sound experiences on tapes and records which give realistic replication of outdoor soundscapes: "Among the Giant Trees of the Wild Pacific Coast," "Spring Morning on the Prairies," "Ocean Landscapes," "Canoe to Loon Lake," and "Dawn by a Gentle Stream."[3] These sound experiences invite listeners to use their hearing sense as a gateway to all their other senses. The poems resulting from this kind of listening experience are as valid as those written in the natural setting. The imagery is as stunning, and the perceptions as keen, so that teachers and students in urban settings should not feel there is a reduction in the intensity of the experience by using these tools.

The following fifth grade poetic response to "Among the Giant Trees of the Wild Pacific Coast" gives eloquent credence to the impact of the listening experience.

---
student poem

A JOURNEY THROUGH THE FOREST

The waves are hitting against the
rocks, and the birds are chirping,
like a squeaky instrument, and
over and over again it happens,
and the thunder starts softly,
and the wind is blowing, and

the sky is getting dark
like the soft fur of a black cat,
the birds stop
singing and go away,
and we can smell the
dampness of

[1]*The Pocket Book of Verse,* "I Wandered Lonely as a Cloud," William Wordsworth, p. 99, Pocketbooks Publishers, 1956.
[2]*The Pocket Book of Verse,* "My Heart Leaps Up When I Behold," William Wordsworth, p. 103, Pocketbook Publishers, 1956.
[3]See the Sound Sources section of the Bibliography.

the ground, and now
the rain starts, more
thunder and some lightning,
and the trees are waving
in the wind, our hair is
sopping wet, and it pours
harder and harder and
then there is some more
lightning, and it
sounds like a flying
saucer flying,
through the sky over us,
and the rain starts to
go away, and the sun
is coming out of
the sky, and the
ground is muddy like
sand at the beach, and
the air smells beautiful
like roses in the
garden, and there are
crickets who sound like
someone who has the
hiccups, the sound
is getting louder, it
sounds like squeaking
hinges, the leaves are
dropping drizzles
of rain on our heads, and
all the bugs are chirping,
like violins in an
orchestra, and we come
to a lake, it sounds
like a waterfall as the
waterfall hits the rocks
the spray goes up in the
air, and we hear a noise,
like a bicycle's squeak
when it needs more
oil, and the birds are
coming out again, chirping
happy songs, and it is
so quiet except for the birds . . .

L. K., 5th grade

TEACHER IMPETUS IN STUDENT OUTDOOR WRITING ——————

A nature or seasonal extension lesson might begin with a walk outdoors on a spring morning, or after a snowstorm, to tune in. Each child would have pencil, paper, and clipboard. Upon stepping outside, students might be asked to stand perfectly still, not moving, not talking, but simply absorbing the atmosphere around them. It would be suggested that as soon as one of their *senses* becomes acutely aware of a sensation, to jot it down. Very often their first reaction would be to the tactile: the cold air on their skin, the warm sun on their face and bare arms.

This introductory phase, where students are gently eased into becoming solitary receptors, might last from five to ten minutes. Following this, we begin to seek specifics through teacher suggestions such as the following:

T: Observe the sky colors, cloud formations, movement of clouds across the sky, the position of the sun, the intensity of color contrasts; observe the ground, its color, the sound when you walk on it, the feel of it

The up-close experience of nature on a
spring day.

Discovering a beech tree's ''beard.''

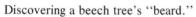

Touching the leaves.

Learning to know with our hands.

Exchanging ideas and images.

Becoming a tree.

Taking root

Reaching for the sun.

Composing our thoughts—becoming one with nature.

Finding that special place where creative thoughts flow most naturally.

Brainstorming/conferring in the natural setting.

Sharing the words: student with teacher.

underfoot and to your hand; smell the air deeply with your eyes closed; listen to the sounds of nature around you and of your movement through the natural environment; feel the bark of a tree, rub a leaf against your cheek; "taste" winter or spring on your tongue.

All the while, the impressions are being preserved by students on paper. At the conclusion of the walk, which may last for a half hour or more, students may, if the area is suitable, find a quiet outdoor place to write, or move back into the classroom to extend their impressions into images, and images into poetry.

One student poem, "Autumn," begins with a series of impressions: "Autumn is leaves of brilliant colors . . . Autumn smells like Chinese food . . . it sounds like a child crying." Prior to the writing of the poem, it was suggested to the student poet to look for metaphors and similes which might extend and enhance her original impressions. Of *what* did the brilliant autumn colors remind her? What does Chinese food *smell* like? And how could she extend the image of autumn being a "little child crying" into something that we, the reader of her poem, could experience through our senses? Included in the poems that follow, "Autumn" is the culmination of this process.

student poems

A JOYFUL WINTER

The winter is cold,
And snowy too
It is white as a dove
And wet as can be
The dew is sparkling
in the sun and dripping
one by one;
The sun's reflection is
very pretty while
riding on a sled upon
the snow or sitting
in the house with the
fireplace blazing all
cozy and warm.

Snowball fights, cannon
wars, igloos, and ice
hockey are things I do

for winter is fun
in many ways.
The water is frozen and as
shiny as silver.
The snow is soft and
I sink in every step
The snow tastes like
an apple, fresh and new . . .
moist.
It reminds me of love and
happiness.
It's a rowdy sort of
season, full of laughter
and joy—a perfect season
for a 10-year old boy,
WINTER!

D. C., 4th grade

AUTUMN

Autumn is the time
of year when the
leaves turn brilliant
colors. Some are the
color of a golden
corn muffin, the sad
look of a whimpering
puppy's eyes, a crackling
fire in the fireplace.

It is a time of mourning and
of memories, like a
dreary, cold day.

Autumn smells like
Chinese food, creamy
and saucy, a freshly
cooked turkey, like
a thick custard
pumpkin pie.

It sounds like a
little child crying
quietly in a corner,
wind whipping
the leaves out of the
trees, the sound of a
faraway echo in a
grassy valley.

That is autumn.

A. L., 5th grade

THE SEASON WINTER

Winter is as cold as
a demon's heart and as
beautiful as a red apple
in full bloom, and smells
like the morning dove
brushing through the sky.

L. G., 5th grade

UNTITLED

During winter you can taste
the white sweet snow fall
in your mouth. Then you
can taste a cold chill throughout
your thoughtful body.

You can feel the snow come
down on your face. You can
almost feel the bottomless snow.

You can almost hear the snow
falling on your houses. It almost
sounds like little voices talking.

You could see the end of winter,
Then you could look back at
all the good things winter has.

K. N., 5th grade

SNOW

I am the color of
a blank piece of
loose-leaf paper
without lines.

I am the smell of
the fresh air when
it is cold out.

I look like a pile of
mashed potatoes and
little white balls
falling from the sky.

I am the taste of
sweet sugar, potatoes and
soft creamy vanilla
ice cream.

I am the feel of
an ice cold ice cube,
smooth blond hair
and as soft as a
cushioney pillow on
a water bed.

S. D., 5th grade

MY SUMMER POEM

Summer looks like a
piece of shiny gold in a
pot at the end of a rainbow,
a cloud after a sunshower.

Summer tastes like a
bowl of ice cream melting
in the sun, a tall glass of
lemonade by the edge
of a pool.

Summer sounds like the
soft purr of a cat,
the chitter-chatter of
crickets on a
dark night.

Summer feels like a
cool soft wind on a
warm night, a
feather drifting
through the air.

Summer smells like a
beautiful rose on a cool
morning,
like perfume and
crystal clear wind. . .

J. C., 6th grade

A FALL DAY

Birds singing
In the trees
Grass around the field.
Bugs on my arm
like leaves flying around me.
Flowers in a garden
Kids playing.

T. V., 3rd grade

SUMMER

Summer is the
season of hot
days and
splashing water,
of sweating
children.

Summer is
the sound of
birds singing,
bees buzzing,
and children
playing in
the yard.

The smell of
fresh air, the
ocean water,
and people
having barbeques
outside their
houses.

Summer is
the hot
season that
comes every
year, that
brings us
cheerful
voices and
makes it hot
and sunny
so we are
able to go
swimming and
plants are
free to grow.

M. A., 5th grade

SPRING

The spring is as bright
as a buttercup gleaming
in the sun.

The spring air
smells as beautiful
as a young orange.

The spring birds
chirp as beautifully
and as loud as you can sing.

The spring taste
of lemonade,
is as delicious as
a professional pianist
playing a tune.

The spring smell
of roses fills
the air, as if people
breathe the smell of roses.

The spring taste
of honey-suckle tastes
wonderful, just
like an orange soda.

Now this is a SPRING!

G. M., 3rd grade

FALL

Fall is hearing wind blowing
Leaves of trees, and then watching
Them turn colors like a rainbow
Fall is smelling the cold fresh air
And tasting the new honey.
And then you can sit down and
Feel the rocky ground.

G. P., 3rd grade

FALL IN NYACK

Fall is
red
yellow
and
orange.
Fall is
dead
leaves
crackling
under
our feet.
Fall is
a
little
chill
in
the
air.
Fall is
trees
with
no leaves on them.
Fall is
a
nice
warm
fire in the
fireplace.
Fall, October 31,
is leaves falling
on Halloween night.
Fall is
birds
flying
south
for the
winter.
Fall is Thanksgiving.

A. W., 3rd grade

FALL

Fall is the time for
the leaves to change colors
and fall off the trees.
And the rain washes
all the leaves away and
it becomes winter.

M. T., 2nd grade

SPRING

Birds.
flowers.
Rabbits.
Rainbow.
Ride Bikes.
Leaves grow on trees.

L. R., 1st grade

SUMMER[4]

The surfboards were like
slithery, sneaky snakes
Sliding over a
desert's sand.
As the big bright green
ocean swallowed the
sand the scared
seashells came out of
their hiding places
like rabbits in a hole
underneath the
ground.

T. R., 4th grade

WINTER

Snow is like white gloves.
Ice is like brilliant snow.
Ice skates are like tiger's claws.
Water is a big blue dragon.
A snowman is like a magic hat.

M. L., 5th grade

A JOURNEY
THROUGH THE FOREST[5]

The ocean beating on
the rocks, birds with
feathers like
beautiful rainbows,
thunder roaring like
lions, trees waving in
the wind, lightning like
a streak of laser;
rain beating down as
if a flood were coming,
leaves are wet like
shining stars, frogs
croaking like
bugs, mud going
slosh when
I walk, a stream
that sounds like
a faucet running,
a waterfall that sparkles
in the sun, moist air like
sticky caramel, soil as
soft as
a pillow, leaves as
wet as a stream,
birds chirping like
a person playing

---

[4]This was done as a movement piece, on "sliding," "swallowed," and "came out of their hiding places," using levels, body shapes, and vocal sounds as each shell emerged. The poem was first spoken after which the movement part began.

[5]This was a poetic response to listening to: *Solitudes: Environmental Sound Experiences,* Vol. III.

a flute, the ocean as
loud as a tiger, the ocean as
blue as
the sky, the ocean smells
like salt water, the
breeze soft against my
face, rainbows as
colorful as a

box of crayons,
seagulls cawing near
the sea, baby bird
chirping in his nest,
the ocean as
calm as
a breeze.

P. P., 6th grade

USING A SINGLE SENSE:
THE SOUNDS OF THE SEASON

Sometimes, to achieve a sharper focus, it is helpful to concentrate on a single sense. The following poems are examples of an assignment which required students to listen to the season and write a poem entitled, "The Sounds of the Season."

student poems

THE SOUNDS
OF THE SEASON

yelling people
sledding down a steep,
bumpy hill,
through the
crunching snow,
crackling of the
fire on a cold night,
the honking
of geese,
the slushing
through the snow.

A. S., 3rd grade

THE SOUNDS
OF THE SEASON ARE

the crunching of
my sleigh roaring down
the hills, the
singing and carolling
on Christmas Eve,
the popping
of popcorn popping
on Halloween,
the creaking and
banging of the
shutter on Halloween
night, the laughing
of Santa
coming down the
chimney, the crunching
of the leaves under
my feet when
I go out to
rake them.

N. M., 3rd grade

THE SOUNDS
OF THE SEASON

The crackling of
the fire as
we throw
Christmas wrappings
in the fireplace,
the whistling of
the wind
as it
blows against
my house,
the laughing
of children
jumping in the
leaves,
the ringing of
Santa's reindeer
soaring through
the air,
the rustling
of leaves in the
wind before they
fall,
the crunching of
leaves on the
ground as I
walk.

B. A., 3rd grade

SOUNDS OF THE SEASON

I hear roaring sounds in the
winter and it is the wind.
I hear crunching sounds in the
fall and it is dead leaves.
I hear people saying
I'm hot in the summer
because it IS so hot
in the summer.
I hear birds singing to their
babies in the spring.

C. L., 3rd grade

THE SOUNDS
OF THE SEASON

The slapping
of a beaver
hitting his tail
on a piece
of wood,
the crunching
of someone walking
in the cold
white snow,
the blowing
of the wind in the
cold winter,
the chirping of birds
flying south
for the winter,
the crackling
of deer running
around the snow,
the whispering
of the singing
carollers next to my
window on Christmas.

C. H., 3rd grade

THE SOUNDS
OF THE SEASON ARE

The crackling of
witches on Halloween,
the whistling of
a kettle while making
hot chocolate,
the crackling of
a fire on a cold,
windy winter night,
singing Hebrew songs
on the first night
of Hannukah,
the tearing of
wrapping paper
from my gifts,

zipping all around
the ice skating rink,
laughing at
one of my dad's

terrible jokes
at a Thanksgiving feast.

B. P., 3rd grade

USING THE NATURE AND SEASONAL EXPERIENCE AS A SCHOOL PROGRAM FORMAT _____

Frequently in the course of the school year, a particularly exciting or innovative idea for a lesson will present itself. At Upper Nyack Elementary, Upper Nyack, New York, the following all-school focus resulted in a poetry, music, and movement experience. This Apple Festival happening reached far beyond the walls of the general classroom and ended up entering the curriculum through art, music, math, language arts, and science. It also reached into the community, involving a variety of people and resources.

The following is a sample teacher/administrative discussion that preceded the actual fall unit at a faculty meeting:

"What about an all-school apple festival for next fall?"

"We could borrow the 150-year-old apple press from the Historical Society."

"My car will hold it."

"Who would write to the Apple Institute of America for free materials, and perhaps a film if they have one?"

"We could use apples this month in math, in classroom cooking."

"The Poet-in-the-School will be here in September; we could ask her to focus some of her lessons with the third graders on apples."

"Let's have an all-school assembly culminating the full-day event with freshly squeezed apple cider!"

"We could ask the PTA for volunteers and to foot the bill for the apples."

"I'll man the press."

"I was going out to the Davies orchards this year anyway."

"Know any apple chants?"

"And what about extending it to the following week in the evening for parents by hiring an English Country Dance caller?"

"Why not put together another throw-together chorus like we did for Bach-to-Bach night? . . . do Early American music."

The actual event bonded children, parents, and teachers into a creative unity. The following program illustrates the fusion of improvisation, movement (using English Country Dances and English Wassailing songs), original poetry, music, orchestration, and joyful all-school singing.

THE APPLE FESTIVAL MUSIC/MOVEMENT/POETRY PROGRAM _____

The Program

Opening read by the principal: "The apple is the loveliest of earth's fruits. There is no flavor like that of a ripe apple. It is the children's fruit, cherished in the school bags waiting for recess, or given over to a special teacher. Apples have always been children's favorites, and for good reason: They put sparkle in their eyes, polish on their teeth, joy in their stomachs, and health all over! As for grown-ups, apples make the great culinary triumph of these United States—apple pie. That in itself is enough to call for this hymn of praise." [The hymn is by Dr. Angelo Patri.]

Apple callers (improvisation) five children throughout auditorium

Apple wassail song, Carhampton, England
    (Sung by the quintet, then all-school as the curtain
    opens to first grade on stage; third and fourth graders
    singing the counter melody:)

"Winding up the Apple Tree" (as in the "Twelfth Night" in England), Traditional, first grades

"Old Roger Is Gone and Buried and Dead," English Traditional Chant, second grades

"Haste to the Wedding," English Country Dance, third grades

Original apple poems by selected third graders (read between the fourth original song)

APPLES

As sticky as honey
Falling out of a beehive,
As red as a
Red, red, cherry,
As smooth as the
Color of pink,
A secret you
Won't tell anybody,
A treasure buried
Under the sand,
A golden bracelet
Twirling around the
Queen's wrist,
A heart beating
With love,
A lovely unicorn
Flying through the air,
I LOVE APPLES.

J. D., 3rd grade

INSIDE APPLES

As white as
A headband in your
hair.
A seed trapped
Inside a cocoon,

As smooth as a
Piece of chalk,
Skin as silky as fur,
As light as the
falling snow.

A unicorn flying
in the clouds,
As white as a
Cloud on a sunny
day.

As fluttery as
hair in the wind.
As soft as a
piano playing
in the night.

C. B., 3rd grade

(Apple poems written with poet, Susan Katz, Poet-in-the-Schools program)

"Look for the Star in the Center of the Apple"
  (Fourth grade original text and music, harmonized with a i, VII
  harmony and orchestrated for Orff instruments)

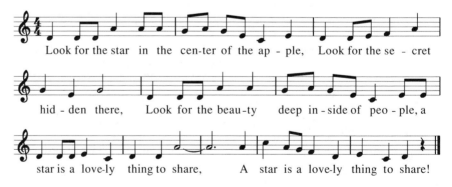

Reprise of "Old Apple Tree, We'll Wassail Thee," followed by a fresh cider-making demonstration.

The Star in the Center of the Apple

written collectively by a 4th grade class
words, melody, and orchestration.

In the same way that students were inspired to write poetry and music by discovering the secrets within the hearts of apples, the resident poet was inspired by the secrets revealed within the student poetry. Each poem contained some of the same magic that filled the classroom, as the hearts of apples were exposed. Just as art inspires art, the honesty and vulnerability students revealed through their poetry inspired a heart-felt response.

THE HEARTS OF APPLES

Beneath the shiny, smiling
skin of apples the hard flesh
holds secrets, wishes,
dreams: in silent chambers
the future waits
to be born.

Within the seed, black
and bottomless as a doll's
eye, a life holds
on to itself, holds on
to instinct's memory
of sun and soil.

In the souls
of children, there lives
the energy of love
and laughter, the high-
stepping life that marches
to the beat of trumpets
and drums.

In the eyes
of children there is
a light that speaks
of things that we,
who store our dreams
in boxes, only half
remember; a light
that shines beneath
the surface, that penetrates
the clouds, that tempts
the robin into song.

In the hearts
of apples, there is
magic and mystery, there
is the tree's core;
in the hearts
of children, forgiveness
and truth and, much,
much more.

Susan A. Katz
November 8, 1986
for the Apple Festival
Assembly

SUMMARY: THE NATURE/SEASONAL LESSON

Using Excerpts from Spring Writing Task as a Showcase for Student Work

Highlighting student work results in positive feedback to the student. Publication also generates an intimate communication with classmates, fellow students, and parents, and provides the student authors with a sense of pride and accomplishment. School newspapers, newsletters, bulletin boards, and all school programs are all vehicles for this type of student-work celebration. In the Upper Nyack School, each creative effort resulting from a "Spring Is" writing assignment was first published in its entirety in the individual classroom. To make these works more visible, excerpts from each poem were later selected to appear in a group poem, which was presented in a fourth-grade "Moving Up" Program.

"SPRING IS" GROUP POEM

— Spring Is . . .

the little white flowers that surround you as you lay on a hill looking at the sky . . . Melissa

strolling in a big field when the sun begins to rise . . . Alexandra

playing in a tree . . . Lateak

the sun playing hot spot lights on you . . . Michelle

spring feels like the soft, wrinkly skin on a baby . . . it smells of wind, flowers, roses . . . Susannah

laying on a beach, pushing my hands through the crystal clear sand . . . Susie

is the taste of ice cream and the sound of crickets singing loudly . . . Derrick

feels like the wind blowing in the trees . . . Tony

tastes like watermelon . . . Natalie

tastes like the starting of a new life . . . Tara

looks like a red-breasted robin with a worm and her young . . . Julie

is the creak of a swing going back and forth, back and forth . . . Debi

is rolling down a steep, flowered hill . . . Andre

is green grass stretching up to the sky . . . Sean

is bugs biting people! . . . Thad

spring tastes like green apples just being picked . . . Dina

is taking a stroll on the beach with the moon lighting your path . . . Mindy

feels like one rose petal that fell slowly to the ground . . . Wendy

spring is like a gold coin sitting in the sky, like a flow of birds come back from the south . . . Marlene

is a baby in the field . . . Ursula

tastes like wild cherries . . . Joseph

is the wind telling you to "come here" . . . Lisa

feels like a very comfortable grass pillow . . . it is leaves falling and finding a new home . . . Jenni

smells like my father just mowed the lawn . . . and sounds like the grand canyon . . . Nicole

smells like a cherry pie just taken out of the oven . . . Stephanie

sounds like paper bags crumpling up as the wind blows against the trees . . . Griff

sounds like a lily pad in a breeze . . . Jon

tastes like lime soda . . . Dennis

looks like an ant lifting up the world like it was a round picnic basket . . . Matthew

sounds as graceful as a California condor soaring through the air . . . Peter

spring is with me like a dog following you through your lovable and cherished life . . . Njiriri

spring has a wonderful feeling! . . . Julie

chapter 12

extended current events experience

EXTENSION: CURRENT EVENTS LESSON

In the broadest sense, extended experiences that come out of a class which is exploring current events can run like a river in any direction—moving forward to explore the future, moving backward in time to redefine the past. Newspaper articles, local events, world issues—all are fodder for the creative interplay of ideas that may result in poems, movement pieces, or musical presentations.

Writing assignments that led into further explorations were, for our students, thought expanders. Acting like the spokes in a wheel, the process began with a central focus ("We the People"; "The American Flag"; "Freedom"; "Hands Across America") and often extended far beyond the original point of inspiration. On many occasions, themes overlapped and "We the People" became the window through which "Freedom" was explored; and "Hands Across America" illuminated the pride in "Being a Citizen of the United States of America."

The following is a selection of poems and music/movement experiences inspired by current events topics (discussed in history and social studies classes). The poetic focus within the context of these vast themes was the personalization of subcategories, such as citizenship, world hunger, and national pride. Flexing their knowledge of poetic techniques, each student was asked to adapt his or her own experiences into the scope of the central theme. For example, a teacher introduction might have been:

T: Having been brought up in an environment where freedom is a comfortable given, we tend to take it for granted. Can you imagine a life where freedom does not exist? where the simplest of goals cannot be achieved? where your life and your actions are directed by others? Now, explore personally and poetically, within the framework of your own life, what freedom is, and what it means to you.

The continuation of the extended lesson might be introduced in the following way:

T: Taking your classmate's poem "We the People Means" as one example, what simple melody might we put to the essence of her first stanza, "Freedom feels like . . . raindrops?" Can anyone sing the beginning of a set of tones we might use? Can R. G. read the inside of her stanza after we sing the lead line? Could her other stanzas be treated similarly? Should the rest of the poem be sung as a recitative or spoken? etc.

student poems: extended

We the People

WE THE PEOPLE MEANS . . .

Freedom feels like
the tiny pitterpattering of
soft wet raindrops
falling on a new
white and sweet-smelling
rose.

Freedom tastes like an
appetizing
breakfast on
a cool clear summer
Fourth of July.

Freedom smells like
the newly-sewed
and crisply-ironed
red white and blue
flag.

Freedom sounds like
the rusty colored
Liberty bell ringing
for you for the first
time.

Freedom feels like
holding the
white feathery
quill when you
sign the
constitution.

R. G., 4th grade

EXTENDED VERSION CREATED FROM CLASS SUGGESTIONS

Fixed melody, agreed on by class to be sung by the group

Group in Canon:

Free - dom   feels   like   rain - drops . . . (Both groups
hum through
spoken text.)

Solo: (spoken over hum) . . . the tiny, pitterpattering of soft, wet, raindrops
. . . falling . . . on a new white and sweet-smelling rose.

Free - dom   tastes   like   break - fast . . . (hum)

Solo: (spoken over hum) . . . like an appetizing breakfast on a cool, clear,
summer Fourth of July . . .

Free - dom   smells   like a   new   flag . . . (hum)

Solo: (spoken over hum) . . . like the newly-sewed and crisply ironed red,
white, and blue flag . . .

Free - dom   sounds   like the Li-ber-ty   bell . . . (hum)

Solo: (spoken over hum) . . . like the rusty colored Liberty bell, ringing for
you for the first time . . .

Free - dom   feels   like a   feath-er- y   quill   (hum)

Solo: (over hum) . . . like holding . . . a white, feathery quill, when you
sign the constitution . . .

Group: Freedom (sung on low D and held) Freedom (sung on A and held)

FREEDOM

Freedom feels like
a French bread pizza
fresh from the oven
hot and flaky
with herbs and spices.

Freedom smells like
a delicious turkey feast with
rich, brown gravy
poured all over it.

Freedom looks like
two huskies playing
joyfully in the
cold winter snow.

Freedom feels like
the affection of a
fluffy, snow white kitten.

Freedom sounds like
Christmas carollers
singing merrily on
Christmas Eve night.

                N. P., 4th grade

WE THE PEOPLE

Is making good plays in baseball.
Playing ghost in the grave yard.
Getting toys on Christmas.
Having a good family like mine.
Watching TV and having freedom.
Playing video games and having fun.
Going on vacation
and swimming in the pool.
Learning in school is as fun as
playing kickball with my friend.
Winning the baseball game and
getting the trophy.

                V. D., 4th grade

"WE THE PEOPLE"
MEANS TO ME:

To explore
  the place
    I want to
      explore like
        Christopher Columbus.
To go on
  strike when
    I want to
      like a bird
        that doesn't
          want to fly.
To go to
  school where
    I want to.
To catch
  snappers when
    I want to.
TO BE ME!!!!!

                S. S., 4th grade

WE THE PEOPLE

America is as sweet
as the sweet smell of roses.

I like the freedom of speech
in America.

You're allowed to do
what you want in America.

The Constitution makes everything free:
  Free to hit a golf ball.
  Free to play baseball.

                M. S., 3rd grade

"WE THE PEOPLE"
MEANS TO ME:

To be able
  to pick any
    school in
      the world,
like a computer
  in the library,
to pick any job,
  like the butterflies
    picking their own
flowers,
To be as
  brave as a pup
    trying to get
      away from
        the cats.
to have any
  kind of money
    that I want
      to have like
the birds picking their
  babies in the nest,
to be as
  brave as an
    eagle flying
      in the sky,
to play
  wherever I
    want to play
like a bird
  playing in
    his nest,
to speak
  whenever
    I want to
      speak like
a tiger
  yawning in
    its sleep.

       T. R., 4th grade

WE THE PEOPLE

Freedom feels like
being in an open field
with the green grass
waving in the sun.

Freedom smells like
garlic bread
crunching and crackling
in my mouth.

Freedom to love feels like
a fresh piece of paper
and your fingers rubbing on it.

Freedom to worship tastes like
bread and wine
melting in your mouth
when you make your communion.

Freedom sounds like
a bald eagle
gliding on a current of wind
crying for freedom.

       K. P., 4th grade

WE THE PEOPLE MEANS . . .

Freedom feels like
a slave
being released.

Freedom tastes
like turkey
roasting in the oven.

Freedom looks
like the colorful
American flag flying
in the air.

Freedom sounds like
red, white and blue
fireworks in the sky.

Freedom feels like
slaves being
set free.

       M. P., 4th grade

WE THE PEOPLE

We the people means ————————
    we have freedom so we can go to
    the store when we want to go.

We the people means
    love so
    we can love anyone
    we want to love.

We the people means
    food so
    we can go to the
    store and eat hot dogs
    and drink soda.

We the people means ————————
    clothes we can go out and go
    shopping so that we can look
    pretty for school tomorrow.

We the people means
    Thanksgiving so we can
    celebrate and eat
    turkey and stuffing.

We the people means
    we only have to feed who we
    want to feed.

That's called freedom.
We have it here
in America.

             N. P., 4th grade

*There is a strong repetitive
framework here that lends itself
to group movement, contrasted
with solo improvisation.
All-class movement choir,
repeating refrain in ensemble
each time it appears.*

"We" the   "people"   "means"
(pointing   (turning,   (palms up—
to self)   all-encom-   freezing motion
          passing   while solo moves
          gesture)   stanzas in
                    between.)

Solo: (speaking/moving the poem in between
the group refrain with improvised movement)

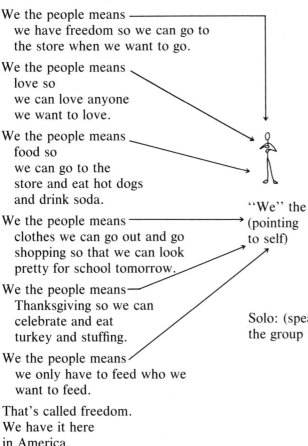

THE AMERICAN FLAG

I'd be waving in the sky
like a red, white, and blue bird
I was first made by Betsy Ross
I'd stand for my country
I was held by George Washington
in the Revolution
I'm the leader of my country and
stand for the United States:
The American Flag.

             J. H., 5th grade

I HAD A DREAM

I am George Washington.
I had a dream I'd be the leader
of the country who led the
American Revolution.
I would hold the flag and be the
first president of the United States
and have the victory of defeating
the British and be on a
one dollar bill.

             J. H., 5th grade

WE THE PEOPLE
MEANS TO ME . . .

To choose friends
   who fit together
      like paint and a brush.

To worship freely
   as leaves
      flying through the air.

To choose the
   school I want.

To live where I want to
   as freely as chipmunks
      building their nests.

Lucky to
   be an American.

         L. R., 3rd grade

WE THE PEOPLE

Freedom looks like
a Red-tailed hawk flying
gracefully over a mountain.

Freedom sounds like
a timber wolf
howling in the woods.

Freedom feels like
a queen wood-bee
stinging you.

Freedom tastes like
a delicious apple
that has just been picked.

Freedom smells like
a delicious bowl
of turkey soup with vegetables.

Freedom feels warm and
comfortable like
the red hot ball of
fire in the sky, the sun.

         J. T., 3rd grade

WE THE PEOPLE MEANS

   . . . having to pick what you
want to do.
It means being able
to talk about anything.

It means having people
celebrate things
in their cultures
without being
bothered.

         P. G., 3rd grade

WE THE PEOPLE MEANS . . .

Going to school
to learn like
a caterpillar learns
to turn into
a butterfly homes
for shelter like a
bug snug in a
rug food and
water to survive
like flowers need
rain to live
we need
love to live
understanding teachers
to teach us
lovely warm sweaters
to keep us warm
sleeping over
at Honor's house
and dancing to
labamba.
We the People.

         V. R., 3rd grade

WE THE PEOPLE MEANS . . .

Freedom feels proud like
the red, white, and blue fire works bursting
into flames over my head on
the Fourth of July night.

Freedom tastes like
a feast of sweet, juicy, buttery turkey
when it's ready to be eaten by
a thousand people.

Freedom looks like
Betsy Ross adding another
white, sparkling star onto our
striped red, white and blue flag.

Freedom sounds like
the gold and copper Liberty bell
ringing clearly for the
hundredth time.

Freedom makes me feel proud
as a silk, soft, smooth
bright flag
swaying over the
capitol in a
cool, frosty fall wind.

> K. M., 4th grade

"We the People" means to me
to be brave as a
lion saving her cubs.
To be free as
a butterfly in the sky.
To read any book
I want as a tiger roaming.
To do anything
I want to do
as an eagle flying.
To go to any school
I want as a butterfly.
To have picnics where
I want as an ant.
To watch any movie
I want as a bear
watches the fish
in the water.

> G. K., 3rd grade

"We the People" means to me
to be as
free as
a cat
in the woods,

to be as
brave as a lion
saving its cubs
from a bear,

to be an
adult, to
go where I
want to go
like a dog,

to go
running in the
leaves on an
autumn
day,

to go to the
school
I want to,

to go like a bird
in the sky.

> H. C., 3rd grade

WE THE PEOPLE

is learning at school
toys to play with
freedom to do
what I
want to
do
having a mom
and dad
choosing what I want to do
a family to love me
being with my family
on holidays and
traveling
anywhere I
want to go.

> M. M., 3rd grade

"We the People" means . . .
freedom, feels like
running your hand
through a crystal, clear river.

Freedom tastes like
feeding a newborn puppy,
and then having it
cuddle up against you.

Freedom sounds like
the cry of the bald eagle
soaring in the air
looking for his prey.

Freedom smells like
my mom putting
a lot of effort into her garden
and cutting one rose off a
rose branch.

Freedom looks like
someone spending all day
at the orchard picking apples,
then going home and making
apple pies.

Freedom feels like the
great pride I feel
when I raise the flag
humming "God Bless America."

M. H., 4th grade

Freedom feels like
a copper coin deep inside of
you, filling your body with
heat, making you burst into
flames.

Freedom smells like
a red and white flower
growing in the
hot, dry desert where
the sun glows and
the sometimes rain
falls to make
plants grow.

Freedom tastes like
a cinnamon apple pie just
coming from the red, crackling
fire outside of my house.

Freedom sounds like
a noisy party on
Main Street.

Freedom looks like
a colorful rainbow with
everlasting colors.

Freedom feels like
the sick getting well and
the dead people rising
for a new life.

C. E., 4th grade

"WE THE PEOPLE" MEANS . . .

Freedom feels as
though I can
always be
comforted by the
power of the pen
that I hold in my hand.

Freedom tastes like
sweet nectar
from a blooming snowwhite
honeysuckle in midsummer.

Freedom looks like
one of my best friend's
black and white patched
cats, stretched out on the
door mat
in the warm, butter-like sun.

Freedom sounds strong like
my poetry teacher's voice
when she is telling us
how to mix poetry and freedom.

Freedom smells like
sweet fresh hay
at harvest time
when the red country barn
is bursting full.

Freedom is being able to
plunge deep into my thoughts
and joyful memories.

G. I., 4th grade

————————————— **student poems** —————————————

Hands Across America

HANDS ACROSS
AMERICA IS . . .

As colorful as
A rainbow with
Red, white, and
Blue. As helpful
As a teacher
Helping a class.
As loving as
Your mother
Hugging you!
As joyful as
Christmas
As exciting as
Meeting
Boy George! As
Happy as me getting
A new skateboard! As
Proud as being
A citizen of
The United
States of America.

R. B., 3rd grade

HANDS ACROSS
AMERICA IS . . .

Loving like a
Mama bird cleaning
Its baby bird.
It's as jolly
As a cheerful party.

It's the American
Flag in the wind.
It's alive like
A wild, wild, wildcat.
As colorful as
A rainbow riding
On a motorcycle.
It's loving like
A mother cat.
It means to me to be
The best helper
for the helpless
And the homeless.

W. H., 3rd grade

HANDS ACROSS
AMERICA IS . . .

As colorful as a rainbow
Fluttering in the sky.
As lovely as birds
Singing a cheerful tune.
As loving
As everybody
Loving each other.
Happiness flowing
Across the world.
Everybody cuddling up
And trying to give.

Everybody trying to give
Something special to
One another.
Something that the whole
World can participate in.
Helping one another
Experience a whole new
Life!

                    M. O., 3rd grade

HANDS ACROSS AMERICA

The human line looking proud,
Is as helpful as a strong hand
And is happy to help the hungry and
homeless.
Holding hands with the world,
makes me delighted to do the country
of America a good deed.
Hands across America
tastes like the things we take
for granted, and smells sour,
like it might feel to be homeless, or hungry.

                    S. J., 4th grade

SUMMARY: CURRENT EVENTS LESSON

There will be times when the teacher must use his or her creative instincts to enhance student works. At these times, the teacher should not hesitate to join in the process of change, being mindful to not malign or overpower the spirit of the original student work. In the following example, complexity and length prompted the teacher to set the poem melodically. (The student was consulted for final reaction and approval.) The enthusiasm engendered by "Hands Across America," which was a prime example of teacher/student collaboration, propelled the work beyond the class level to an all-school focus.

Due to scheduling demands, teachers often do not have the luxury of using class time to enhance those works deemed by the class as worthy of enhancement. A workable solution to this problem is for the teacher to assert his or her creative talents. The teacher is *always* a contributing and integral member of the process and need never feel reluctant to participate.

Hands Across America

J. Thomas

chapter 13

extended environment experience

EXTENSION: ENVIRONMENT LESSON

In this chapter we share with you a culminating experience which rose above the sum of its parts to become a moving, memorable, all-encompassing school event. We selected a single, relevant theme that could be extended over a period of weeks within the structure of routine school and classroom activities. We were able to play with all the skills and techniques addressed in the first section of this book. Further, our intent was to move beyond the classroom into the special resources available in the music room (i.e., Orff instruments and nonpitched percussion). It was the intention of the music specialist to enhance the poetry writing experience through possibilities inherent in the Orff Schulwerk approach.

We were working in an elementary school (kindergarten through fourth grade) and selected second, third, and fourth grades to be participants in this experience. The third-grade students, already primed in poetic skills through the five workshop sessions scripted in the first section, were targeted to receive the environment workshops. Meetings were held with classroom teachers who would be involved in the total process, and a focus was agreed on. The lessons were designed to run for eight weeks; six poetry classes spread over three weeks; six editing and refining sessions spread over three weeks; and a two-week follow-up period to ready the music extension phase. Our ultimate goal was to present an assembly which framed the student poetry in melody, movement, instruments, and vocalization, as well as creating structures to showcase individual works in a dramatic and meaningful format.

The theme ultimately selected was influenced by a number of factors:

— The school itself was in the midst of building expansion, which resulted in a chaotic environment inside and out.

— Community efforts (sponsored by the local garden club) were under way for creating natural habitats and beautification of school grounds.

— Environmental issues dominated the news (i.e., oil spills, acid rain, ozone depletion, endangered species, conflict over fishing practices, etc.).

— In previous months, emphasis had been placed on Black History Month and an awareness of individual worth.

— The school was involved in efforts to create an awareness within students of their own powers to effect positive change in their world.

With these elements in mind, a far-reaching theme of "This Is My World: I Choose" was decided on. We opted to begin with something simple in the way of stimulus. The familiar subjects, colors and feelings, were selected, since they had been used earlier to teach poetry techniques. It was hoped that these comfortable subjects would be dealt with on a more personal level. Classroom discussions attempted to establish the intimate relationship between the subject, the student, and his or her world. The following outline became the worksheet from which we began:

OUTLINE FOR SIX POETRY WORKSHOP SESSIONS

1. THEME: THE COLORS OF MY WORLD will explore the colors of the natural world and encompass the use of basic poetry techniques.

2. THEME: THE FEELINGS OF MY WORLD will deal with exploring emotions that are evoked through an awareness of the world around us: seasons, holidays, environment, etc.

3. THEME: THE PEOPLE OF MY WORLD will deal with the differences and similarities between people; will define the people of our world and their roles in our world through imagery, as well as common denominators between people (i.e., brotherhood, Black History Month, etc.). Discussion will emphasize the benefits of differences, similarities, contributions as individuals and as groups, etc.

4. THEME: THE CREATURES OF MY WORLD will deal with endangered species, the living world around us, and our role in it. We will attempt to coordinate with planned school programs (Garden Club planting, habitat; Carnival of Animals; "Horton the Elephant" fourth-grade Recorder Club Musical).

5. THEME: THE PLACES OF MY WORLD will deal with environments: mountains, deserts, oceans, etc. Discussion will be geared toward environmental issues, threats to the environment world-wide and locally, and our individual responsibilities and abilities to make a difference.

6. THEME: THIS IS MY WORLD: I CHOOSE will deal with our individual place in the world; what we love about it, what we need to do to make a better world for the people and creatures in it; and our responsibility toward the environment.

While these lessons were carried out by a language specialist, the techniques used could just as easily have been implemented by the classroom teacher. All the techniques had been introduced earlier, and the real emphasis in these lessons was on classroom discussion, student participation, and a meaningful personalization of pertinent themes. Students were asked to explore, in depth, their feelings about each subject. Poetry became the vehicle through which ideas and feelings were explored and ultimately took shape.

In between the poetry sessions (which were on Mondays and Wednesdays), classroom teachers worked with students to refine and edit their poems. Further work was done during the language arts time. This involvement with the poems became part of the normal language arts class, using poetry to teach whatever was on the teaching agenda: punctuation, spelling, etc. These revised copies were then passed on to the music teacher, who culled through the works with an eye toward those poems which would best lend themselves to extension. The student groups made the decision which ultimately shaped the presentations of the (teacher-selected) poems—that is, melodic setting? rhythmic setting? soundscape-behind-word setting? extended form? etc. In the four 35-minute music periods (over the two weeks), roughly two poems were expanded in each of the three third grades. The three fourth grades chose an excerpted format, using a collaborative music refrain (text by them, music by the teacher) to highlight individual lines from approximately fifty student works.

The ideas spilled beyond the classroom and became:

— Bulletin boards in the hallways focusing on environments: air, sea, land and subsequent pollution.

— Individual student suggestions for ways to improve home and neighborhood environments.

— Plans to raise monies to contribute toward saving the elephant, adopting whales/wolves, as classroom and school projects.

— Student-published poetry arranged into topical booklets, suitable for selling.

— Donations requested upon admission to fourth-grade elephant-theme musical for donation to environmental agencies.

A particularly educational facet of the bulletin board happening was the idea by one of the teachers to set up school-wide bulletin boards reflecting various environments: ocean, desert, mountain, sky.[1]

---

[1]Marion Anderson, third-grade teacher, Upper Nyack Elementary School.

Environmental bulletin boards.

Underwater environmental bulletin board.

Wildlife environmental bulletin board.

The idea was to begin with a clean environment (students did the work for these bulletin boards in art class, involving yet another discipline), and then litter them by tacking up the type of litter collected from their own schoolyard. This illustrated visually, for the entire school body, the devastating effects of various forms of litter:

— Bottle tops
— Candy wrappers
— Plastic soda connecting rings
— Styrofoam packaging
— Plastic bags.

The learning exercise involved the devising of methods to affect the real world (neighborhood and school). These community actions would then entitle students to clean up: remove litter and restore the original bulletin board environment.

Through all of these plans and activities, it became apparent that there was excitement throughout the school which required teachers to follow their students' lead, and new student ideas were discussed and acted upon on a daily basis. This kind of spontaneous creative combustion is perhaps the most exhilirating of all teaching experiences.

student poems

This Is My World

THE COLORS OF MY WORLD

Blue is as loud as rain
beating on the city sidewalk,
as sparkling as a pond
in the evening wind,
as cold as the whistling wind
in the chilling winter,
as sweet as sugar
from the sugar bowl.
Blue is a tear
on a baby's face.

A. L., 3rd grade

THE FEELINGS OF MY WORLD

Loneliness is as blank as
One piece of paper
In a stack of 1,000.
Happiness is as soft as a
Filly that is one day old.
Unhappiness is as sad as
A duckling that waddled
Away from its nest
And never came back.
Sadness is one blue tear
Rolling down my cheek.

Frightfulness is something
In the fog
That you can't make out.

L. H., 3rd grade

THE COLORS OF MY WORLD

Pink is as sweet
as strawberries in a bowl.
Gold is as shiny
as a gold medal in a box.
Blue is as silent
as a cow in a meadow.
Black is as sticky
as tar on the ground.
Silver is as pungent
as garlic bread on the table.
White is as cold
as snow on the ground.
Yellow is as round
as a golden sun.
Brown is as dark
as clouds in the sky.
Red is as hot
as a fire in a fireplace.

C. C., 3rd grade

THE FEELINGS OF MY WORLD

Angry is a
roaring tiger in
the jungle.
Angry is as dry
as a desert,
as sharp as a sword,
as rough
as sandpaper.
Angry is as
heavy as a bar
of lead.
Angry is a
sour lemon.

D. P., 3rd grade

THE PEOPLE OF MY WORLD

Carpenters are as busy
as beavers in the woods.
Teachers are as smart
as owls at night.
Children are as curious
as monkeys in the zoo.
Parents are as caring as
cats with their kittens.
Babies are as happy
as a laughing hyena.
Poets are as sweet
as strawberries in a bowl.

D. G., 3rd grade

THE CREATURES OF MY WORLD

Dolphins are
as beautiful as a
bright rainbow
in the sky,
birds are as
musical as a flute,
raccoons are as soft
as clouds floating in the sky,
seals are as smooth
as a baby's skin,
fish are as helpful
as rain,
horses are as
playful as kittens
playing with yarn,
deer are sweet,
luscious lollipops,
bear cubs are
as cute as puppies when they play.
Animals make me
feel special
and without them,
I wouldn't
feel special.

J. L., 3rd grade

THE PLACES OF MY WORLD

The forest is
The howl of a wolf.
The polar places are as cold
As the freezer.
The city is a huge
Gooey, gloppy, glue of mud
On the ground.
The desert is as dry as my throat
After I haven't had water
For a long time.
Mountains are beautiful sea gulls
Soaring swiftly
Through the air.
Towns are as peaceful as
The ocean crashing
Against the rocks.
Oceans are as beautiful as
A flock of birds
Flying over my head
On a warm spring day.
Beaches are as beautiful as
A rose in the spring.
Swamps are dreary,
Dark, dangerous dungeons.
The country is
A smooth piece of glass.

D. B., 3rd grade

THE PEOPLE OF MY WORLD

Teachers are as kind
as loving parents;
doctors are as helpful
as the sun and the rain;
a pilot is like
a butterfly in the sky;
principals are as
busy as beavers;
firemen are as daring
as fierce tigers;
parents are as sweet
as blossoming roses.

C. H., 3rd grade

THIS IS MY WORLD, I CHOOSE

I choose to love the sound
of the birds
as sweet as strawberries
that have been dipped in sugar.
I choose to love the clean,
clear complexion of
a SPARKLING ocean
as clean as the air
on a hot summer day.
I choose not to like
the gallons of toxic waste
that change the color of the water
like ink in a glass of water.
I choose to care for the earth
like a newborn baby's cared for
by its mother.
I choose not to see
homeless people
roaming the streets like lost dogs.

G. B., 3rd grade

THIS IS MY WORLD, I CHOOSE

I choose to love poetry
which is as bright as
a flickering candle
in a dark cave.
I choose to hear animals
eat the fresh green grass
that smells as pleasant
as fruit.
I choose to see birds
as gentle as playful kittens
romping with a piece of yarn,
a dancer gliding
across the stage,
the trees to stand
as big and strong
as soldiers
standing at attention.

A. A., 3rd grade

THIS IS MY WORLD

I choose to love the
forest that
hides the hidden streams.

I choose to love
the mountains
that reach the
morning sky.

I choose to love
the feeling
of the
world
being a cleaner place.

I used to love
that big blue ball in
space before it
was
polluted.

This is my world
and yours.
Let's clean
our world.

      N. P., 3rd grade

THIS IS MY WORLD, I CHOOSE

I choose to have
A world as free from
Drugs as a bird
Flies freely
Through the air,
As clean as a stream
In the woods.
A turquoise ocean
as big, bright
and beautiful as
Green growing grass,
As unpolluted as
A red rose.
My world is like
A magician
That changes a gun
Into flowers.

      S. C., 3rd grade

THIS IS MY WORLD, I CHOOSE

I choose to love
a sparkling blue ocean
as clean as a fluttering butterfly
With the burning hot sun
beating down on the ground
like an elephant
walking in the jungle.
I choose fresh wet rain
falling like crisp,
colorful autumn leaves.
I choose to love
waking up in the morning
and hearing birds sing
as softly as a bird's feather.
I choose to change
pollution to a pleasant,
beautiful rose
blooming in a garden.
I choose animals
to live as long
as the blue clear sky.
I choose to live in
a beautiful world.

      B. B., 3rd grade

THIS IS MY WORLD, I CHOOSE

I choose to stop
The litter.
I choose to love the singing
Of the birds.
This is the world
I choose to love.
I choose to recycle
Cans and styrofoam.
I choose to help
The environment
By planting flowers.

      C. L., 3rd grade

STUDENT ORCHESTRATION
OF "MY PEOPLE" BY LANGSTON HUGHES ————————————————

The student excitement and delight in their written work carried over into the creative task of intensifying the poems through music and movement. In reality, this music process began not with a student work but with a Langston Hughes poem ("My People") learned in a second-grade language arts class. Having memorized it as a choral reading, the class, still full of the moment, shared their accomplishment with the music teacher. It was decided (by the class with approval from the music teacher) to work with this poem and turn it into "poetry-plus" as an introduction to the planned "This Is My World: I Choose" assembly.

MY PEOPLE

The night . . . is beautiful
So the faces of my people.
The stars are beautiful
So the eyes of my people.
Beautiful also is the sun.
Beautiful also are the souls . . . of my people.

Langston Hughes

Upon first hearing this poem, the music teacher was struck by the key words and asked the students to recite it again and listen for those words and others which *they* felt were key to the meaning and feeling of the poem. They found *night, stars,*

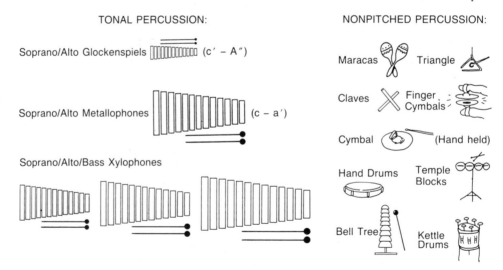

TONAL PERCUSSION:

Soprano/Alto Glockenspiels (c′ – A″)

Soprano/Alto Metallophones (c – a′)

Soprano/Alto/Bass Xylophones

NONPITCHED PERCUSSION:

Maracas   Triangle

Claves   Finger Cymbals

Cymbal   (Hand held)

Hand Drums   Temple Blocks

Bell Tree   Kettle Drums

sun, and *souls.* The next task was to find musical sounds which paralleled their word selections. The instruments[2] shown at the bottom of page 312 were available to the students. For *night,* one child invented a four-note theme on the bass xylophone which the group agreed sounded dark:

For *stars,* they chose an improvised motif on the glockenspiels (tuned to: E GAB D). The *sun* became the sound of the sustained cymbal; and the *souls* became the sound of the bell tree. The children felt a short melodic pattern would be nice at the end of each line, and a number of these were invented and shared. Ultimately the class chose this one:

Scored, the completed work looked like the following and became the introductory piece in the assembly:

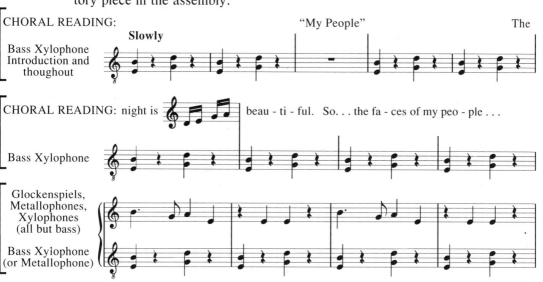

[2]These instruments were developed by composer Carl Orff after world models, such as the gamelan found in Indonesia, and the drums and nonpitched percussion found in Africa. The instruments make it possible for young children to play in ensemble at an early age. The instruments provide accompaniment to the children's singing and movement and enable them to improvise and compose in a wide variety of melodic patterns and elemental harmonies. Carl Orff intended that his approach be taught in a way which integrates movement, singing, speech and rhythmic play, the playing of elemental instruments, and improvisation. In the teaching of musical concepts, he also offered the possibilities of enhancing poetry, dramas, and general learning through use of his approach.

For one of the selected poems in the "Creatures of My World" category, a musical refrain was decided on after the class built four layers over the pattern supplied by the teacher.

This resulted in a piece which was driven by the insistence of the patterns created by the students (drum included) and the reiterative melody of the refrain sung by the students. Scored, the resulting student creation looked like this:

The Creatures of My World

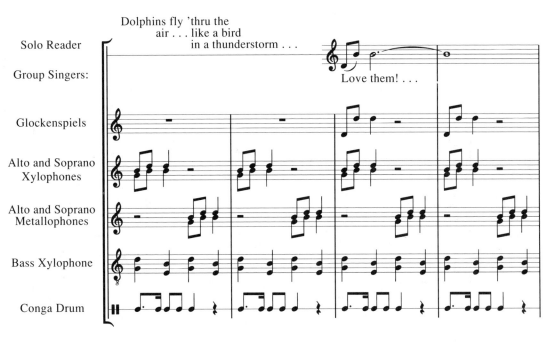

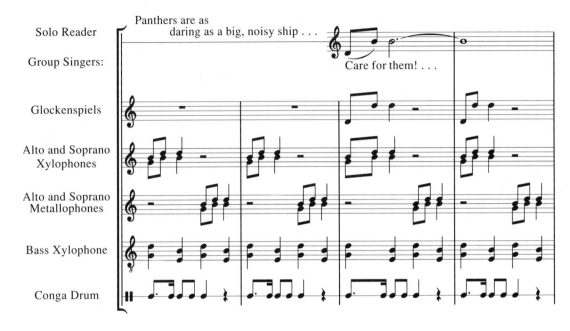

The second selection for "The Creatures of Our World" category involved dolphins and lent itself to a simple format of the student reading over the metallophone's musical punctuation.

DOLPHINS

Dolphins* are as gentle as
a new baby* and
as soft as
The water they live in*
They are as gentle as
Quiet whispers,*
But tomorrow*
They will be

As nothing.*
Dolphins* are as sweet
As sugar,*
but the water
That they live in*
Is sour . . .

A. L., 3rd grade

The third "Creatures of Our World" selection was treated as a movement poem with the jubilant arched dolphin leap as the impetus for finding choice sustained sounds. The children then took words from the poem as guideposts for their movements: "dolphins jump like dancers" . . . "glide over the water," etc. They designed a movement interpretation which played with large pieces of billowy chiffon and scarves to duplicate the shimmery underwater effect.

Students used locomotion, air space, and floor patterns, and the qualities of float, flick, glide, dab, press in their choreography. The score follows:

Score of Dolphin Movement Piece

DOLPHINS
N. K., 3rd grade

Solo: DOLPHINS!
(metallophones) (arched
leap)

JUMP like dancers and FLY like birds over the water . . . they seem to have wings!

DOLPHINS!

. . . sing and dance, and
laugh . . .

"Dolphin" movement piece.

DOLPHINS! . . . keep them in your world
. . . let them sing for you. Let
them dance, and glide over the
water for you. Don't kill them . . .

DOLPHINS! . . . love the world.

DOLPHINS! . . . love the sea.

DOLPHINS! . . . love you . . . please love
them. Their eyes twinkle
[glockenspiel improvisation]
like stars that fall from the sky
that you found in your back
yard . . . that you found,
shining in the dew [add
metallophone glissando].

DOLPHINS! . . . enjoy the world, but with
you, they can't enjoy it for
long. They are dying
. . . from you . . .

Poem: Vocal and Movement Extension

The "Feelings of My World" were conveyed through a poem (by S. F., 3rd grade)
to which movement and vocal sound were added by the class. The narrator
controlled the length of the movement by hitting the hand-held cymbal to indicate
everyone was to freeze.

Narrator: Uncomfortable . . . is being squeezed into a tight place:

> Students converged with disjunct, automatic movements into a center spot,
> accompanying the crunch with appropriate ad libs and sounds.

Narrator: Bored . . . is having nothing to do . . . on an exciting day.

> Group melted apart and floated into disparate shapes all over the stage with
> bored sounds.

Narrator: MAD . . . makes you want to tear your pillow apart and then throw it out the window.

> Group made punching/slashing motions in all directions with accompanying loud sounds.

Narrator: Sadness . . . is losing something . . . you really loved . . .

> Group all walked toward stage front with arms outstretched, then crossed them, then put their heads down with a sad sound and held the final motion (no cymbal sound).

> Students used the Orff instruments as sound effects for "The Places of My World" by S. C., 3rd grade. A single triangle sound was the signal agreed on to hold the movement for the next stanza.

Narrator: The ocean . . . is a wavy, wonderful, wacky, watery rain forest . . .

> Metallophones did glissandos. One solo wave used his whole air space from the lowest to the highest, while the group waves stayed low and undulating.

Narrator: Mountains are as high as skyscrapers . . . as they seem to touch the sky.

> Xylophone and temple blocks played ascending improvisation at the same time. At the triangle, the group froze with arms in skyscraper positions.

Narrator: Clouds [metallophone glissando] are as white and wondrous as a desert . . .

> Group, using high air space, floated in slow-motion.

Narrator: The desert [guiro/xylophone pattern]

> is as deserted . . . as an empty cookie jar . . .

> The group feigns thirst for cookies, saying the word *cookie* at all speeds and vocal ranges . . . reaching outward with their hands.

Narrator: The ice caps [sound of the bell tree] are as cold and slippery as a 200 below zero day . . .

Musicians played glissandos on metallophones and bell tree, as movement group slid and slipped on the stage.

Narrator: These are the places of my world. [Group holds final point for approximately three seconds.]

The third-grade students who were considering R. S.'s "The People of My World" poem for expansion agreed that the author's words sounded very rhythmical, which led them to the need for a short, layered rhythm pattern in between lines. An African piece from Ghana using hand drum, maracas, claves, small drum, and large drum had been learned earlier by the class, and it was this piece which ultimately found a new usage in "The People of My World."

RHYTHM PATTERN:

("o" means to let drums ring; "+" means to mute them by not letting the hand rebound.)

A triangle was used to embellish four of the lines, and to add contrast. The poem was read over the heartbeat of the African piece, as follows:

Introduction: The instruments came in, one layer at a time until all were playing, and then stopped together to let the narrator begin:

Narrator: Policemen . . . are like . . . blue . . . soldiers.

RHYTHM PATTERN:

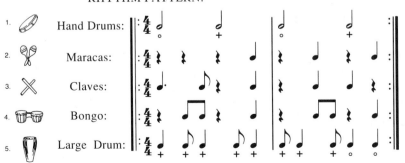

Narrator: Teachers . . . are like . . . junior . . . scientists!

(Rhythm pattern)

Narrator: Nurses are bandaids, barbers are scissors.

(Rhythm pattern)

Narrator: Presidents are bosses, mailmen are letters.

(Rhythm pattern)

Narrator: Neighbors are the next thing, children are toys

Fishermen are people who catch . . . nature.
Doctors are germ killers, bankers are money.
Soldiers are gates that are locked.

Narrator: Baby sitters . . . are baby cradles.

(Rhythm pattern)

Narrator: Friends . . . are on the same . . . rope

(Rhythm pattern and one more beat all together to end)

Melodic Improvisation

In setting two fourth-grade poems from the "This Is My World" theme, the first task became one of singing recitative in a scale (mode) recently studied with the fourth graders: dorian (D E F G A B C D).

A i IV harmony was borrowed from another dorian song, and a group-invented melody was found for the first line of each stanza of the poem by M. P. (fourth grade).

Instruments:

Metallophones

Bass Xylophones
(tremolo throughout)

Soprano and Alto
Xylophones

Glockenspiels

Group:
My world is clean, health-y air . . .

Solo:
a - gainst my face . . . see-ing blue skies and white clouds . . . al - most tast - ing

Cry - stal clear, clean health-y air . . .

Group:
My world is tall, grow-ing grass . . .

Solo:
With no lit - ter - bugs in sight, food and can-dy wrap-pers ex - tinct . . .

Solo:
Peo-ple clean-ing up af - ter joy - ful pic - nics.

Group:
My world is whale herds . . .

Solo:
Keep-ing to-geth-er, dot-ting the sur-face as if to say, "we're free, we're free" . . .

Swim-ming up to boats say-ing "hel - lo" to man who is kind.

Group: My world is clean, health-y air,

Solo: Land un-touched by man; wild life run-ning free; friend-ly whales, swim-ming

in o - ceans ... Man and earth ... friends ...a - gain ...

(The preceding piece approximates the improvisation done by the fourth graders.)

Poem With Related Sounds

Another complete fourth-grade poem shared in the assembly was one which had great contrast in the stanzas. The students decided there should be a set of good sounds, whatever that constituted, and a set of rougher, more strident bad sounds to parallel the poem. The good chosen were as follows:

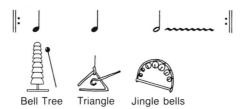

Bell Tree   Triangle   Jingle bells

This pattern was played slowly under the brighter parts of the poem.

The students with sounds representing the bad parts of the poem assembled and, playing in tandem, found four different drum sounds, followed by maracas, single bell, and guiro. The pattern became

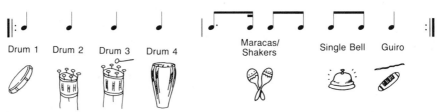

Drum 1   Drum 2   Drum 3   Drum 4   Maracas/   Single Bell   Guiro
                                        Shakers

The sequence of the poem and good sounds and bad sounds follows:

This Is My World
E. S., 4th grade

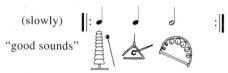

Narrator: [reading over above sounds]

This is my world . . .
I love the nature,
And I love the rain . . . [sounds stop]

Narrator: NOT THE JUNK AND ACID RAIN! [bad sounds follow]

Narrator: [over good sounds]

I love to watch the birds fly . . .
In the clear sky . . . [sounds stop]

Narrator: NOT THE JUNK ALL AROUND AND THE DUST IN MY EYE

[Bad sounds]

Narrator: [over good sounds]

I would love to live
A long life
And have picnics on the clear ground . . . [sounds stop]
NOT A LIFE 'TIL I GET TO 16
[Bad sounds]

Narrator: [over good sounds]

I love watching the stream go past
And the wind blowing the grass [sounds stop]
NOT THE MUDDY STREAM OR THE DIRT FLYING AROUND [bad sounds].

Excerpted Poetry Using a Rondo Form

In an effort to allow as many students as possible to share their wonderful insights and wishes for their world, a large rondo was created for the finale of the assembly. Approximately fifty fourth graders chose a stanza or two from their completed poems to read, one after the other, stopping every eight people to sing the A theme of the rondo with the whole school. This A theme song, though written by the teacher, had words written by the students. It could easily have been written totally by students, and it was only the limited time frame in putting the program together which prevented this. So the form of the final segment became:

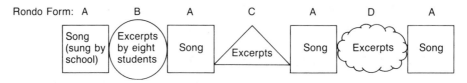

The A theme song follows, with selected "This Is My World" poems and excerpts.

Words: 4th grade
Music: J. Thomas

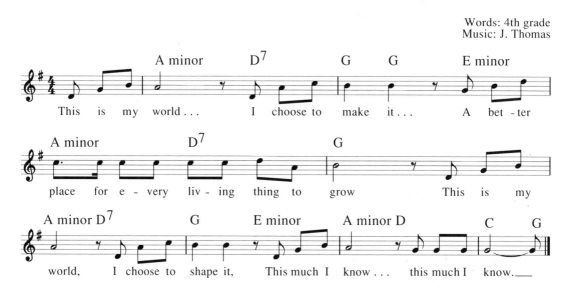

MY WORLD: I CHOOSE . . .

A program of original poetry
by Upper Nyack students
March 30, 1990, 9:30 A.M.

INTRODUCTION: Susan A. Katz, Poet

1. MY PEOPLE, Langston Hughes
      Setting for instruments: 2V

2. THE CREATURES OF MY WORLD
      Poem by L. H., 3A,
         with music setting by class
      Poem by A. L.: "Dolphins"
      Poem by N. K.: "Dolphins"
      (movement and song)

3. THE FEELINGS OF MY WORLD
      Poem by S. F., 3S
         (movement and vocal sound)
      Poem by S. C.
         (for speech and instruments)

4. THE PEOPLE OF MY WORLD
      Poem by R. S., 3M
         (setting using Ashanti rhythm)

5. THIS IS MY WORLD
      Poem by M. P., 4S
         (setting in dorian recitative)
      Poem by E. S., 4H
         (for nonpitched percussion)

"This Is My World" sung by A. S., 3S
Poem by A. L., 3A
Poem by Y. M, 3S
Poem by A. B., 3S

Excerpts of "This Is My World," poems by all fourth graders.

Music/movement directed by Judith Thomas

Culmination program (one scene).

My World . . . I Choose, singing.

Students accompanying their singing on Orff instruments.

Reiterating the assembly theme song: "This Is My World."

student poems

"This Is My World: I Choose . . ."

My world is a place of peace,
A place of joy,
A place of beauty.

It is not a place of war,
A place of sorrow,
Or a place of pollution.

My world is cared for and loved.
Not vandalized, and ripped apart
at the roots.

I want my world to be
Everyone's world,
Every moment of the day.

This is my world.

> A. L., 4th grade

This is my world!
I love the sound of birds and doves in the sky.
I hate looking
At the rivers and ground
Covered with trash.

This is my world in spring;
I like to smell clean, clear air
And smell flowers
In one big sniff.

This is my world!
I love to smell pine trees
In the dark, black night
of the winter sky.

This is my world.
I would love to see
killing stopped,
and drugs stopped.
It's a nightmare to see
those things going on
in this world where we live.

This is our WORLD, just OURS.

> N. M., 4th grade

This is my world of nature,
Fresh and clean,
The woods dark and muddy.

This is my world of spring,
Fishing in a fresh water pond,
Feeling the breeze of the cool wind.

This isn't my world,
Where there is pollution
And the smell of gas
Filling the air.

This isn't my world,
Where there is litter
Scattered all over the place.

This isn't my world,
Where animals are dying
From garbage thrown in the
Blue, sparkling ocean.

> C. R., 4th grade

It is a world of green grass,
Of valleys, and mountains
Tall and high.

It is a world of peace,
Love and kindness,
With no more wars.

It is a world of caring
For whales, seals and all fish.
It is a world of free land
For people who are free,
Or not free.

It is a world of no pollution
Or any more violence.
This is my world
And no one else can change it!

> E. C., 4th grade

excerpts

This is my world
Living peacefully
The sun shining in my face
Everybody's face . . .

> K. F., 4th grade

This is my world
The beautiful world
No crime
No ugly drugs.
This is my world
A wonderful sun
Shining down on us
With the warmth of summer . . .

> K. J., 4th grade

. . . A world with a Spring breeze
An area full of trees with leaves
A non-polluted air.
My world would be a hand shake
For every man you meet . . .

> J. L., 4th grade

This is my world
The bright golden sun
This is my world
The day that just begun
This is my world
Birds that sing in the Spring
There are so many
Beautiful things . . .

> M. S., 4th grade

In my world
Cities will be clean,
People will have homes . . .

> E. D., 4th grade

This is my world
A world of understanding
Seeing the birds fly south
Seeing the sun set
The dolphins jumping in the air
Lots of peace . . .

> A. A., 4th grade

This is my world
I choose to like
The sun setting over the ocean
Not coffee cups and beer bottles
On the streets.

This is my world
I choose to like seagulls
Soaring over the ocean
Not seeing on the news
That someone got shot.

This is my world
I choose to like seeing the snow
Fall from my window
Not seeing homeless people
On the streets of New York City.

> T. F., 4th grade

This is my world
Where people recycle
They stop other people
from polluting . . .

> C. S., 4th grade

In my world
Lovely bluejays fly freely on
The crest of a new day . . .
In my world
A morning dove sings out
As if he were in a concert . . .

> J. C., 4th grade

In my world
Deer run freely in
Open fields.
Salmon spawn in
Crystal clear water
In my world
pine trees

reach to
billowy clouds.
Brooks run
freely through
rough mountains.

A. B., 4th grade

excerpts and complete poems

I see my world of fresh air
crystal clear lakes
reflecting the warm
comfortable sun.

I hear my world
a beautiful white swan
cooing in a pond.

I smell my world
of fresh mountain air,
while skiing down a
slope as white as a dove.

I taste my world
of fresh spring water,
soothing my tongue.

I feel my world
of salty ocean water,
cooling my refreshed face.

This is our world.
Can we keep it this way . . .
for it is the ultimate
challenge.

M. W., 4th grade

This is my world
where birds fly in
crystal clear air,
All trees, far from
extinction.
Rivers flow with
fresh spring water.

This is my world
where fish swim
freely in endless circles
through fresh, blue water . . .

K. C., 4th grade

Once sea was peaceful with man
Now sea is almost destroyed
by man;
a friend once . . .

S. S., 4th grade

In my world
There is clean, fresh air
Like a crystal ball,
Gleaming in the sunlight . . .

R. H., 4th grade

This world, our world,
overtaken by black, unwelcoming smoke
encircling our once beautiful world . . . .

T. S., 4th grade

This is my world,
With happiness, peace, glory.
A world of meadows filled with
Daisies, wild flowers.
A world of care; beauty; colors of happiness.

This is my world.
A world with no war, smoking, acids, odors
That fill the air,
A world without crime,
Murder.

This is my world:
Where whales roam freely
Without man's dangerous touch.
This is my world.
with animals of all kinds,
With mountains topped
By dove white icy snow;

This is my world.
A world with big, beautiful birds,
Chirping in the trees,
With a sun like a golden coin,
Shining through clouds as silvery and
Shiny as glass.
A world with streams, brooks, and creeks,
flowing with shiny
Blue water.
This is my world,
With no oil spills,
With no pollution places or waters.
This is my world.
With meadows to run in,
Tall grass to play in,
Creeks and ponds
To catch frogs and fish in.
With windows to look
At the silvery rain drops
Smiling faces of children,
A world of understanding
Of life and colors, a world of love.
This is my world.

                    T. M., 4th grade

This is my world,
Lakes sparkle in the sun to flying geese
Up above.

Tall grass sways gracefully from
side to side.
Springs of water spurt up here
And there.

Fish jump freely around the
Ball of life.

The eyes of Indian children amazed
At magic they hear.

Whales stay near the surface
Close to man.

Bells on a horse-drawn sleigh
ring in the snow.

Baby seals sleep with no
Worry for hunters.

This is my world
We should take care of it.

                    B. T., 4th grade

In my world
the wilderness is like
the clear crystal
Hudson River that flows
throughout New York's
wondrous land.

Free animals discovering
unexpected adventures in the
clear world around them.

In my world whales in pure blue
water swim free from
harpoonists,
far from extinction.

                    A. B., 4th grade

My world would be
oak trees gleaming under
the life giving sun.
Roses blooming in the
misty dawn.

My world is
mournful whales dying before us
and greasy chips wrappers
and soda cans
floating down our murky streams . . .

                    J. B., 4th grade

This is my world
where I choose to love and care.

This is my world where I
choose to breathe the fresh, sweet
air of spring and
summer, like a
bird lost in its dreams.

I choose to see all the beautiful
wildlife perched in a tree
like the clouds
or swimming deep
in the sea like
the sand.

This is my world where I choose
to walk on clean streets,
now covered in soda cans and
candy wrappers.

I choose to love every speck of it,
even though it is filled with smoke,
glazed in oil, and
swept up in candy wrappers,
broken glass and soda cans.
Even my love,
everybody's love,
can't stop this from happening.
This is my world where
babies are dying from their mothers
taking drugs . . .

J. S., 4th grade

SUMMARY: ENVIRONMENT LESSON _____

The point of concluding with this particular extended environment-related experience is to illustrate the positive aspects of educational layering. For us, this all-school happening reinforced the degree to which cross-curriculum teaching can affect, and enhance, the total learning gestalt. The goal throughout this book has been to strive for this level of teaching using creative techniques in a way that is curriculum-kind (those which permit the teacher to work within his or her own format without additional material interjection).

Within the framework of "This Is My World: I Choose," the process was designed to be an ongoing one. When the language and music specialists completed their input, environmental themes were projected into all of the various school disciplines. Possible math projects were considered, science lessons designed, and even history lessons planned which would compare past/present/ and future environments. Earth Day activities were on the agenda, and a follow-up outdoor spring poetry/music day was planned for just prior to the end of the school year.

An exciting, energized classroom combines teacher skills, student participation, a bit of faith, and a bit of magic. By yielding to this evocative process, one is able to let go creatively, and in so doing find delight in "working the word."

appendix

INTRODUCTION: SUPPLEMENTARY MATERIAL _____

We hope it is obvious to the reader of this text that it would be virtually impossible to include all the lessons with which the authors have experimented over the years. The poetry presented in Sections I and II is representative of the sequential growth of language skills and the naturally inspired flow of music and movement activities. In this appendix we offer supplementary material which may provide the reader with additional ideas for the expanded lesson experience through poetry (language).

Included with these student poems (which were selected because they were representative of types of responses to the individual writing assignments) are occasional suggestions for possible direction/departure points for further development. These suggestions provide a viable opportunity to use these poems as a focus for which teachers may want to write their own scripts, which could then be transposed into actual in-class lessons. The openness of these suggestions is the invitation for the teacher to move as creativity dictates.

SUPPLEMENTARY LESSONS

1. I-oriented poems
   — "I Seem to Be/But Really I Am"
   — "I Used to Be/But Now I Am"
   — "I Am"
   — "I Was"
   — "Ways of Me"
   — "I Am Lava"

2. "Poetry Is" poems (five poems)

3. "The Things I Like Best" Poems

— "The Things I Love"
— four poems entitled "The Things I Like Best"

4. ABC poems (two poems)

5. "Before I Was Born" poems (five poems)

6. "The Things I Do, The Places I Go" poems
— "Skiing"
— "The Beach"
— "Hunting"
— "The Outdoors"
— "City"
— "The Ocean"
— "One Day at the Park"

7. Guessing poems
— "White"
— "Yellow"
— "Clear"
— "Untitled"

8. Storms poems
— "Snowflake"
— two poems entitled "Storms"

9. Holiday poems
— "My Thanksgiving"
— "Valentine's Day"
— "Christmas"
— "Last Year's Chanukkah"

10. Similes poems (three poems)

11. Miscellaneous poems
— "The Silence Sings in the Wind"
— "Growing Up"
— "The World to Us"
— "Cowboy on a Horse"
— "The Graveyard"

annotated student poems

All of the poetry lessons explored in this supplemental section presuppose that the student has had an introduction to poetry techniques.

i-oriented poems

Motivation: In this poetry assignment, students were asked to explore "self" using poetry techniques. They came at the assignment from a number of different creative directions.

I SEEM TO BE/BUT REALLY I AM[1]

I seem to be a dog chasing a cat
But really I am a kitten purring
gently.

I seem to be the sun shining brightly
But really I am the moon glowing
in the midnight sky.

I seem to be a broken dish
But really I am a china tea cup.

I seem to be mud
But really I am a rose.

I seem to be a chicken in a
farmyard
But really I am a little lamb.

G. B., 4th grade

Extensions: The disparity between lines suggests using a disparate extension treatment. Students might experiment with "I seem" being sung, contrasting with "But really" spoken, or the reverse.

I USED TO BE/BUT NOW I AM

I USED TO BE

I used to be a rainbow
But now I am a flower
I used to be a puddle
But now I am a sea
I used to be a rock
But now I am a mountain.

J. C., 4th grade

Extension: The steadiness of the word rhythm of this poem invites playing with body percussion ostinato accompaniment (or nonpitched percussion). To lengthen the work, interludes of rhythmic material might be inserted every two lines.

[1]The ideas for this poem and "I Used to Be/But Now I Am" were suggested in *Wishes, Lies and Dreams,* Kenneth Koch, Vintage Books/Chelsea House Publishers, 1970.

I AM . . .

I AM A ROSE

I am a rose in a meadow
Someone just picked me
I am sitting in a house
People are looking at me
I feel like a beautiful decoration
on a table.
I am in a diamond glass vase
I am all alone.

J. C., 4th grade

*Extension: The simplicity of
this poem might be enhanced
with only a simple sound
happening behind the reading,
at regular intervals.*

I WAS . . .

I WAS . . .

I was as rough as rocks
at the seashore in the
hot blazing sand.

I was the sound of
crackling thunder in
the sky.

I was the taste of
the salty ocean
after it rained.

I was the smell of
the bitter lemon and
lime.

I was the dream of
a boy at night time.

D. S., 5th grade

*Extension: "I Was" begins
with strong language that
mellows as the verses progress.
It would be interesting to let
students find sounds which
follow that diminishing
sequence to underscore the
poem's imagery.*

I SEEM TO BE/BUT REALLY I AM

WAYS OF ME

I seem to be mean and fresh
    but really I am sweet and polite.
    I see myself as a cotton ball
so delicate
    others see me as a globe
turning and turning.

I seem to be a piece
of dirt
but really I am a president.

I seem to be a ripped up
book
but really I am "bran" new.

I see myself as a
daffodil
others see as
an Oak tree.

I seem to be a broken
crayon
but really I am a
gold pen.

I seem to be
a purple kid
but really I am pale.

I see myself as having a
big heart
others see me as
having none.

D. N., 4th grade

I AM LAVA

I am lava
I chase people off land
and kill animals and people
I feel like I am hot as the sun
I am the most powerful thing
on earth.

J. S., 4th grade

"poetry is . . ." poems

Motivation: Working to develop poetic skills is a process that stretches over a number of introductory lessons. At some point it seems natural and inevitable to ask students to put into words their feelings about the poetry they have been writing. "Poetry Is" is an assignment designed to help students define and articulate their feelings about poetry.

POETRY IS . . .

Poetry is a
meadow of flowers
daisies and buttercups dancing about
with joy.
It feels like a
smooth piece of silk
waiting to be felt.
Poetry is the soft
sound of
sea gulls
calling at the beach.
It is
summer in words.
Poetry is
a lovely thing.

E. F., 3rd grade

Comment: Note the lines, "It is/summer in words." This type of ethereal student insight into the magic of imagery is the reward that brightens the teaching experience.
Extension: The first four lines of this poem abound with a natural and undeniably strong rhythm. This sets those lines apart from the rest of the poem, so an extension consideration might be to create a melody for these four lines and bring them back into the poem as a rhythmic, melodious refrain.

POETRY IS . . .

Poetry is a rainbow
covering the sky.
I see a glittery
story in it.
It is a mocking bird mocking.
I taste a blossom
on a tree.
It is soft
as cotton.
It is happy
as a smiling face.

C. S., 3rd grade

POETRY IS . . .

A nice big donut
It is sugar.
It smells like milk
all over the donut.
It is a big waterfall
splashing down a mountain.
It is as soft as a kitten.
I LOVE IT!

M. S., 3rd grade

POETRY IS . . .

  The sun coming up
My cat's purring
The taste of a chocolate cupcake
The feeling of fur coats
The smell of my mother's perfume.

S. M., 3rd grade

POETRY IS . . .

I see in Poetry
the "glooming" moon
glowing in the dark.

I hear in Poetry
trumpets blowing
in the air.

I taste in Poetry
the fresh taste
of cold freezing water.

I touch in Poetry
the smooth ice
around me.

I smell in Poetry
the nice smell of
juicy turkey.

J. S., 5th grade

POETRY IS . . .

Poetry looks like a
big colorful rainbow
with clouds in
the sky.

Poetry sounds like
a big angry tiger roaring
after someone teased
it.

Poetry tastes like a
big bowl of candy
at a Halloween
party.

Poetry feels like
the feel of a big
soft pillow with
feathers you sleep
on at "nighttime."

Poetry smells
like the sweet
smell of a garden
of pretty flowers.

M. B., 5th grade

*Extension: Because each
stanza of this poem explores a
new sense and is therefore
different, it might be good to
emphasize that difference by
separating the stanzas with
some sort of interlude, perhaps
just a melody simply sung or
played on a recorder.*

"the things I like best" poems

Motivation: Students were asked to reflect in silence on the things in their lives which gave them the most pleasure. They were then asked to make a list of ten things in their lives that they liked best. Selecting from that list, those things which could best be worked through imagery into poetry resulted in the following poems.

THE THINGS I LOVE

I love the
morning smell of
the breeze making
the trees whistle.
I love seeing a
menagerie of
purple, green, white, red,
blue, and orange flowers
dancing with the wind
and the trees playing
their leaves.
And the Blue Jays
singing.
I love watching
a half sun at
sunset stretch
down to Asia.
I love the sound of
my mother whispering
in my ear.
I love feeling the soft
wind pushing my hair to a jingle.
I love touching
smooth white silk.
I love you and me!

                    S. S., 5th grade

*Extension: This poem seems
like it could simply ride over a
short, soft melody, played as
an enhancement to the words.
It would be a challenge for the
class to find those sets of
sounds (key sounds) which
would best capture the rather
soft and nostalgic quality of the
poem.*

I love to hear
the sea gulls flying
in the air.
I love to taste
lemon meringue pie
on my tongue.
I love to feel satin
on my face,
moving back and forth.
I love to see my best friend
Chrissy.
I love to be me!!!!!

                    A. W., 3rd grade

THE THINGS I LIKE BEST

I love to play
by the shore
of the Hudson River.
I love to smell
the salty sea
while sitting on the beach.

THE THINGS I LIKE BEST

I like to see rainbows as colorful as
an autumn painting, roses as red
as a heart, seagulls flying over the
ocean, blue as a bluebird flying

over a blueberry. I like wolves
howling on the bright white ball
in the sky, as bright as a light
bulb burning in the night. I like
softball. I like that big fat
ball coming right at my
bat. I love my friend Alethea!
But, the thing I like most
is just being me!

                   C. P., 3rd grade

THE THINGS I LOVE BEST

I love to see
pretty red violets
on a prickly stem.
I love the sound
of the hot crackling fire!
I love the smell of a
daisy in a flower pot
just waiting to
be picked.
I love the taste
of cool orange juice.
It feels like
Allegra's hand
brushing through
my lovely big black afro.

It's like having your
first new born
child. Now wasn't that
a sweet poem.

                   C. P., 3rd grade

THE THING THAT I LOVE BEST

I love the morning sun
as bright as a light,
I love sound
when the flowers pop up
and the roots pop down,
love the smell
of sweet flowers,
of all the colors
of red, yellow,
pink, green,
orange, purple and blue.
I can see a rainbow
too,
surrounding the world,
If I could
I would name them all
rose,
As the wind passes on my cheek,
Spring is beautiful!

                   M. A., 3rd grade

"abc" poems

Motivation: This poem is an exercise in creating images using metaphors and similes. Students were asked to go through the alphabet, choosing a word for each letter in the alphabet, and then creating an image for the chosen word. They were also expected, whenever possible, to use other poetic skills such as alliteration, etc.

ABC

A is an alligator
green as grass.

B is a bishop
solemn as a soul.

C is a color
black as a shadow.

D is a dart
swift as an arrow.

E is an eight
oval as an egg.

F is a fool
dumb as a dog.

G is a group
big as a room.

H is a hole
empty as a pot.

I is an Igloo
round as a ball.

J is a jug
thin as a string.

K is a kangaroo
jumpy as a jack.

L is a law
as strict as a teacher.

M is a moon
big as a bun.

N is a nut
small as a mouse.

O is an orange
orange as an O.

P is a pig
fat as a fig.

Q is a queue
long as a line.

R is a road
wide as a witch.

S is the sea
deep as the ocean.

T is a tradition
common as a spoon.

U is an umbrella
up in the rain.

W is the wind
howling in the night.

X is a xerox
round as a zero.

Y is a yo-yo
going up and down.

Z is a "zygone"
going in the wind.

A. B., 5th grade

Extension: The short, consistently rhythmical lines make this a poem which would be fun to move. Students could invent a four- or eight-beat step movement ostinato, using arm motions, claps, etc., and then chant the poem above their movement.

ABC POEM

A is an apple
shiny as snow.

B is a barrett
as flat as a rock.

C is a cat
as soft as cotton.

D is a dog
as fast as a car.

E is an elephant
as big as a tree.

F is a friend
as nice as a kitten.

G is glass
as smooth as a chalkboard.

H is a horse
swift as a train.

I is an ice cream cone
as cold as the snow.

J is a juggler
as funny as a clown.

K is a kitten
as playful as a friend.

L is a lemon
as yellow as the sun.

M is a Martian
as wierd as a monkey.

N is the north pole
as cold as a blizzard.

O is an octopus
as big as a car.

P is a pencil
straight as a stick.

Q is a queen
as pretty as a flower.

R is a rose
as red as a heart.

S is a sun
as yellow as a banana.

T is a turtle
as ugly as a frog.

U is an umbrella
as wet as a stream.

V is a van
as big as an elephant.

W is white
as white as snow.

X is an x-ray
as scary as a monster.

Y is Yorktown
a very busy city.

Z is a xylophone
as sweet as a bird.

D. W., 5th grade

"before i was born" poems

Motivation: It is always rewarding to give students an opportunity to stretch their imaginations; to play with an idea in an outrageous way, imagining the unimaginable. This assignment is presented in the spirit of fun. Students are invited to create images that delight the mind and the senses . . . to enjoy the process.

BEFORE I WAS BORN

I was:
A pony asleep in the fields
near a barn and an owl in the
forest. Before I was born
I smelled like perfume in a
bottle. Before I was born I
sounded like waves, coming down on
the sand at the beach. Before
I was born I tasted like fresh
blueberries and butterscotch candy
before I was born I felt like a
wet sea shell in a jar and as
smooth as a blade of grass
and a four leaf clover.

L. K., 4th grade

Extension: "Before I was born" is the reiterative refrain in this poem, and so can be highlighted in any number of ways:
—By the group speaking/singing the words, before I was born.
—By various solo voices speaking/singing the words.
The melody can be linear or textured. If a thicker version is desired, "before I was born" can be sung in canon with two groups.

BEFORE I WAS

Before I was
Born I was the
first one to see
Earth.

Before I was
Born I was
the first one
to hear E.T. say
"Ouch."

Before I was
Born I tasted
like licorice.
Before I was born
I touched the stars.

Before I was born
I smelled like a hug!

J. M., 4th grade

BEFORE I WAS BORN

Before I was born I was a leopard
leaping in the deep blue sky I
smelled like a flamingo floating in the
blue sea I sounded like a penguin
swimming in the cold and windy lake I
tasted like a pumpkin pie just baked and
bought I looked like a new born baby
in a crib crying my cry sounded like
rain drops falling on the ground.

Y. C., 3rd grade

BEFORE I WAS BORN

Before I was born
I was the sun rising.
Before I was born

I could hear a bee buzzing
my hair.
Before I was born
I could see a snake
eating. Before I was born
I could hear the angels singing.
Before I was born
I tasted like a pear.
Before I was born
I felt like a smooth unicorn.
Before I was born,
I smelled like chocolate
candy.

R. J., 4th grade

BEFORE I WAS BORN I WAS

Before I was born I was
the smell of a pretty yellow flower
in a big field.

Before I was me I was a beautiful
silk dress worn by a beautiful
queen.

Before I was myself I was
a beautiful rainbow with a pot of
gold at my side.

Before I was born I was the
taste of pizza.
And now I'm me!

Anon., 3rd grade

"the things I do, the places I go" poems

Motivation: Poetry can be found in the realm of one's own realities. These poems are based on the students' individual experiences and memories. The assignment is introduced as an open writing task, allowing students to choose the personal subject (thing, place) they wish to explore poetically. Teacher input is minimal, except to remind students *not* to abandon their poetic skills even though the poems will be about *real* places and happenings.

THE OUTDOORS

We were approaching the highest part
of my life. We were on a mountain
facing the wilderness, and the clear
blue sky, the clouds were casting a
shadow upon the ocean currents,
flowers were scattered along the
mountain top. The people swam
along the ocean waves. The waves were
as tough as a brick wall.

G. F., 7th grade

THE OCEAN

The silent salty water
washes against
the smooth sandy
sand like tears dripping
down from a shy, bashful
girl crying for help.
The scared seagulls diving
from the windy breeze right
into the bright blue ocean
the rough seashells moving
back and forth from the
courageous waves crashing
at the tip of the shore.
The sun beginning to set at
the shore when the people
dusting off their silky sandy
blankets set off for home.

I. S., 5th grade

CITY

The streets ran like children hurrying to the
park. The signs hung like spider's cobwebs
after they've been spun. The cabs drive like
children sliding down a slide. The building
stands tall like an elephant after it's been
scared. The traffic lights stared at night
like the stars.

L. T., 5th grade

ONE DAY AT THE PARK

One day at the park
The bird's concert was sold out
Chipmunks were jumping about
The trees were swaying
Squirrels were playing
Dandelions were moving
Flying leaves were grooving
Ant holes were spread around
Like peanut butter and jelly on bread
The air was as fresh as a strawberry.

M. E., 5th grade

*Extension: From the line "the
trees were swaying," this
student wrote in a semi rap
mode, where the rhythm
became driving. Thus, the first
three lines might be spoken
arhythmically, adding some
sort of rhythm accompaniment
for the lines:*

> *the trees were swaying . . .*
> *squirrels were playing . . .*
> *dandelions were moving . . .*
> *flying leaves were grooving*
> *. . .*
> *ant holes were spread around*
> *. . .*
> *like peanut butter and jelly*
> *on bread . . .*

*The rhythm could be comprised
of complementary body
percussion patterns, found
sounds, or be in a jazz style,
i.e., composite of vocal
rhythms on "seat" syllables
(e.g., bee BAH doo dah), or
simply plosive sounds. The last
line might be set apart by
having a solo voice speak it
freely, nonrhythmically, without
any accompaniment.*

"guessing" poems

> **Motivation:**   In this assignment, students are asked to write poems rich in imagery. The imagery itself should reveal the subject of the work. In the examples presented here, color was the theme; but any subject could have been used. Upon completion of the task, students read their creations aloud, and classmates are asked to guess the inspiration for the poem.

WHITE

I am the color of a freezing snowy day,
like a furry kitten playing and as clean
as a fluffy cloud floating in the sky.

I am the sound of snow falling to the ground,
chalk screeching on the board,
and a duck swimming in a pond.

I am a fragrance of a beautiful daisy,
of foam from the sea, and the smell of
a bright new day.

> M. M., 4th grade

YELLOW

I am a juicy pineapple, a popcorn kernel that hasn't been popped and a sour lemon.

I am mustard in a jar, a cut up grapefruit, a golden apple and a delicious rose.

I am a bright carnation, a singing canary, blonde hair on a head.

I am a golden leaf in the fall, a piece of sponge cake, frozen lemon ices.

I am a pear being bitten into, a lion roaring, an egg being beaten up with a fork.

> K. W., 4th grade

Extension: This poem would be fun for exploring found sounds as accompaniments, because of the plosive sounds created by many of the bouncing, bounding words and combinations. Selecting the right color/timbre of found sound to complement a particular stanza would be challenging. Ostinato patterns using more than one found sound could be created as accompaniments, or used as segues between verses—or both.

CLEAR

I look like a
tear on a crying
child's face, a
new chap stick,
new braces on someone's face
and carbonated
water.

I feel strange
as water, cool
as a summer
breeze, and as
cold as snow.

I smell like
rain, a fountain
for birds and
a puddle on
the street.

I taste like the
ocean's water,
seltzer and
white chocolate.

I sound as
pretty as a
bird chirping,
as young as
a year-old baby,
and like
water dripping
from a sink.

M. N., 4th grade

UNTITLED

I look like a tear dropping from the sky,
I look like a dark lonely night, and I
look like the midnight sky.

I smell like a big beautiful weeping willow
tree swaying in the breeze, I am the smell
of a daisy just starting to grow.

I am the sound of a gloomy child dying, I
am the sound of a funeral passing down the
street.

I taste like a rotten apple, I taste like
mold sitting in a dark cabinet.

I feel like a pointy pin, I feel like a
sharp knife going into someone's heart.

L. B., 4th grade

"storms" poems

Motivation: Teachers are always looking for ways to inspire students to write. Sometimes the stimulus is found in the classroom within content areas. Sometimes the natural world around us provides a source of inspiration. This trigger stimulus is both intriguing, capturing our attention, and rich in imagery and poetic implication. The variables of weather, in particular the violent and intense nature of storms, lend themselves to translation into the poem.

SNOWFLAKE

A snowflake is broken glass shattered all over the
floor.
It is a big crystal bowl with little designs
on it.
A snowflake is the rich thick soap lather
surrounding me.
It is little drops of water falling from the
cloud above.
It is blowing across my face and it is falling
on my head.

J. S., 4th grade

STORMS

The tall trees swaying in
the storm looked like
ballerinas dancing.

The angry thunder growled
like a mad dog.

The galloping lightning
flashed across the sky as
if it was running in a race.

The big rain drops were
like an elephant's tears.

The dark clouds were as
gloomy as a sad person.

The blowing wind went
wildly through the sky as
if it were a cat chasing
a mouse.

The white snow slowly
fell as if it was a turtle
walking over a huge
mountain of rocks.

The whirling tornado
roared like an angry
lion.

The cold ice crackled
like a person dropping
a crystal glass.

R. R., 6th grade

Extension: *The brevity of
"Snowflake" coupled with
active, moving images make
this a good poem for a
movement activity. Finding
ways to use the Laban
movement qualities (slash,
press, punch, glide, wring,
float, flick, and dab) to express
"broken glass shattered"
"little designs,"
"surrounding," "drops of
water falling from the cloud
above," and "blowing across
my face" would make for an
interesting movement
exploration game—perhaps
later adding found or small
percussion sounds to enhance
those images.*

STORMS

The storms slowly walked
silently through the country.

The wind wondered wildly
when the long winter would end.

The snow slept softly like
a snow white polar bear in
hibernation.

The thunder roared like a
lonely lion lying down to sleep.

B. F., 6th grade

"holiday" poems

Motivation: The universal quality of holidays makes them a subject which has been used repeatedly by teachers in writing assignments and class discussions. One is always looking for a new approach to dealing with the subject; a way of making it more personalized and less commercial. Toward this end, the emphasis is on the poignancy of the experience: "How do *you* celebrate the holiday?" "What makes it special for you?" "What memories do you carry with you long after the holiday has ended?" "What images stay in your mind—images of taste, touch, scent, sight, and sound?" The attempt is to move beneath the surface of the event and to delve into the individual perceptions of the rituals and interactions. It may be helpful to point out when initiating this writing experience that we, as a class, are all hoping to learn something new when the poems are shared. This may inspire students to try to find something unique in their experiences.

MY THANKSGIVING

Thanksgiving looks like
getting out of bed to
sunshine. It smells like
a flower blooming.
It feels like a blanket
cuddling me under the
bed. It tastes like a
juicy, big, round drumstick.
Thanksgiving makes me feel
alive.

D. W., 3rd grade

VALENTINE'S DAY

Valentine's Day is like a day of
love.
Hearts are like a rainbow with hearts
dropping off.
Love is like a feeling you get when you
like someone.
A kiss is like a kiss from your mother
and getting a lipstick mark on your face.
Lips are as red as a cherry lollipop.
A cup of hot cocoa on a winter day
when it is 28 degrees out and you are in a nice
warm house.

M. P., 2nd grade

LAST YEAR'S CHANUKKAH

There was snow like bundles
of white pillows last year at
Chanukkah when I got a beautiful
stereo shining as bright as the
sun in summer up above the
sky.

One of my favorite dolls I wanted was
set before me in a box with shining
wrapping paper like a star up above
the sky.

We lit the
Menorrah and sang the
prayers like
sparrows on a tree.

I smelled the
Chanukkah cookies
in the oven and
they reminded me of
the fresh
flowers on my
birthday in
summer.

T. W., 4th grade

CHRISTMAS

Christmas is white
Christmas is in December.
Christmas is a holiday. I
Like Christmas.

L. M., 2nd grade

Extension: Reading this poem

•

in a duple meter—"Christmas

•   •   •   •

is white" (rest). | "Christmas

•   •   •

*is in December"(rest)—makes
it possible to imagine a space
of four beats coming after each
line in which to create a
rhythm. This rhythmic interlude
would lengthen and strengthen
the poem as well as highlight
the strong rhythm of the words.
The rhythm could be played on
the body or small percussion.*

"similes" poems

Motivation: The more students write, the more comfortable they become with using writing skills. In the case of poetry, the emphasis is on developing an exacting word sense. Through repetition and practice, learned techniques become automatic. In asking students to emphasize the image rather than the idea in the simile poem, we give them the opportunity to flex their linguistic abilities.

The set-up for this poem was to feed students the bulk of the image (e.g., "water was smooth . . ." "her touch was light . . ." etc.) and then have them complete the image in the form of a simile. Placing the individual images within the context of a poem demonstrates that even unconnected ideas can come together through form to become the embodiment of poetry.

SIMILES

The water was as smooth as a
flowing lake
The cat's tongue was as rough
as steel
Her touch was as light as a
little baby dog
She was as gay as
my laughter
The sunset was as red
as fire

The snow was as high
as the Rockies
We were bundled up
like grizzly bears
The tip of my nose was as red
as the brightest red in the world.

M. K., 4th grade

SIMILES

The water was as smooth as velvet
The cat's tongue was as rough as sandpaper.
Her touch was as light as a feather
She was as gay as a jolly clown.
The sunset was as red as fire
The snow was as high as a mountain cliff.
We were bundled up like a suitcase.
The tip of my nose was as red as fire.

C. F., 4th grade

SIMILES

The water was smooth as a soft, windy breeze
The cat's tongue was as rough as sharp hard rocks.
Her touch was as light as a soft falling feather.
She was as gay as a happy little cat.
The sunset was red as a moon's dark blood.
The snow was as high as the Swiss Alps.
We were bundled up like a soft furry bear.
The tip of my nose was as red as a
Bright flaming fire.

M. S., 4th grade

Extension: The attention this student paid to balancing the lines and making them feel symmetrical gives this poem the potential for song. However, to attempt to set the whole song would constitute a task which would probably slow down the lesson pacing. A solution might be to set the first four lines in melody, bringing them back at the end as a reprise, and speaking the remaining middle section.

miscellaneous poems

Motivation: In a sense these are the poems which reflect the end result of the process. The students represented here (seventh graders) have, through repeated exposure to writing assignments using poetry techniques and skills, become comfortable with the process. At some point the teacher needs to assume that students are ready and able to fly.

The poems presented here were the result of students selecting and exploring their own chosen subjects. There is a great deal of *feeling* evident in the language of the poems, and one senses the enormity of the investment on the part of the student.

The motivation for beginning this assignment was quite simply "write a poem."

THE SILENCE SINGS IN THE WIND

The powdered snow is so beautiful
that it could be a sign of oncoming
God.

The two children playing in the
powder, not realizing the Godliness
in the atmosphere;

and two starved cows searching,
scratching at the snow for a blade
of grass to eat;

and the wandering cowboy dreaming as
the silence sings in the wind.

J. T., 7th grade

THE WORLD TO US

The world is so big to us,
The trees are so far away,
The birds fly so high above us.

The ground is so close,
The flowers are so near,
I can't wait until we get the size
of grownups.

Then the trees won't be so far away.
The flowers won't be so close,
and birds won't fly so high.

J. S., 7th grade

COWBOY ON A HORSE

The silence of being alone
The mystery of the white
snow lying ahead.
The fate of starving
in the cold.
The fate of your horse
dying leaving you alone.
The unpredictable sky
hanging heavy above.

A. G., 7th grade

*Extension: The imagery is so
exceptional in the title and
denouement of this poem that
it might be nice to highlight it
melodically. Isolating that
phrase in melody, "the silence
sings in the wind," and
interjecting it at the beginning
and in between stanzas would
be effective.*

GROWING UP

When I was young,
very young, I believed in:

Santa Claus,
the Tooth Fairy,
& the Easter Bunny.

The world goes around like a
ferris wheel, things get harder
as we grow up, they're not like they
used to be. Like in Friendship,
Friendship is like sand—it slips
through your fingers; and school's
like working out calculation problems.
At home when I was little all I
did was watch Sesame Street and
eat peanut butter & jelly. Now I
face reality and reality is hard
as stone
and heavy to carry.

S. V., 7th grade

THE GRAVEYARD

The gravestones so tilted and grey,
To think in the future here I will lay,
The bodies that lay there under the ground,
Without moving, or making a single sound.
I know once in our lives we all must die,
But then we'll be free as birds in the sky.

K. R., 7th grade

Following is a list of books representing a variety of classroom possibilities for poetry, music, and movement enrichment which the authors have used and found inspirational over the years.

Perceptive Possibilities

These are good reference books for teachers who want to introduce new ideas and possibilities into the classroom in terms of creative curriculum expansion, and for looking at the familiar in new ways.

Applegate, Mauree, *When the Teacher Says, "Write A Poem,"* Harper & Row, New York, 1965.

Bagley, Michael T., and Hess, Karin K., *200 Ways of Using Imagery in the Classroom,* Trillium Press, Inc., New York, 1984.

Gensler, Kinereth, and Nyhart, Nina, *The Poetry Connection: An Anthology of Contemporary Poems with Ideas to Stimulate Children's Writing,* Teachers and Writers Collaborative, Inc., New York, 1978.

Leff, Dr. Herbert L., *Playful Perception: Choosing How to Experience Your World,* Waterfront Books, Inc., Burlington, Vt., 1985.

Murphy, Richard, *Imaginary Worlds: Notes On a New Curriculum,* Teachers and Writers Collaborative, Inc., New York, 1974.

Wallace, Robert, *Writing Poems,* Little, Brown and Co., Boston/Toronto, 1982.

Walsh, Chad, *Doors Into Poetry,* Prentice-Hall, Englewood Cliffs, N.J., 1962.

Wendt, Ingrid, *Starting with Little Things: A Guide to Writing Poetry in the Classroom,* Oregon Arts Foundation, Salem, Oreg., 1983.

Zavatsky, Bill, and Padgett, Ron (eds.), *The Whole Word Catalogue II,* McGraw-Hill Paperbacks, published in association with Teachers and Writers Collaborative, Inc., New York, 1977.

Movement

The following books give the teacher excellent movement vocabulary for evoking interesting, expressive, and varied movements from students. They deal with movement qualities, time, and weight, and space—and with words that prompt movement.

Gray, Vera, and Percival, Rachel, *Music, Movement, and Mime for Children,* Oxford U. Press, London/Toronto, 1962.

Laban, Rudolf, *Modern Educational Dance,* MacDonald & Evans, Ltd., London, 1963.

Mettler, Barbara, *Materials of Dance as a Creative Art Activity,* Mettler Studios, Tucson, Ariz., 1960.

Orff-Schulwerk Philosophy and History

The following is from the autobiography by Carl Orff and deals with those years in which the Schulwerk was developed.

Orff, Carl, *Das Schulwerk,* Schott, 1970.

Children's Original Work

These books may be helpful in providing teacher focus on expansion themes and may provide valuable examples from which students may be able to depart.

Benig, Irving (ed.), *The Children: Poems and Prose from Bedford-Stuyvesant,* Grove Press, Inc., New York, 1971.

_____ "it is time for the trees to get big in spring," a project of Community School District 6, New York, N.Y., The Arts in General Education Program, Dr. Paul Treatman, Community Superintendent (may be purchased from Bureau of Curr. Development, 665 W. 182nd St., New York, N.Y. 10033), 1977.

_____ *I Caught a Snowflake in My Hand,* poems and prose by the children of District 6 (see above); Academically Gifted Child Program, 1977–1978.

_____ *Forever Is a Carousel: An Anthology of Children's Poetry from the Gateway District 22,* Ralph T. Brand, Community Superintendent, 2525 Haring Street, Brooklyn, N.Y., 11235, 1979.

Koch, Kenneth, *Wishes, Lies and Dreams: Teaching Children to Write Poetry* (by Koch and the students of P.S. 61, New York City), Vintage Books/Chelsea House Publishers, a Division of Random House, New York, 1970.

_____ *Rose Where Did You Get That Red? Teaching Great Poetry to Children,* Vintage Books, a Division of Random House, New York, 1974.

Evocative Teaching

This is not only a book about drama as a learning medium, but it also deals with teaching registers and creative ways of dealing with class-created tasks.

Wagner, Betty Jean, *Drama as a Learning Medium,* Dorothy Heathcote, NEA, 1970.

Reflecting on Masterwork Poetry

The following books may prove helpful in providing threads from masterwork poetry which might be woven into the fabric of teaching. These books also familiarize teachers with the kinds of contemporary writing they hope to illicit from students.

Altenbernd, Lynn, and Lewis, Leslie L., *Introduction to Literature: Poems* (3rd ed.), Macmillan Publishing Co., Inc., New York, 1975.

Ellmann, Richard, and O'Clair, Robert (eds.), *Modern Poems: An Introduction to Poetry,* W. W. Norton, Inc., New York, 1973.

Kostelanetz, Richard (ed.), *Possibilities of Poetry: An Anthology of American Contemporaries,* Dell Publishing Co., Inc. a Delta Book, New York, 1970.

Littell, Joy (ed.), *Poetry Lives,* McDougall, Littell and Co., Evanston, Ill., 1979.

Moffi, Larry (ed.), *Intro 13,* The Associated Writing Programs, Norfolk, Va., 1982.

Van den heuvel, Cor (ed.), *the haiku anthology,* English Language Haiku by Contemporary American and Canadian Poets, Anchor Books, Anchor Press/Doubleday, Garden City, N.Y., 1974.

Williams, Miller (ed.), *Contemporary Poetry in America,* Random House, New York, 1973.

Gestalt

The following books cross lines—some using classical works, some using contemporary works, some a combination thereof, some offering ideas and suggestions for how to interpret and use poetry, and some discussing masterwork poets, analyzing their works and contributions.

Hunter, J. Paul (ed.), *Poetry: Norton Introduction to Literature,* W. W. Norton, Inc., New York, 1973.

Kennedy, X. J., *An Introduction to Poetry* (3rd ed.), Little, Brown and Co., Boston/Toronto, 1974.

Packard, William (ed.), *The Poet's Craft: Interviews from the "New York Quarterly,"* Paragon House Publishers, New York, 1987.

Riding, Laura, and Graves, Robert, *A Survey of Modernist Poetry,* Haskell House Publishers Limited, first published 1928, new edition 1969.

Shawcross, John T., and Lapidas, Frederic R., *Poetry and Its Conventions: An Anthology Examining Poetic Forms and Themes,* The Free Press, a Division of the Macmillan Co., New York, 1972.

Reference Books

These books help to standardize the definitions of poetic form. They also deal with vocabulary, grammar, punctuation, poetic terms, elements of literature, and writing techniques.

Bernstein, Theodore M., *The Careful Writer: A Modern Guide to English Usage,* Atheneum (a Leonard Harris Book), New York, 1965.

Brittain, Robert, *A Pocket Guide to Correct Punctuation,* Barrons Educational Series, Inc., Woodbury, N.Y., 1981.

Deutsch, Babette, *Poetry Handbook: A Dictionary of Terms* (4th ed.), Barnes and Noble Books, New York, 1974.

Fernald, James C., *Funk and Wagnalls Standard Handbook of Synonyms, Antonyms, and Prepositions,* Harper & Row, New York, 1947.

Foley, Stephen Merriam, and Gordon, Joseph Wayne, *Conventions and Choices: A Brief Book of Style and Usage,* D. C. Heath and Co., Lexington, Mass. and Toronto, 1986.

Freeman, Morton S., *A Treasury for Word Lovers,* iSi Press (a subsidiary of the Institute for Scientific Information), Philadelphia, Pa., 1983.

Johnson, Edward D., *The Handbook of Good English,* Facts on File Publications, New York, 1982.

Levine, Harold, *Comprehensive English Review Text* (4th ed.), Amsco School Publications, Inc., New York, 1962.

Lewis, Norman, *Word Power Made Easy,* Pocketbooks, New York, 1975.

Roget, *Roget's International Thesaurus* (3rd ed.), Thomas Y. Crowell Co., New York, 1962.

Scholas, Robert, Klaus, Carl H., and Silverman, Michael, *Elements of Literature,* Oxford University Press, Inc., New York, 1978.

Sisson, A. F., *Word and Expression Locater,* Parker Publishing, Inc., West Nyack, N.Y., 1966.

Williams, Miller, *Patterns of Poetry: An Encyclopedia of Forms,* Louisiana State U. Press, Baton Rouge and London, 1986.

Zinsser, William, *On Writing Well: An Informal Guide to Writing Non-Fiction* (3rd ed.), Harper & Row, New York, 1985.

Sound Sources

The following records and tapes are useful classroom tools for building imagery through aural stimuli and are inspirational in enriching the classroom experience and in offering sound examples which may be used as points of departure.

NATURE AND NATURAL SOUNDS:

"Deep Voices: The Second Whale Record," Capitol Records, Inc. *ST 11598.

"Missa Gaia: Earth Mass: A Mass in Celebration of Mother Earth Recorded Live in the Cathedral of St. John the Divine, and the Grand Canyon," Paul Winter, Living Music Records, Inc., *LMR-2, Box 72, Lichfield, Conn., 06759.

"O'cean (oh-see-on): Flute Music through Larkin," Windsung Sounds, P.O. Box 7227, Stanford, Calif., 94305.

"Paul Winter: Common Ground," A&M Records, Inc., SP4698, P.O. Box 782, Beverly Hills, Calif., 90213.

"Solitudes: Acoustical Environmental Sound Experiences without Music or Voice," Volume I, Dan Gibson Productions Limited, P.O. Box 1200, STN.Z, Toronto, Ontario M5N2Z7.

"Solitudes: Environmental Sound Experiences," Volume III (see above).

"Songs of the Humpback Whale," Capitol Records, Inc. Stereo 620, Hollywood and Vine Streets, Hollywood, Calif.

CLASSICAL:

"Deep Breakfast," Ray Lynch, Ray Lynch Productions, P.O. Box 252, San Rafael, Calif., 94915-0252.

"Johann Strauss' Greatest Hits," Ormandy, Philadelphia Orchestra, MS7502, Columbia Records, CBS Inc., 51 W. 52nd Street, New York.

"The Newest Sound of Debussy: Snowflakes Are Dancing, Tomita," RCA *ARL 1-0488, New York.

"The Young American Virtuoso: Christopher Parkening in the Spanish Style," S36020, Capitol Records, Inc., Hollywood and Vine Streets, Hollywood, Calif.

"Tschaikovsky, Highlights from the Ballet, Sleeping Beauty," Andre Previn, London Symphony Orchestra, Capitol Records, S-37261, Hollywood and Vine Streets, Hollywood, Calif.

credits

Jerome Kirk, *Orbit* (1972). Stainless steel, 144″ H. × 72″ W. × 72″ D. Storm King Art Center, Mountainville, NY. 1972.10.

Tal Streeter, *Endless Column* (1968). Steel painted red, 62′ 7″ H. Storm King Art Center, Mountainville, NY. Purchased with the aid of funds from the National Endowment for the Arts 1977.2.

Isaac Witkin, *Kumo* (1971). Cor-ten steel, 16′ 3″ × 13′ 4″ × 12′ 2″. Storm King Art Center, Mountainville, NY. Purchase 1971.3.

Grace Knowlton, *Spheres* (1973–75). Concrete, large 96″ diameter, small 36″ diameter. Storm King Art Center, Mountainville, NY. Gift of the artist 1977.4.

index